UK Parallel '96

Springer

London
Berlin
Heidelberg
New York
Barcelona
Budapest
Hong Kong
Milan
Paris
Santa Clara
Singapore
Tokyo

C.R. Jesshope and A.V. Shafarenko (Eds)

UK Parallel '96

Proceedings of the BCS PPSG
Annual Conference, 3-5 July 1996

Published in collaboration with the
British Computer Society

Springer

Chris Jesshope, PhD, MSc, BSc
Shasha Shafarenko, MSc, PhD
Department of Electrical Engineering
University of Surrey
Guildford, Surrey GU2 5XH, UK

ISBN-13: 978-3-540-76068-9   e-ISBN-13: 978-1-4471-1504-5
DOI: 10.1007/978-1-4471-1504-5

British Library Cataloguing in Publication Data
A catalogue record for this book is available from the British Library

Typesetting: Camera ready by contributors
Printed and bound at the Athenæum Press Ltd., Gateshead, Tyne and Wear
34/3830-543210 Printed on acid-free paper

PREFACE

UK Parallel 96 is the first in an annual series of national conferences covering the broad area of parallel and distributed computing. The first conference was held at the University of Surrey in July 1996 on behalf of the BCS Parallel processing Specialist Group.

It is rather sad that parallelism in computers no longer seems to have the support that it used to enjoy. Indeed there are many who will have noticed the shift in emphasis away from parallelism towards distributed computing, especially if the research contained the three magic letters "www" in its description. It is sad because now, more than ever, parallelism in computer architecture is more important than ever. Not only in super computers or symmetric multi-processors, which seem to be dominating the server and database markets these day, but also in the plain old uni-processor, which is no longer a sequential computer. Multiple instruction issue, pipelining and the latency of memory systems, compared to the aggressive speeds at which today's microprocessors run, mean that the uni-processor must exploit significant levels of parallelism if efficient execution is to be expected.

Thus it may be seen as bucking the trend to introduce a new conference series in this area, given the above trend. However, we confidently expect this area to flourish and to require a venue for the presentation of results in the UK as well as in the international arena. In this way we hope to encourage bright young British researchers to present their research without having to pay the large fee associated with an international conference. Although the industrial sessions are not included in this proceedings, we do not diminish the significance of disseminating these results to the wider industry but simply acknowledge the pressures under which most industry is operating. This proceedings therefore is the publication of the academic programme from this conference and contains work from a number of Universities within the UK. The scope of the proceedings illustrates the breadth of the work being undertaken in the UK and includes a variety of papers covering the following areas. There are papers on compiler development for both data-parallel and message passing languages, in which the over-riding goal is high efficiency; it is no use developing tools if they can not compete with the efficiency of the low-level approach. There are also papers covering the development of software tools for more application specific applications, including both BSP and genetic algorithms as a basis for the tools. In addition to this there are a number of important applications papers.

For more information concerning the BCS Parallel processing Specialist Group, the sponsor of this event, please contact Dr Nigel Tucker at the following email address: paradis@cix.compulink.co.uk (Dr Nigel Tucker).

Chris Jesshope
Conference Chair

CONTENTS

Simulation Modelling of Parallel Systems in the EDPEPPS* Project

Thierry Delaitre, François Spies, & Stephen Winter

Centre for Parallel Computing, University of Westminster

London, United Kingdom

Abstract

In this paper, a simulation model for incorporation within a performance-oriented parallel software development environment is presented. This development environment is composed of a graphical design tool, a simulation facility, and a visualisation tool. Simulation allows parallel program performance to be predicted and design alternatives to be compared. The target parallel system models a virtual machine composed of a cluster of workstations interconnected by a local area network. The simulation model architecture is modular and extensible which allows a re-configuration of the platform such as the hardware layer. The model description and the validation experiments which have been conducted to assess the correctness and the accuracy of the model are presented.

1 Introduction

The key obstacle to the widespread adoption of parallel computing is the difficulty in program development. Firstly, an application has to be decomposed into parallel objects (processes, or tasks) according to the computational model underlying the programming language. Secondly, the parallel hardware configuration has to be specified. Finally the processes are then mapped onto the hardware. The range of design choices available to the parallel program designer at each of the three stages can be immense. This has tended to produce highly-optimised platform-specific solutions, which are not easily ported to other platforms.

A lot of work has been done to create standard and relatively user-friendly interfaces at the message-passing layer, enabling programmers to decompose their applications into standardised processes which will run on a wide range of hardware (offering the standard message-passing platform). In principle, a program developed for a cluster of workstations should run correctly on a distributed-memory multiprocessor machine such as an SP2. Parallel Virtual Machine (PVM) [1] is such a message-passing environment, widely used by researchers and engineers, which permits a heterogeneous collection of networked computers to be viewed by an application as a single distributed-memory parallel machine. However, developing a *high performance* parallel application remains a specialist task, since parallel programs present complex modes of

---

*This project is funded by an EPSRC PSTPA programme, Grant Number : GR/K40468 and also by EC Contract Num: CIPA-C193-0251, CP-93-5383

behaviour which are difficult to predict *a priori*. In particular, the issues of partitioning the application into processes, and subsequently mapping those processes onto processors of the target computer system, to achieve optimal performance, remains the responsibility of the program designer. Optimality of performance is not guaranteed following a port to another platform, which may have very different characteristics. In essence, the application must be re-engineered for every platform. The problems can be exacerbated in the case of network programming, where there is a need to account for the variable workload of the network which is not dedicated exclusively to the processing of a single application.

Rapid prototyping is a useful approach to the design of high-performance software in that algorithms, outline designs, or even rough schemes can be evaluated at a relatively early stage in the development life-cycle, with respect to possible platform configurations, and mapping strategies. Modifying configurations and mappings will permit the prototype design to be refined, and this process may continue in an evolutionary fashion throughout the life-cycle. Appropriate techniques for evaluating performance are required at each iteration however.

There are three principle approaches to *performance evaluation* of a distributed application: *measurement, analytical modelling and simulation* [2]. Measurement can only be achieved on existing systems and results are affected by a range of run-time environmental factors arising within the system and the measurement process itself. Analytical modelling – the development and study of models whose solutions are tractable to mathematical techniques – enable exact descriptions of system behaviour to be developed, but restrictions on system functionality and workload must usually be introduced to make the model solvable, resulting in loss of accuracy. Simulation – of models which are often analytically intractable – overcomes both these difficulties, enabling the behaviour of arbitrarily complex software and hardware systems to be tracked to any level of detail. Modelling abstractions are needed only to improve the performance of the simulation, but these are generally less restrictive than in the case of the analytical approach. Simulation thus helps the designer to identify those components which limit the capacity of the system (bottlenecks), and allows performance estimates of the application from the early stage of its conception to be obtained.

In the next section, we describe the state of the art on modelling tools. Then, in section 3, we present the technique used for developing simulations. Finally, our simulation model is presented and its validation in sections 4 and 5.

2 Parallel System Performance Modelling Tools

The current trend for parallel software modelling tools is to support all the software performance engineering activities in an integrated environment [3].

A typical toolset should be based on at least three principal tools: a graphical design tool, a simulation facility, and a visualisation tool. The last should coexist within the same environment as the first to allow information about the program behaviour to be related to its design. Many existing toolsets are comprised of only a subset of these tools and often, visualisation is a separate tool. The target parallel system is typically a transputer-based multiprocessor machine and the modelling of the operating system is usually not addressed (except in the PEPS toolset [4]).

One of the earliest toolsets for parallel programming was the Transim/Gecko [5, 6] toolset, developed under the Parsifal project at the University of Westminster. The designer can rapidly evaluate different designs of an occam-like program running on transputer-based multiprocessor with an animation-based representation of the resulting trace. Also, Gecko allows occam processes to be remapped graphically and to re-simulate the application. The Transim/Gecko approach has been the model for simulation based environment projects such as MIMD [7, 8] at the University of Edinburgh. MIMD (Multiple Instruction stream, Multiple Data stream) is a modelling environment to study the performance of parallel programs. MIMD is built on top of DEMOS [9] and Simula. DEMOS is an extension to Simula which contains classes suitable for discrete event simulations. MIMD provides classes for modelling message passing parallel programs on distributed memory architectures. The existing classes allow occam programs running on Transputer machines to be modelled. Both toolsets have similar features in common except that in MIMD an experimental framework has been defined in order to investigate the effects of varying certain parameters characterising a parallel program on its run-time behaviour. A more recent toolset, the HAMLET Application Development System [10] is a development environment for real-time applications based on transputers (primarily) and PowerPCs. The HAMLET toolset combines graphical design tools, simulation techniques, and performance traces. In particular, it consists of a design entry system, DES, a specification simulator, HASTE, a debugger and monitor, INQUEST, and a trace analysis tool, TATOO. The DES tool generates the design used for simulation which is identical with the design for target code generation. A key feature of HAMLET is the ability to produce a code suitable for the simulator and a code suitable for real execution from the same graphical design. Also, performance traces obtained from the simulation and from the monitoring tools have the same format, therefore the visualisation tool is suitable for simulation and monitoring. The limitation of this tool is with its hardware and software libraries which are restricted to transputers and PowerPCs. Another toolset developed at the University of Vienna is the PAPS toolset [11] (Performance Analysis of Parallel Systems) which aims to predict the performance of parallel programs running on parallel transputer architectures. The input models are the parallel program represented as a directed task graph, the specification of the multiprocessor system and a description onto which processor each task graph is mapped. The PAPS toolset automatically generates a discrete deterministic timed Petri net out of the parallel system specification. The simulation of the Petri net model produces a trace

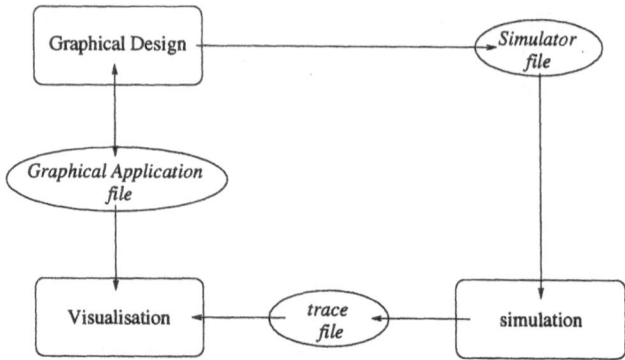

Figure 1: The EDPEPPS Architecture.

file and some statistical information about the program execution. The major differences between PAPS and the toolsets cited above are that the input models and the simulation model use a different formalism. Moreover some statistical information about the program execution is produced.

In the next projects, the target parallel system is assumed to be a virtual machine whereas the previous toolsets assume a physical machine. The PEPS project [4] aims to investigate benchmarks, modelling, characterisation, and monitoring of PVM programs for Transputer-based platforms. The aim of performance modelling in PEPS is to develop a tool for the performance evaluation of computer architectures. PEPS uses the Simulog simulation toolset including MODARCH which offers a range of software and hardware components. The library of objects allows PVM programs running on a network of transputers to be modelled. In this case, the model of PVM is much simpler than PVM within a heterogeneous distributed computing environment in which all nodes share a single communication medium and where contentions occur. One of the major challenges in PEPS is the modelling of the micro-kernel on each transputer. Also, a similar experimental framework such as in MIMD is provided. The SEPP project [12, 13] (Software Engineering for Parallel Processing) has developed an overall architecture based on five principal tool types: Static Design Tool; Dynamic Support Tools; Behaviour Analysis Tools; Simulation Tools; and Visualisation Tools. The programming model is a subset of the PVM programming paradigm.

3 Simulation in EDPEPPS

EDPEPPS [14] (Environment for Design and Performance Evaluation of Portable Parallel Software) is a tool research project at the University of Westminster which intermeshes with the SEPP project. EDPEPPS is based on a rapid prototyping philosophy, in which the designer synthesizes a model of the intended software, which may then be simulated, and the performance subsequently analysed using visualisation. The toolset combines a graphical design tool (PVM-

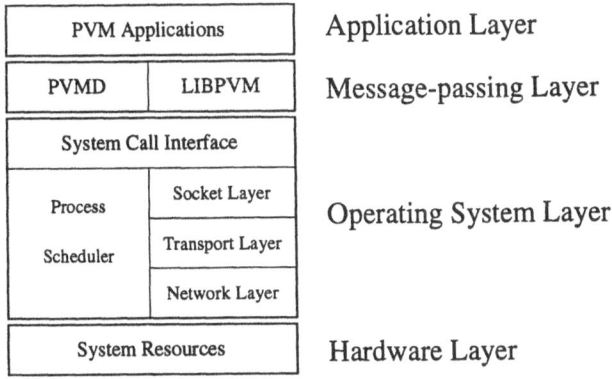

Figure 2: Simulation model architecture.

Graph), a simulation facility, and a visualisation tool (PVMVis). The same design is used to produce a code suitable for simulation and for real execution. The results of simulation are an event trace file and some statistical information about the virtual machine. The graphical design tool is based on the PVM programming model. Simulation of the PVM platform in EDPEPPS is built using the state of the art simulation environment, SES/Workbench^{TM} [15, 16].

Simulation in EDPEPPS is based on discrete-event modelling – a technique well-proven in the simulation of computer hardware and software. Discrete-event models underpin Transim for example, which achieves a remarkable degree of accuracy. The technology is well-established, and sophisticated modelling tools are available commercially. SES/Workbench, has wide functionality meeting the requirements of computer system modelling, a time-saving graphical design interface, and animation-based visualisation capabilities. Techniques for parallelising discrete-event simulation programs are well-established, thus providing a route for optimising the run-time performance of the simulator. The workbench is used both to develop, and simulate platform models. Thus the simulation engine in the workbench is an intrinsic part of the prototype EDPEPPS toolset. The design of the platform simulator is described in the following sections.

After developing our simulation model, a verification and validation step is necessary, in order to be sure that it gives relevant performance evaluation of the real system. Parts of our model validation have been conducted from the system resources layer to the application layer. Validation takes the forms of comparative measurement. In the case of Ethernet we compare our results against published measurements [17, 18].

4   Simulation model

The EDPEPPS simulation model consists of the PVM platform model library and the PVM programs for simulation. The PVM platform model is partitioned into three layers (Figure 2): the *message passing layer*, the *operating system layer* and the *hardware layer*. Modularity and extensibility are two key criteria in simulation modelling, therefore layers are decomposed into modules, which permits a re-configuration of the entire PVM platform model. The initial modelled configuration consists of a PVM environment which uses the TCP/IP protocol, and a cluster of heterogeneous workstations connected to a single 10 Mbit/s Ethernet network.

A PVM program generated by the PVMGraph graphical design tool, is translated and passed to the workbench, where it is integrated with the platform model in readiness for simulation. The next section defines the interface between PVMGraph and Workbench which is the SimPVM language.

4.1 SimPVM – A Simulation Oriented Language

PVMGraph allows PVM applications to be developed using a combination of graphical objects and text. From this description, executable PVM programs may be generated, but to *simulate* program execution, annotations must be inserted into the graphical/textual source to control the simulation. This allows both an executable and a "simulatable" version of the program to be generated from the same graphical/textual source. All simulation models in EDPEPPS are based on queueing networks. The "simulatable" code generated by PVM-Graph is predominantly a description of the software rather than the execution platform. To simulate the application, a model of the intended platform must be available. Thus, a simulation model is fundamentally partitioned into two submodels: a dynamic model automatically generated from the PVMGraph description, which is comprised of the application software description and some aspects of the platform (eg. number and type of hardware nodes); and a static model which represents the underlying parallel platform, to a suitable level of detail. By building the static descriptions into the simulation system itself, the service is transparent to the application designer, yet provides a virtual, simulation platform for the generated application.

The SimPVM language basically contains the following elements:

- the list of processes to be initially executed (*exec*), and the host (identification) number where they execute;

- the description of processes (*process*) and functions (*function*). In this version, processes cannot be parameterised;

- C instructions for variables declaration, loops (*for* and *while*), conditional instructions (*if else*), and assignments;

- PVM functions for process management (e.g. pvm_mytid and pvm_spawn), buffer management (e.g. pvm_getsbuf) and for point-to-point communication (e.g. pvm_send);

- simulation constructs such as computation delay function and statistical variables.

```
exec Master(0,1);                       process Master() {
                                          int mytid, tc, i, v[100];
process Slave() {                         mytid=pvm_mytid();
  int mytid, i;                           pvm_spawn("Slave", NULL, 0, NULL, 1, &tc);
  mytid=pvm_mytid();
  for (i=0; i<6000; i++)                  for (i=0; i<6000; i++) {
    pvm_recv(-1,-1);                        pvm_initsend(PvmDataRaw);
  pvm_exit();                               pvm_pkint(v,100,1);
}                                           pvm_send(tc,1);
                                          }
                                          pvm_exit();
                                        }
```

Figure 3: A SimPVM version of the Master-Slave program

SimPVM lies above the *libpvm* level of the platform model but some special functions are also provided that direct interaction with the kernel model. A SimPVM program is translated into an SES/Workbench simulation model where lines of the program are interpreted as simulation objects[1], which can be a *Reference* for a process, a *Call to a Reference* for the PVM functions, or a *Specific Node* for C instructions.

Figure 3 shows a detailed SimPVM version of a *Master-Slave* program.

4.2   The PVM Platform Model

The PVM message-passing layer models a single (parallel) virtual machine dedicated to a user and is composed of a daemon which resides on each host making up the virtual machine and the library which provides an interface to PVM services. The daemon acts primarily as a message router. It is modelled as an automaton or state machine which is a common construct for handling events. The life-cycle of the state machine corresponds to the main function of the daemon. It enters this loop after configuring itself. The library allows a task to interface with the daemon and other tasks. It contains functions for packing/unpacking messages, managing multiple buffers, message passing and process control. The library is structured into two layers. The top level layer includes most of the programming interface functions and the bottom level is the communication interface with the local daemon and other tasks.

The major components in the operating system layer are the System Call Interface, the Process Scheduler, and the Communication Module. The Communication Module is structured into 3 layers: the Socket Layer, the Transport Layer and the Network Layer. The Socket Layer provides a communications endpoint within a domain. The Transport Layer defines the communication protocol (either TCP or UDP). The Network Layer implements the Internet Protocol (IP) which acts as a message router.

---

[1] The SES/Workbench simulation model language is defined by graphical nodes

The Hardware Layer is comprised of hosts and the communications subnet. Each host is modelled as a single server queue with a time-sliced round-robin scheduling policy. The communications subnet is taken to be ethernet, whose performance depends on the number of active hosts and the packet characteristics. Resource contention is modelled using the CSMA/CD (Carrier Sense Multiple Access with Collision Detection) protocol. The basic notion behind this protocol is that a broadcast has two phases : propagation and transmission. During propagation, packet collisions can occur. During transmission, the carrier sense mechanism causes the other hosts to hold their packets.

5   Platform Model Verification and Validation

Model verification and validation are crucial steps in the simulation process. Functional modelling aims to reproduce the logical flow of the system being modelled (the target system). Functional model verification, whose aim is to ensure that the simulation program performs the target system functions correctly, is therefore similar to ordinary program debugging; program tracing and animation are two valuable techniques for this purpose. Once the functional model is verified, the next step is to model performance. The purpose of performance modelling is to establish timing and other parameters (by measuring the target system). This model is validated by exhaustive experimentation on the target system and the model with the aim of obtaining comparative measurements between the two.

The methodology adopted to validate the PVM platform model is a bottom-up approach. The components of the Hardware Layer are first separately validated in isolation from the other layers. Then the Operating System Layer is added and finally the Message-Passing Layer. For each layer, appropriate performance measures are defined and statistical components are added on top of each functional model to form a performance model.

Two sets of experiments have been conducted on the ethernet model. The configuration was as follows: 15 active nodes; 2500 meter cable length; 10Mb/s bus bandwidth. In the first experiment, the ethernet simulation model is compared with expected results published in the scientific literature [19, 20]. A Poisson arrival rate for a fixed packet length is assumed. In Figure 4, the ethernet offered load corresponds to the global load generated by each node. The diagram shows a collection of curves representing different packet lengths. Results from the literature correspond almost exactly to our simulation results (measured error less than 1% in all cases). The second experiment introduces a realistic ethernet workload [21] which is modelled as a bimodal distribution. In this case, we also observed similar results between simulation and published papers (again, measured error less than 1% in all cases). These experiments, although not conclusive, provisionally indicate a high degree of confidence in the validity of our ethernet model.

Experiments on the Communication Module within the Operating System Layer consisted of measuring the throughput of the UDP and TCP protocols on

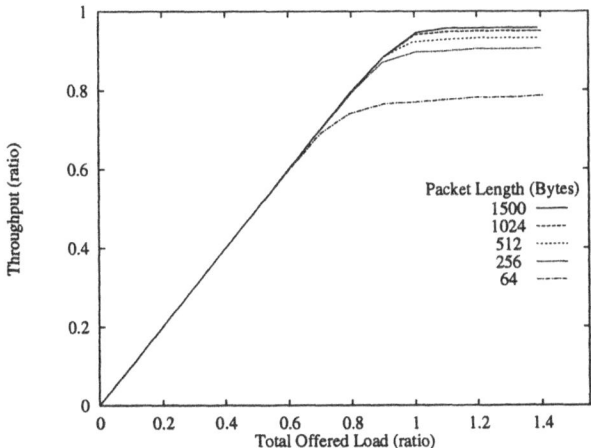

Figure 4: Simulated Ethernet Throughput.

both the existing network, and comparing with the simulator predictions. The communication rate of these protocols must be addressed because the Message-Passing Layer relies on both. An application consisting of two processes using sockets was developed to gather the measurements. The hardware configuration consisted of Sun with Solaris 2.4 (SS20) and Pentium with FreeBSD (P5-BSD) workstations. Three sets of tests were performed to obtain communication rates: two on TCP (one set inter-workstation and one set intra-workstation); and one set on UDP (inter-workstation). The UDP protocol is used to communicate between daemons and the TCP protocol is used to communicate between a daemon and its local tasks. The results of the UDP experiment are reported in Figure 5. This experiment was performed sending 6000 messages for each size on a load-free network. The communication time is divided into three parts: protocol time (UDP/IP) for the sender and for the receiver and the Ethernet time. The curve called *Communication model* represents the heterogeneous communication time in our simulation model. It is the sum of both *Protocol layer model (SS20 and P5-BSD)* and *Ethernet model* curves, which is the estimated time to communicate between an SS20 and a P5-BSD. The protocol layer model has been extracted using a multiple linear regression model by substracting the *experimental results* from the *Ethernet model*. The protocol layer model has been established using linear segments to represent the packet fragmentation. From Figure 5 it may be observed that in all cases, the results from the simulation runs and the real network matched to an error mean of 0.7% with a standard deviation of 0.25. We are really satified with the accuracy of this layer, because the error is mainly in the interval [0.45%, 0.95%].

Some validation of the Message-Passing Layer has also been carried out. Point-to-point PVM functions rely on the communication layers, and these functions were modelled faithfully in the simulation. To achieve some control over the experiment, a CPU time cost was substituted for all other PVM func-

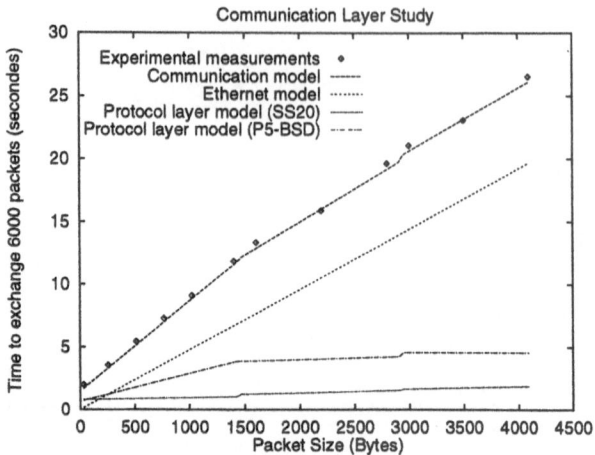

Figure 5: Example of a heterogeneous communication model for UDP protocol over Ethernet

PVM application	Communication Intensive	Computation Intensive
Real workstations in sec	30.5	1.5
Simulation model in sec	30	1.48
Differences (%)	1.7	1.3

Table 1: Execution time observed with two types of PVM application

tions (eg. packing functions) in the simulation. These costs were taken from earlier measurements on PVM. Experiments for two types of synthetic applications were conducted: one computation-intensive; and one communication-intensive. In the latter, two processes in a master/slave configuration (Fig. 3) exchange messages in both directions with multiple packet sizes. Measurements were taken for a virtual machine of two hosts. From these results (Table 1), it may be observed that the error was less than 2%. Although more validation experiments are planned, these early indications lead us to conclude that our PVM platform model is a reasonably accurate representation of the actual PVM message-passing environment.

6 Conclusion

This paper has described the simulation subsystem underpinning EDPEPPS, a toolset to support a performance-oriented parallel program design method. The toolset supports graphical design, performance prediction through modelling and simulation, and visualisation of predicted program behaviour. The designer is not required to leave the graphical design environment to view the program's behaviour, since the principal visualisation facility is an animation of the graphical program description, and the transition between design and visualisation viewpoints is virtually seamless. It is intended that this environment will encourage a philosophy of program *design*, based on a rapid synthesis-evaluation design cycle, in the emerging breed of parallel programmers.

Success of the environment depends critically on the accuracy of the underlying simulation system. Preliminary experiments for validating the PVM-based platform model have been very encouraging, demonstrating accuracy of the model to within 1-4%. Speed of simulator response, which is also a critical factor, will be addressed through parallelisation of the simulator.

Acknowledgements

The authors acknowledge Dr. George R.R. Justo for his participation to the EDPEPPS project. One of the authors (Thierry Delaitre) wishes to acknowledge the support and contributions of his supervisor, Dr. Stefan Poslad, in the simulation aspects of the work reported in this paper.

References

[1] A. Geist, A. Begueling, J. Dongarra, W. Jiang, R. Manchek, and V. Sunderam. *PVM: Parallel Virtual Machine*. MIT Press, 1994.

[2] Raj Jain. *The Art of Computer Systems Performance Analysis*. Wiley, 1991.

[3] C.M. Pancake, M.L. Simmons, and J.C. Yan. Performance evaluation tools for parallel and dsitributed systems. *Computer*, pages 16–19, November 1995.

[4] PEPS Partners. PEPS bulletin, the bulletin of the performance evaluation of parallel systems project. EEC PEPS Esprit 6942, May 1993.

[5] E.R. Hart and S.J. Flavell. Prototyping transputer applications. In *Real-Time Systems with transputers*, pages 241–247. IOS Press: Amsterdam, 1990.

[6] M. Stephenson and O. Boudillet. GECKO: A graphical tool for the modelling and manipulation of occam software and transputer hardware topologies. In C. Askew, editor, *Occam and the Transputer–Research and Applications*. Occam User Group Amsterdam, IOS press, 1990.

[7] N. Skilling. Mimd: A multiple instruction stream multiple data stream computer simulator. Technical Report TR9107.ps, University of Edinburgh (Dep. of Chemical Engineering), july 1991. chemg.ed.ac.uk:/pub/TechReports/91/tr9107.ps.

[8] R. Candlin and N. Skilling. A modelling system for the investigation of parallel program performance. *Computer Performance Evaluation*, 6(1):1–32, February 1992.

[9] G.M. Birtwistle. *Discrete Event Modelling on Simula*. Mamillan, London, 1986.

[10] P. Pouzet, J. Paris, and V. Jorrand. Parallel application design: The simulation approach with haste. In *High–Performance Computing and Networking*, volume 2, pages 379–393, International Conference and Exhibition, Munich, Germany, April 1994.

[11] H. Wabnig and G. Haring. PAPS: The parallel program performance prediction toolset. In *7th International Conference on Modelling Techniques and Tools for Computer Performance Evaluation*, 1994.

[12] S. C. Winter and P. Kacsuk. Software engineering for parallel processing. In A. Pataricza, editor, *The Eight Symposium on Microcomputer and Microprocessor Applications*, volume 1, pages 285–293, Budapest Technical University, october 1994.

[13] T. Delaitre, E. Luque, R. Suppi, and S. Taylor. Simulation of parallel systems in sepp. In A. Pataticza, editor, *The Eight Symposium on Microcomputer and Microprocessor Applications*, volume 1, pages 294–303, october 1994.

[14] T. Delaitre, G.R. Justo, F. Spies, and S. Winter. An environment for the design and performance evaluation of portable parallel software. Technical Report of the EDPEPPS project, EDPEPPS/6, University of Westminster, UK, Februrary 1996.

[15] Scientific and Engineering Software Inc. *SES/Workbench User's Manual, Release 2.1*. Scientific Engineering Software Inc., 4301 Westbank Drive, Austin TX 78746, February 1992.

[16] Scientific and Engineering Software Inc. *SES/workbench Reference Manual, Release 2.1*. Scientific Engineering Software Inc., 4301 Westbank Drive, Austin TX 78746, February 1992.

[17] N. Shacham and V. B. Hunt. Performance evaluation of the CSMA/CD (1-persistent) channel-access protocol in common-channel local networks. In *Local Computer Network, IFIP*, pages 401–414, 1982.

[18] D.K. Choi and B.G. Kim. The expected (not worst-case) throughput of the ethernet protocol. In *IEEE Transactions on Computers*, volume 40, pages 245–252, march 1991.

[19] N. Shacham and V. B. Hunt. Performance evaluation of the CSMA/CD (1-persistent) channel-access protocol in common-channel local networks. In *Local Computer Network, IFIP*, pages 401–414. North-Holland, 1982.

[20] F. A. Tobagi and V. B. Hunt. Performance analysis of carrier sense multiple access detection. In *Proceedings of the LACN symposium*, pages 217–245, May 1979.

[21] J.A. Hupp J.F. Schoch. Measured performance of an ethernet local network. *Comm. of the ACM*, 23(12):711–720, December 1980.

On Potential Software Support for a Three-Phase Development Process for Parallel Large-Scale Applications*

W.H.F.J. Körver

Computer Systems Research Group
Dept. of Electronic & Electrical Engineering, University of Surrey
Guildford, United Kingdom

J.P. Geschiere

High Performance Computing Division
Department of Computer Science, Leiden University
Leiden, The Netherlands

Abstract

In earlier work we presented a structured process for the development of large-scale parallel applications and a supporting underlying formal framework which is based on a DAG-like structure extended with data- and control-dependences. The applicability of this process strongly relies on the manageability of the diverse steps which, for this reason, concentrate each on one development aspect only. This paper proposes a number of tools which can support the process in each of the three main stages and which allow a further precision and structure of various steps, thereby leading to an improvement of the decisions that need to be made. It also discusses subsequent improvements on the process which become feasible by the proposed software support and explains how this will eventually lead to an interactive software support for the entire process.

1 Introduction

The development of parallel large-scale application codes is a challenging problem, not only because of the large number of mutually dependent parallelism aspects involved, but also because it requires a combination of application, parallelism, and software engineering knowledge. It will be clear that the manageability of such a development process is extremely important, especially due to the complexity caused by the input-dependences in large-scale applications and the required platform-dependences in the parallel algorithm.

In [3, 4], we proposed a structured software engineering methodology for the development of large-scale parallel application software, including an underlying, supporting formal framework to express and manipulate potential parallelism, directed to the distributed and shared memory machine models.

---

*This research was supported by the EC 'Eurochip' project.

The research reported in [3, 4] on this three-phase development process, and the extensive case studies presented in [4], can be regarded as an exploration of the validity, manageability, and applicability of the process. The current state of the development process turned out to be a valid one and proved its applicability in practice, where the formal framework demonstrated its value both as a conceptual tool and by providing formal guidelines.

The applicability of the methodology relies on the organised structure of the process, the manageability of the various steps, and the successful support by the underlying formal framework. However, in view of this manageability, a number of mutually related parallelism aspects have been directed to different (consecutive) steps, whereas combining them could improve the design decisions that have to be made. In order to combine these aspects without affecting the manageability of the individual steps, this paper proposes software support for the various phases of the development process.

The paper advocates a structured, stepwise development of the supporting software. It initially proposes three separate tools which fit in the current structure of the development process and whose implementation does not require further research. These tools are subsequently combined and extended to offer additional support for the most crucial steps of the process.

The first tool administrates the analysis data and generates the DMDAG, which expresses the potential parallelism in the application. Since this data and the DMDAG are required and updated throughout the process, this tool supports the process in all phases. The second tool supports the scheduling of the DMDAG by three types of simulation: *task-based* to detect the critical factors for the scheduling; *cluster-based* to make a pre-selection of scheduling-options; and *mapping-based* to evaluate these options. The third tool computes the parallelism-specific implementation requirements for the DMDAG per implementation step and thereby structures the iterative implementation and verification steps of the process. It is important to note that the tools also enable an automatic generation of the design documentation of the diverse steps.

The extensions of the tools lead to restructuring the process and are related to the following steps: the choice of tasks for the DMDAG; the estimations for the execution times and delays in the DMDAG; and the scheduling of the DMDAG. The paper explains how, in the restructured process, the combination of the initial tools together with these extensions will eventually lead to a well-balanced interactive development environment.

Organisation of the paper

Section 2 gives a short overview of the underlying formal framework and the structure of the development process from [3, 4]. The three initial tools are described in Section 3, where the formal framework is used to explain their validity and feasibility. Section 4 explains how the three most crucial decisions in our development process are supported by the initial tools, suggests further software support, and re-considers the structure of the process. Finally, Section 5 makes a number of concluding remarks.

2   The development process

The development process described in [3, 4] consists of three main stages: analysis, parallelisation and optimisation. These phases are divided in a number of well-defined steps, contain feedback-loops, and are strongly supported by the underlying formal framework which provides a medium to express the information that is required for the development process and which defines the rules or structures the heuristics used in the individual steps. By the latter the formal framework lays the basis for well-specified software to support the diverse steps. This section gives an introduction to the formal framework and discusses the structure of the development process based on it.

2.1   The formal framework

In [3, 4] we extended the traditional notion of DAGs (Directed Acyclic Graphs, [6]) in order to express and manipulate potential parallelism. The extensions are directed to distributed and shared memory for which they are called DMDAG and SMDAG respectively, and capture both conditional execution order as well as a variant of the traditional data dependences (eg. [1, 8]). The nodes in these graphs are either *tasks* or *selections*, where a task represents a computational unit that reads input initially and produces output eventually, and a selection represents a control unit which determines which part of the graph is to be executed. The possible execution orders are determined by the (directed) edges in the graph which represent control- and data dependences, where the former connect selections to tasks, and the latter connect tasks to tasks and selections. The task-to-task dependences come in two flavours: *hard dependences*, which prescribe a strict execution order independent of the scheduling of the tasks; and *soft dependences*, which prescribe an execution order only when the same memory is used. A DMDAG is defined as follows[1].

A DMDAG is a quintuple $\langle T, S, tt, ts, sp \rangle$, where

T and S are the sets of tasks and selections respectively;

$tt \subset T \times \{h, s\} \times T$ denotes dependences between tasks, where $u \xrightarrow{h} v$ denotes a hard dependence, and $u \xrightarrow{s} v$ denotes a soft dependence from u to v;

$ts \subset T \times S$ denotes (hard) dependences from tasks to selections;

$sp \subset S \times \mathcal{P}(T \cup S)$ denotes control dependences, which may be labelled with a guard. Elements (s_1, U) and (s_2, V) of sp must satisfy

$$(\{s_1\} \cup U \subseteq V) \vee (\{s_2\} \cup V \subseteq U) \vee (U \cap V = \emptyset);$$

$\langle T \cup S, tt \cup ts \cup sp' \rangle$ is a DAG, where $((s, u) \in sp') \Leftrightarrow (\exists U : u \in U : (s, U) \in sp)$.

A tt-dependence indicates that the tasks in question use a common data set. A *hard* dependence $u \xrightarrow{h} v$ indicates that v requires the version of the common data that is produced by u. Consequently, a hard dependence induces a strict execution order of the tasks, and if the tasks are allocated to different processors

---

[1]The interpretation of the notions that are explained is slightly different for SMDAGs, but these differences are irrelevant for this paper; for details we refer to [4].

also a communication action. A *soft* dependence induces an execution order only if the same copy of the common data set (the same memory) is used; it is required if, for instance, u has to consume an old version of the common data whereas v produces a new version. A *ts*-dependence $v \longrightarrow s$ denotes that selection s uses data produced by task v. Selections have at least one outgoing control dependence, where a control dependence (s, U) with guard P denotes that if P holds when s is executed, then the subgraph with nodes U will be executed. The condition on *sp*-dependences that is given in the definition above denotes that selections either have disjoint *sp*-subgraphs, or are nested.

Similar as in DAGs, the execution time of a task u is expressed as $x(u)$ and the communication time of a hard dependence from task u to task v is expressed as $\tau(u, v)$. The (relatively small) execution times of selections and synchronisation times of soft dependences are usually neglected.

The formal framework in [4] expresses high-level protocols which define general implementation requirements for DMDAGs and SMDAGs. These protocols are illustrated below. The formalism is also used to explain how to transform these graphs such that potential parallelism is added at the cost of memory-use. The rules for these transformations are explained in Section 3.1.

Implementation protocols

A *schedule* assigns the DMDAG nodes that must be executed to processors. For a specific execution path given by a subset A of *sp* that selects one outgoing *sp*-dependence per selection, the set of DMDAG nodes that must be executed is called $TS(A)$ and contains all tasks and selections except those in non-selected *sp*-subgraphs: $TS(A) = (T \cup S) \backslash (\cup U : (\exists s : (s, U) \in sp \backslash A))$.

The high-level protocols explained in [4] define implementation requirements for DMDAGs and SMDAGs which are independent of the specific schedule and number of processors and abstract from the specific programming environment. They are illustrated below by the requirements for tasks in case of unique task-allocation ([4] also considers multi-allocation). The complete protocol also contains requirements for communication actions and selections, and dynamically updates: an initially only partly given schedule; set TS discussed above; and 'Finished'-variables for tasks and *receive* actions (which are initially false).

Let the schedule be (at least partly) given as $TP(v)$ for tasks and $SP(s)$ for selections, with $TP(v) = 0$ and $SP(s) = \emptyset$ if v and s are not yet scheduled. Of course, we assume that the schedule is given up to –at least– the first selection, and that *control-directions* are available that prescribe how to schedule further (how to update TP and SP) depending on the selection choices made. The implementation requirements for tasks are now explained as follows.

Processor X is only allowed to execute tasks v with $TP(v) = X$. Whether a task v can be executed depends further on the incoming *tt*-dependences only. A dependence between tasks that are scheduled to the same processor prescribes an execution order, which means that Finished(u) must hold for each $u \longrightarrow v$ with $TP(u) = TP(v)$ before v can be executed. Since external soft dependences do not prescribe an execution order, they have no consequences for the protocol.

For a hard dependence $u \xrightarrow{h} v$ with $TP(u) \neq TP(v)$, the data from u must be received before v can be executed. Consequently, task v must be guarded by[2]

$$
\begin{aligned}
G(v) \;\Leftrightarrow\; &(TP(v) = X) \land \\
&(\forall u : u \longrightarrow v \land TP(u) = TP(v) : \text{Finished}(u)) \land \\
&(\forall u : u \xrightarrow{h} v \land TP(u) \neq TP(v) : \text{Finished}(receive(u,v))).
\end{aligned}
$$

The outgoing tt and ts dependences of task v lead to a protocol that has to be performed after task v is completed. In view of dependences to tasks and selections that are scheduled to the same processor, the value Finished(v) must be updated. For each external outgoing hard dependence (to tasks as well as to selections), the corresponding data must be send to the appropriate processors. This leads to the following exit protocol for task v^3.

$$
\begin{aligned}
exit(v) \;=\; (\,&\text{Finished}(v) := \textit{true}; \\
&(\forall w, i : v \xrightarrow{h} w \land i \in TP(w) \backslash TP(v) : \text{`}send(v,w,i)\text{'}); \\
&(\forall s, i : v \longrightarrow s \land i \in SP(s) \backslash TP(v) : \text{`}send(v,s,i)\text{'}))
\end{aligned}
$$

The complete implementation requirement for task v now becomes

$$
\underline{if}\;\; G(v) \;\; \underline{then} \;\; \text{`execute } v\text{'}; exit(v) \;\; \underline{fi}.
$$

2.2   The structure of the development process

The first of the three main phases of the development process [3, 4] analyses the application and expresses its potential parallelism in a DMDAG (or SMDAG). The second phase determines schedules for this DMDAG and uses the implementation protocols from Section 2.1 to structure and guide a manageable stepwise implementation. The third phase evaluates and possibly optimises the parallel software. This section discusses the global structure of the process (see Figure 1) and points at the causes for complexity. For details on the individual steps we refer to [4]. Where necessary, such details are given in the following sections.

Phase I: analysis

The process starts with a hierarchical algorithmic description ($\top$) of the application in terms of its subsystems and a *sound* execution order. This description is used in phase I to infer a DMDAG (expressing the *necessary* execution order) and additional information required for phases II and III. Steps 1–4 investigate the subsystems and estimate their computation size. Based on that, tasks are chosen as original subsystems (at some hierarchical level) or as groups of consecutive subsystems (heuristics for task choice are discussed in Section 4.1). The data-usage analysed in step 5 (cf. Table 1) is used for the dependence analysis

---

[2]Since only those tasks and selections that are in TS are relevant for the execution, all quantifications over tasks or selections are per default over those in TS.

[3]The *send* and *receive* actions are denoted informally, their general form is *send*(sender-node, message, receiver-node, receiver-processor). The redundant arguments are omitted.

in step 6 and the transformations of the DMDAG in Phase II. The formal rules for the dependence analysis and the transformations are given in Section 3.1.

The complexity in steps 1–5 is caused by a possible lack of detail in T, by the difficulty to judge at this stage which tasks may cause scheduling or performance problems (and should be decomposed further), and by the input- and platform-dependences of computation and communication sizes. It is important to note that the estimates for computation and communication sizes are used to determine the schedules for the DMDAG as a result of which poor estimates will cause poor performance later (see Phase III).

Information	Derived in	Used for (where)
tasks and selections	Step 4	DMDAG nodes
original execution order	Steps 1-4	dep. direction (Step 6)
computation sizes tasks	Step 3	the x of tasks (Step 6)
common data sets	Step 5 ⌐	⌐ tt-dependences and
size of common data sets	Step 5 →|	the τ for the hard
input & output of tasks	Step 5 ⌐|	⌊ dependences (Step 6)
input of selections	Step 5 ⌐→|	ts-dependences (Step 6)
DMDAG	Step 6	(Phases II and III)
alternative DMDAGs	Phase II	(Phases II and III)

Table 1: Analysis data and its purpose

Phase II: parallelisation

Steps 7 and 8 investigate scheduling options with the help of the information derived in Phase I. The scheduling problem is complex for traditional DAGs [2, 6], but even more so here due to the input dependences in DMDAGs and the platform dependences of good schedules. Phase II uses the practical scheduling technique *clustering* [2, 5, 7], which consists of two phases: (1) clustering, which groups tasks in clusters (to be scheduled to the same processor); and (2) creating the various cluster-to-processor mappings. Since parts of both the clustering and the mapping can be input and platform dependent, algorithms are designed to produce (parts of) them at runtime. Their efficiency and the quality of the makespans of the resulting schedules are essential. An additional criterion is the way the cluster choice enables a stepwise implementation.

Heuristics for detecting cluster-options are discussed in [4] and summarised in Section 3.2. They are partly based on the criteria for the clustering evaluation (step 8), of which the most important are the efficiencies of the resulting schedules and mapping algorithms. Secondary criteria are: the relative workloads of clusters; the spreading of the workload per cluster; the relative numbers of clusters and processors; the timing of inter-cluster dependences; the similarity of the clusters; the flexibility (wrt. input/platform) and dynamic nature of the mappings; and the manageability of their implementation (cf. [4]).

In the remainder of phase II, the schedule-independent high-level implementation protocols structure and guide iterative implementation and verification steps. The heuristics for detecting suitable implementation steps (step 9) are discussed in [4]. Software support for steps 9–11 is discussed in Section 3.3.

Phase III: optimisation

The choices in Phases I and II and therefore also the DMDAG and its schedules are based on estimated execution times (x) and delays (τ), whose real values generally are input- and platform-dependent. The derived schedules may therefore lead to performance problems which can only be detected during execution. The evaluation and possibly optimisation of the parallel algorithm takes place in Phase III. For a discussion on the most important optimisation techniques, their implementation, and their verification we refer to [4].

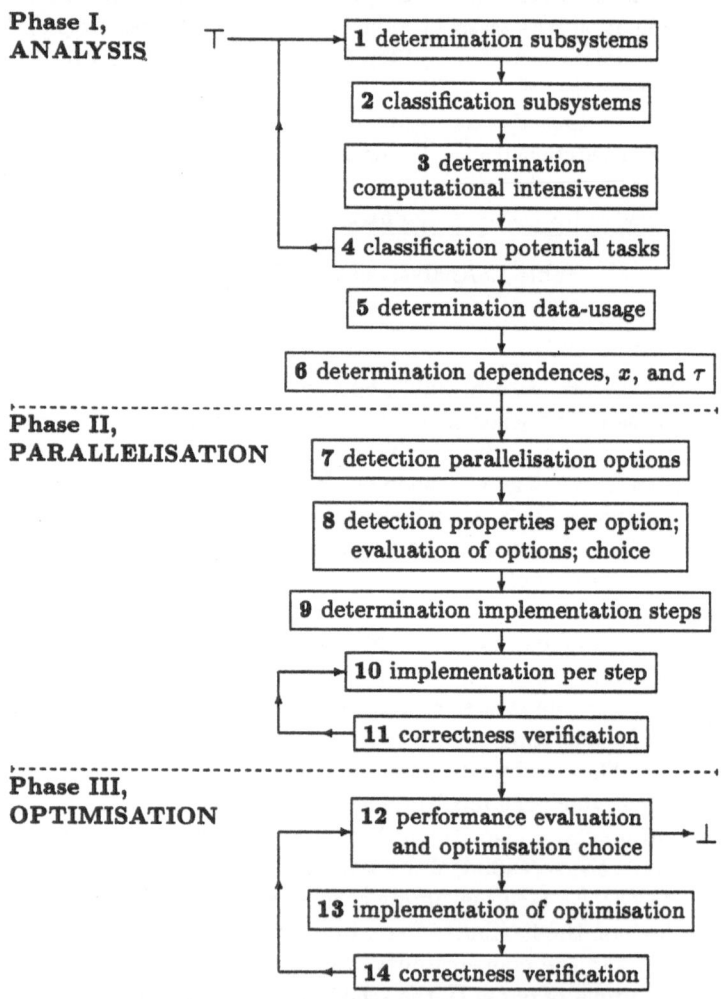

Figure 1: Structure of the Development Process

3 Initial software support

This section discusses initial software support for the development process that can be implemented without further research on the mutual relations of the parallelism aspects involved and without restructuring the process. The intended tools support the analysis, the cluster and mapping choice and evaluation, and the implementation steps respectively. The next section combines these tools, discusses additional, more advanced software to support the various steps, and explains how this then enables us to restructure and improve the process without affecting the manageability of the individual steps.

3.1 Analysis support

Besides the complexity of the analysis phase mentioned in Section 2.2 regarding the choice of tasks and of workable but reliable estimates for the computation and communication sizes (for which support is discussed in Section 4.1), the case studies in [4] also exhibited more practical difficulties in phase I related to the amount of analysis data that is essential for the process, the updating hereof in the next phases, and the routine, but error-prone operations on it.

The initial task of the tool proposed in this section is the administration of the analysis data. Further, the tool can automatically generate the DMDAG for a given choice of tasks (which is based on strict rules) and updates the analysis data and the DMDAG in view of the transformations of the DMDAG in phase II. The latter is essential for the parallelisation and implementation steps. This tool serves as the basis for the tools proposed in Sections 3.2 and 3.3.

The data analysed in phase I is used and updated at various stages of the development process and should be registered by the intended tool. The data analysed in steps 1–5 is the following (cf. Table 1).

A1. The hierarchical structure of the subsystems thus far investigated, their original execution order and rough estimates for their computation time (a graphical representation hereof will structure steps 1–4);

A2. The chosen tasks and selections (the DMDAG-nodes);

A3. The data-usage of the tasks and selections: the common data sets; the input of selections and the in/output of tasks in terms of these sets;

A4. Estimates for the computation sizes of tasks (possibly input-dependent);

A5. Estimates for the sizes of the common data sets per task and selection (possibly depending on the input (-size)).

The dependences of the DMDAG (with *A2* the complete DMDAG) can be generated from items *A1–A3* (explained below). Items *A4* and *A5* are translated into computation times and delays (cf. Section 2.2). The tool should support and verify this translation. Since this information is crucial throughout the process it should also be registered, leading to the following items:

A6. The dependences and complete structure of the DMDAG (a graphical representation hereof will support phases II and III, cf. Sections 3.2 and 4);

A7. The computation times (of tasks, x) and delays (of hard dependences, τ).

The intended tool can generate the dependences (item $A6$) automatically from data items $A1$–$A3$ by strictly applying the following derivation rules.

$R1$. The direction of each dependence equals the original execution order;

$R2$. If task t produces data for selection s, then (ts-dependence) $t \rightarrow s$;

$R3$. If the set of tasks U forms a selection alternative of s, then $(s, U) \in sp$;

$R4$. If u outputs the version of data-set d that v inputs, this leads to a *hard* tt-dependence $u \xrightarrow{h} v$ on d;

$R5$. A *soft* tt-dependence $u \xrightarrow{s} v$ on d exists if either (1) or (2) holds, where
   (1) d is input but *no* output of u and output (possibly also input) of v,
   (2) d is output (possibly also input) of u and output but *no* input of v;

$R6$. The transitive closure of all tt-dependences on d derived by rules $R4$ and $R5$ leads to additional *soft* dependences.

The rules are explained by the interpretation of DMDAGs given in Section 2.1. The tt-dependences are defined per data-set, where the dependences derived by rules $R4$, $R5(1)$, and $R5(2)$ relate to 'flow dependences', 'antidependences', and 'output dependences' respectively in the terminology from [1, 8, 9]. The tt-dependences from rule $R6$ are induced by the others.

The transformations of the DMDAG, by which potential parallelism is added at the cost of memory use, provide a useful technique to improve clusterings (phase II) or to optimise the algorithm (phase III). They are based on data-set renamings and eliminate soft tt-dependences (explained below). Since dependences are essential for the evaluation and implementation of the algorithm, the tool should update items $A3$ and $A6$ when transforming the DMDAG.

Since a soft dependence $u \xrightarrow{s} v$ from rule $R5$ expresses 'only' a requirement on memory access order (in contrast to hard dependences, which express a data-exchange requirement), the dependence can be avoided by using two copies of the common data set: one for u and one for v. This is done by renaming the data-set in the output of task v thereby forcing the implementation of an extra copy (note that $R5$ no longer applies). The renaming carries forth to the successors of v, and leads (via $R6$) to the elimination of other soft dependences. Since both the renamings and the elimination of soft dependences are defined by simple, obvious rules, the tool can easily be extended to update data items $A3$ and $A6$. (For a full discussion on transformations we refer to [4].)

Advantages of the proposed analysis tool

The tool avoids the tedious manual registration of analysis data and the error-prone manual generation of the DMDAG, thereby enabling the developer to concentrate on the main issues of phase I. Further, it becomes feasible to generate a DMDAG for a potential choice of tasks in step 4 to judge its efficiency, an aspect that is discussed further in Section 4.1. In addition to these advantages the tool can easily generate the required design documentation for phase I as items $A1$–$A7$ form the core hereof. In phases II and III, the tool enables the developer to efficiently try out transformations of the DMDAG whereby the graphical representation of the DMDAG provides the required overview.

3.2   Scheduling support

For the scheduling of DMDAGs we use the clustering technique (cf. Section 2.2), which first groups tasks in clusters and then maps clusters to processors. The detection of cluster-options is done by heuristics (see [4] for an overview) which take different perspectives: they can aim at a cluster structure that reflects the structure of the DMDAG (reflection-heuristic, [4]); consider the computation vs. communication costs ratio [2]; aim at minimising the communication costs (eg. the 'owner-computes rule') and eliminating communication bottlenecks; or create independent tasks (transformations of the DMDAG, Section 3.1).

As the scheduling of the DMDAG is crucial for the success of a development process and can be extremely difficult (cf. the second case study in [4]), it is important to have –in addition to the heuristics– as good software support as possible. This section proposes an interactive simulation tool that can assist in detecting the factors that cause the complexity of the scheduling of a particular DMDAG as well as in detecting reasonable cluster- and corresponding mapping options, and which provides a means to evaluate the alternative options without actually implementing them. The intended simulation takes place at different stages of the detection and evaluation of the clusters and mappings, which are described in detail below. Although the tool can indicate the (stage-specific) problem areas and can assist in these steps, the heuristics and evaluation criteria should form the main guidelines. Section 4.1 discusses extensions of this tool that further assist these steps (7 and 8) as well as step 4 (task choice).

Obviously, the simulation is, as the steps themselves, based on the –possibly poor– *estimates* for the execution times and delays (phase I). This partly inherent disadvantage of parallel software design is addressed in Section 4.2.

Task-based simulation

In the first stage, the tool simulates the DMDAG while assuming an infinite number of processors. It uses the computation times x of tasks and the delays τ of hard dependences to compute the critical paths and the makespan (overall execution time) of a schedule for a given (input-dependent) execution path. The simulation takes place as follows: each task is scheduled in time as early as possible in view of the dependences, where the delays of hard dependences of tasks that are not (yet) explicitly scheduled to different processors are taken to be 0 (even if this means that specific processors perform multiple tasks simultaneously). For tasks that are explicitly scheduled to the same processor, the tool provides the option to either perform the tasks simultaneously or use a given priority order. The tool can now indicate the critical tasks (the ones on the longest paths) and compute the makespan. In order to provide as much flexibility as possible the simulation can, besides ignoring the delays of some or all of the hard dependences as described above, also ignore some or all of the soft dependences (important wrt. the DMDAG-transformations).

The main goals of the tool are to provide an overview of the tasks and data-communications that may cause scheduling problems and to assist in detecting reasonable cluster-options. For the latter the following strategies can be used. The first strategy starts with a simulation that ignores all communication delays (regards hard dependences as synchronisations), and then gradually introduces them by deciding on task-to-processor mappings in an order contrary to the execution order while aiming at a minimal makespan at each step. This strategy resembles the proof structure in [6] and generally leads to a reasonable schedule under the assumption that sufficiently many processors are available. The second strategy is similar but concentrates first on the mapping of tasks that are on multiple critical paths (which can be indicated by the tool). It is important to note that these strategies do not guarantee finding a good clustering and are merely intended as additional support when applying the heuristics, in which the strategies indicate the problem factors. By the gradual introduction of the delays and mappings they naturally lead to the following stage of simulation.

Cluster-based simulation

Once a number of cluster-options are selected, each option can be simulated by mapping each cluster to a different processor (still assuming sufficiently many of them) while regarding the inter-cluster delays. The various possible execution orders inside each cluster (of independent tasks) can now be simulated, where the developer should indicate which execution path (dictated by the selections) should be chosen (this is a general aspect of simulation). This stage intends to detect the problematic inter-cluster communications, give an impression as to which clusters can be mapped together, and enable a pre-selection of cluster-options before going to the time-consuming next stage.

Mapping-based simulation

The third stage of simulation offers support for the evaluation of cluster-options and the detection and evaluation of the cluster-to-processor mappings for various numbers of processors. The intended simulation computes the makespan of a specific mapping for a given cluster-option. In this stage it is important to test the quality of the cluster- and mapping options for as many relevant inputs and configurations (incl. the number of processors) as possible. However, the usually large number of input-dependences in a DMDAG will force the developer to indicate priorities in the execution paths to be simulated. In view of manageability it is also important to make a rapid selection of the most promising options by simulating the most common configurations first.

3.3 Implementation support

Step 9 of our development process (Figure 1) determines a stepwise implementation strategy that ensures the manageability of the iterative implementation and verification steps (heuristics for detecting a suitable strategy are given in [4]). The actual implementation steps are not so much theoretically difficult, but are inherently tedious and error-prone (hence the iterative verification by step 11). For the evaluation of an implementation strategy (step 9) and for each implementation step (step 10) it is vital to have a precise overview of the implementation requirements per step. The tool we propose in this section computes these requirements for specific cluster choices and specific implementation steps using the high-level implementation protocols from Section 2.1.

The parallelism-specific implementation requirements for each task and each selection follow directly from the protocols given in [4] (see Section 2.1). For a particular cluster choice or a specific implementation step these protocols can be simplified in that only part of the communications and synchronisations that correspond to tt-dependences needs to be implemented (explained below). Such savings on the general protocol minimise the parallel-specific implementation overhead per step and thereby simplify the corresponding verification.

To illustrate the saving of *communications* (from *hard* dependences), let u and v with $u \overset{h}{\to} v$ be in the same cluster (permanently by the cluster choice or transiently by the implementation step). Since u and v will be scheduled to the same processor ($TP(u) = TP(v)$ in the protocol), their *send* and *receive* actions need not (yet) be implemented (cf. $G(v)$ and $exit(v)$ in Section 2.1). In general, only the *inter-cluster* communications have to be implemented.

To illustrate the saving of *synchronisations* (from *soft* dependences), let u, v and w be in the same cluster and let soft dependences $u \overset{s}{\to} v$ and $v \overset{s}{\to} w$ exist by rule *R5*. Since the tasks will be scheduled to the same processor, the dependences lead to explicit synchronisations 'v after u' and 'w after v' (enforced in the protocol by the 'Finished(u/v)' in the guard $G(v/w)$ of v/w). Consequently, the induced dependence $u \overset{s}{\to} w$ by rule *R6* is vacuous in that u and w are already synchronised, and therefore the implementation requirement resulting from it, 'Finished(u)' in $G(w)$, need not (yet) be implemented. In general, the transitive closure in *R6* need only consider the paths of *R4*- and *R5*-dependences where the intermediate tasks are not in the same cluster as the start or the end task. (Note: this rule also avoids the implementation of $u \overset{s}{\to} w$ above if only u and v or only v and w are in the same cluster.)

Notice that whereas the first rule saves the tedious implementation of *send* and *receive* actions (and the corresponding gathering and scattering of data), the implementation effort saved by the second rule seems little. However, it is important for the possible debugging in step 11 to avoid unnecessary code to be able to concentrate on effective operations only.

Advantages of the proposed implementation tool

The tool computes and administrates the implementation requirements for each implementation step. Although the simplifications of the general protocol are defined per cluster choice and implementation step by strict rules, computing them manually is cumbersome and distracts from the main issues of steps 9–11. The proposed tool therefore structures the evaluation of implementation strategies in step 9, helps to minimise the implementation effort in step 10, and as pointed out above, simplifies the possible debugging in step 11. Further, as before, the registration done by the tool is required for the design documentation.

4 Further software support and restructuring of the process

The choice of tasks for the DMDAG (step 4) and the choice of schedules (steps 7 and 8) are two of the most crucial decisions in the development process as the former determines the *potential parallelism* in the DMDAG and the latter determines in how far this parallelism is exploited for the various hardware configurations. Although they are separated in the current process (cf. Figure 1), they are inherently related: it is clearly impossible in steps 7 and 8 to exploit more parallelism than expressed in the DMDAG and moreover, it is difficult to foresee the critical factors for the schedules (in terms of tasks and dependences) at the time of task choice (step 4). Section 4.1 addresses these steps and their relation and discusses how software support can make it feasible (wrt. manageability) to link the steps in an iterative decision process.

The estimates for the execution times and delays (step 6 based on steps 3 and 5) represent the third of the most crucial parts of the development process as the task and scheduling choices and thereby the quality of the parallelism in the algorithm depend on them. They are especially difficult to make because the computation and communication sizes can be strongly input- and platform-dependent (cf. [4]). The latter is the main cause for optimisations in phase III, where, however, it is hardly manageable (and excluded in the current process) to make major changes in the task and scheduling choices. Section 4.2 discusses how the proposed tools structure phase III in general and in particular how they can assist in reconsidering the task and scheduling choices.

4.1 Further analysis and parallelisation support

In the analysis phase, the original description ($\top$) is decomposed into subsystems, tasks are chosen, and their data-usage is determined in terms of common data-sets, whose precision is important to minimise dependences between tasks. The most important criterion for the choice of tasks and the precision in data-sets is the quality of the schedules for the corresponding DMDAG, where restricting factors are the detail in $\top$ and the manageability of a large amount of analysis data. Consequently, the heuristics for the task and data-set choices are related to the heuristics and evaluation criteria for schedules. These heuristics therefore regard the following aspects: the computation sizes of tasks (in view of flexibility wrt. clustering and workload distribution); the number, position, and communication sizes of the dependences (wrt. critical paths, the relative timing of communication actions, and communication bottlenecks); the relative position of tasks in the DMDAG (eg. regarding critical paths); and the global form of the DMDAG (eg. breadth in view of the amount of parallelism).

In view of the manageability of phase I, these heuristics are only partly included in the current process (cf. Figure 1). However, the analysis and simulation tools (Sections 3.1 and 3.2) enable to manage more analysis data and to simulate –at least partially– a DMDAG for a *potential* choice of tasks in order to detect possible critical tasks and dependences. Consequently, it is possible to consider more of the heuristics in the task and data-set choices in phase I. Notice that this leads to an iterative decision process where potential schedules are (partially) regarded at the time of task and data-set determination. An additional advantage of this is that, whereas it is extremely difficult in many cases to decompose tasks in phase I in order to obtain the required information regarding data usage or logic subsystems, the iterative process can assist in deciding whether such an analysis might be profitable and, consequently, whether it should be done. The iterative decision process can be expressed in Figure 1 by a feedback loop from steps 6, 7, or 8 to steps 4 and 5.

The software support for such an iteration can be extended further by formalising the heuristics above within the formal framework (as they are currently partially informal), which will enable us to incorporate them at various stages in the simulation tool. In a similar way, a further formalisation of the heuristics and evaluation criteria for scheduling can lead to extending this tool such that it can advise in detecting or improving good schedules. Current research therefore investigates these formalisations to improve the development process where the tool support must ensure that the manageability is not affected.

4.2 Optimisation support and the process structure

The estimates for the computation time x of tasks and the communication delays τ of hard dependences (step 6) are based on the computation size of tasks (determined in step 3 by functional, procedural, or experimental analysis) and the sizes of the common data sets (step 5) respectively. Their actual values, however, can vary per machine (processor type, latency, bandwidth), per input (characteristics, size) and even per run (in case of collisions), and moreover, they may relate differently per machine. Consequently, the estimates made in phase I (and used in phase II) will often prove inaccurate in the resulting implementation. This drawback leads to the optimisations in phase III, where, however, although it is relatively straightforward to adjust the (cluster-to-processor) mappings, it is difficult to adjust the cluster and task choices.

For manageability reasons, the current process excludes that major adjustments in the cluster and mapping choices are made in phase III. However, due to the tools, such adjustments can become manageable: where the simulation tool can assist in making a rapid evaluation of the possible optimisations, the implementation tool can compute the required changes in the parallelism-specific implementation parts. For the process structure in Figure 1 this means that a global feedback loop from the later to the earlier steps is included.

As a further improvement of the development process, current research aims at combining the implementation and optimisation phases in order to detect and perform optimisations in an as early stage as possible, and to guide the choice of implementation steps to minimise the complexity of the corresponding verification and debugging steps. Together with the changes in the structure of the process proposed in the previous section, this will eventually lead to combined analysis–parallelisation and implementation–optimisation phases, with extended, interactive software support for the entire development process.

5 Concluding remarks

Whereas the work in [3, 4] can be regarded as an exploration of the validity and applicability of the development process and its underlying formal framework, this paper should be regarded as an initial survey on the feasibility of structured software support for the process. This paper described three initial tools which support various development phases and whose validity and feasibility is explained by the formal framework. Further, it discussed software support for the most crucial steps of the process and explained an improved structure for the process wherein the manageability is ensured by the tools. With this, the paper described an essential part of the eventual goal —a complete interactive development environment for parallel software— in which further software support should also regard the analysis of $\top$ itself (step 1), the implementation protocols (step 9) and the verification and debugging (steps 11 and 14).

References

[1] U. Banerjee, *Dependence Analysis for Supercomputing*, Kluwer Academic Publishers, Boston, 1988.

[2] A. Gerasoulis and T. Yang, Efficient Algorithms and a Software Tool for Scheduling Parallel Computation, in P. Chretienne et. al. (Eds.) *Scheduling theory and Its Applications*, John Wiley & Sons, 1994.

[3] J.P. Geschiere and W.H.F.J. Körver, A Formal Framework for Defining and Developing Parallel Large-Scale Applications, in E.H. D'Hollander et. al. (Eds.), *Parallel Computing: State-of-the-Art Perspective (ParCo'95)*, pp 125-131, Elsevier Science Publ., 1995.

[4] J.P. Geschiere and W.H.F.J. Körver, A Practical Development Process for Parallel Large-Scale Applications and its underlying Formal Framework, Technical Report CSRG95-05, Dept. of EE Eng., Univ. of Surrey, 1995.

[5] S.J. Kim and J.C. Browne, A General Approach to Mapping of Parallel Computation upon Multiprocessor Architectures, in *Proc. of Int. Conf. on Parallel Processing, Vol. 3*, pp 1-8, 1988.

[6] C.H. Papadimitriou and M. Yannakakis, Towards an Architecture Independent Analysis of Parallel Algorithms, *SIAM J. on Computing*, 19 (1990), pp 322-328.

[7] V. Sarkar, *Partitioning and Scheduling Parallel Programs for Execution on Multiprocessors*, MIT Press, 1989.

[8] M.J. Wolfe, *High Performance Compilers for Parallel Computing*, Addison Wesley, 1996.

[9] H.P. Zima and B. Chapman, *Supercompilers for Parallel and Vector Computers*, ACM Press, 1991.

Achieving Scalability, Portability and Efficiency in a High-Level Programming Model for Parallel Architectures

P Morrow[†]   D Crookes[‡]   J Brown[‡]   Y Dong[‡]

G McAleese[†]   D Roantree[†]

I Spence[‡]

[†] School of Information and Software Engineering, University of Ulster
Coleraine, Co Londonderry, Northern Ireland, BT52 1SA
Email: pj.morrow@ulst.ac.uk

[‡] Department of Computer Science, The Queen's University of Belfast
Belfast, Northern Ireland, BT7 1NN

Abstract

This paper describes a novel approach to implementing a high-level programming model for parallel architectures. A set of abstractions are provided for an image processing language which can be implemented efficiently in parallel whilst at the same time being portable over a range of parallel architectures. Our approach is to decouple the potentially parallel (and machine dependent) aspects of a system and provide suitable language constructs for these. A *delayed evaluation* technique is used when a program is running whereby optimised instructions can be generated during its execution and used subsequently during further runs of the program. Thus the performance of a program can effectively *evolve* during a series of executions. Although the approach is currently domain specific we hope to demonstrate general applicability to application areas other than image processing.

1 Introduction

The need for machine independent parallel programming languages, compilers and tools for scaleable computers has long been recognised. In addition the boundaries between compilers, languages and run-time systems has become less distinct in recent years with the advent of compiler-compilers, sophisticated interpreter systems and visual programming environments. In general three approaches to providing a parallel processing capability are regarded as appropriate:

1. design extensions to current programming languages and enhance the compiler appropriately;

2. provide a library of routines to accommodate the parallel aspects of a program; or

3. design and implement a new parallel language.

Each of these approaches has its advantages and disadvantages: (1) and (2) require less effort on the part of the language implementor but may not achieve optimum efficiency from the underlying hardware. Approach (3) requires greatest effort during implementation but should be very efficient where utilisation of parallelism is concerned. However programmers will have to learn a new language and the scientific community would be reluctant to rewrite large 'legacy' codes.

To reduce effort in compiler writing it would be advantageous if we could provide language constructs (abstractions) which would appear as, and be used as, part of the language itself but would not require a new compiler or preprocessor to be written for each parallel machine on which the language is implemented. In effect this is a combination of (1) and (2) above. This has important implications not only for scalability but also portability. In addition there is a need to hide parallelism from the user in order that the transition from sequential programming to parallel programming is relatively seamless. The abstractions should be implemented behind the scenes and should utilise the underlying parallel hardware optimally.

The importance of portability for software tools for parallel/scaleable machines has been recognised both in the UK and in the US. The Portable Software Tools for Parallel Architectures (PSTPA) programme of the UK's Engineering and Physical Sciences Research Council has fifteen projects currently running and the Portable Tools (PTools) programme in the US has six. This paper describes the initial findings of a project funded under the PSTPA programme and specifically addresses the problem of designing and implementing an image processing language, for parallel scaleable architectures, which is portable over a range of machines and also retains efficiency of execution.

The primary direct objective of the research described here is to build an environment for developing portable, parallel software systems, initially targeted at image processing applications. An efficient implementation is being produced for scaleable architectures. Our approach is to decouple the potentially parallel (and architecture-dependent) aspects of a program from the remainder by defining an abstract Extensible Parallel Image Coprocessor (EPIC), and developing associated software tools. The extensible nature of the coprocessor is crucial to obtaining optimised execution of programs.

Even as a purely application-specific project, the significance of the Image Processing market makes our approach worthwhile. In recent years it has been recognised that there is a definite need for image processing software development tools (e.g. [1] [2]) for scaleable architectures. In addition the range of applications for image processing technology is expanding rapidly. Ongoing developments in architectures for parallel image processing increase the need for programming models to be more abstract.

Nevertheless, the more long term aim of the research is to contribute to the quest for a *general purpose* abstract programming model for scaleable computers which guarantees efficient implementation. The traditional approach is often to begin with a general-purpose model and to research techniques which make the implementation increasingly efficient. Our approach is instead to begin with an application-specific model, which from the outset guarantees efficiency and portability, and generalise its abstractions to move towards a general purpose model. We wish to show that although we start with domain specific abstractions which we can implement efficiently, these can be generalised to other domains while still retaining the efficiency of implementation. The main objectives of the research project are as follows.

- To identify and define a set of programming abstractions appropriate to parallel (scaleable) image processing systems. This set of abstractions constitute the core of the Extensible Parallel Image Coprocessor (EPIC) model.

- To design and construct an (object-oriented) application development environment, in which users can develop portable (and efficient) image processing applications based on the EPIC model.

- To develop a rule-based transformation system which allows the set of programming abstractions to be extended, i.e. to provide the extensible nature of the EPIC model.

- To identify and recommend how the EPIC model could be applied to other application domains. Even without generalisation of its abstractions, it is not unlikely that the EPIC environment will be applicable to problems beyond the domain of image processing.

The remainder of this paper outlines our strategy for achieving the above objectives. In particular the EPIC model is described followed by an overview and examples of the language abstractions. The strategy of optimising programs through delayed evaluation and evolving performance is then explained. Finally some conclusions are drawn and an indication of the current state of the project is given.

2 The EPIC Programming Model and Environment

2.1 Previous work

Current research into general-purpose parallel programming models is seeing gradual progress, particularly in data parallel programming models. The work of Jesshope, Shafarenko et al on F-Code [3] is well established, though it does not directly give the optimised efficiency obtainable for image processing applications. Data parallel models based on FORTRAN (HPF and FORTRAN

90) are making steady progress on the autoparallelisation front; but progress is hindered by many factors concerning the nature of FORTRAN. Valiant's BSP model [4], relying on parallel slackness to mask the latency of remote accesses, is another unifying model, and data parallel extensions are being developed by McCall at Oxford University. A broader, more practical approach is that adopted by PVM [5] or MPI [6], programming environments in which programs execute on a heterogeneous collection of machines. However, programming using PVM or MPI is undertaken at quite a low-level.

Previous work by some of the authors has resulted in the design and implementation of image processing languages for specific parallel machines (IAL, Tulip, I-BOL) [7], [8]. Other research has also looked at portability through the use of an abstract parallel machine description (PIPA) [9]. In this case a compiler was written (in Prolog [10]) which generated pseudocode for the abstract machine model. This machine code was portable over parallel architectures and subsets were implemented on transputer networks [11] and an AMT DAP.

However although the instructions were defined at a 'high level' (effectively a Reduced Powerful Instruction Set) the range of instructions was limited and thus the range of image processing applications was limited. The current project pulls together much of this research and in particular addresses the issue of providing a mechanism whereby the instruction set can be expanded (by the run-time system) to provide optimised instructions which can be executed efficiently. In addition, earlier work did not consider the issue of generalising to a non image processing domain; nor did it attempt to adhere to industry 'standards' (such as C++). Also the original abstract machine model (PIPA) concentrated on the problem of portability with insufficient attention being paid to individual pixel access and to efficiency of execution. The EPIC model greatly extends previous work and also addresses the issues given above.

2.2   The Programming Model

The programmer's model of the parallel capability of an architecture is defined as an abstract coprocessor. While this is a standard way of achieving portability, the traditional problems with achieving efficiency and optimisation are overcome by enabling the dynamic generation of new, automatically optimised operations. This retains the well-defined model of a coprocessor, but provides the equivalent efficiency of an optimising compiler with knowledge of the architecture. The main features of the EPIC model are as follows:

- The coprocessor is object-oriented in nature. It processes objects defined by a range of classes (e.g. images of different kinds, vectors, templates, etc.) using an extensible set of operations on these objects. A base level layer of primitive operations is provided, on top of which can be built a layer of operations specific to a particular application.

- Parallelism is expressed as performing a given operation on objects. Dependencies are expressible by generating sub-sequences of indices. Index sets and sequences can themselves be structured, for greater power of expression.

- One component of the EPIC model is an instruction builder and optimiser which builds new higher level functions from a specification which is expressed in terms of already-defined functions. Rather than base the new function on calls to existing functions, this component uses a set of transformations which optimises the instruction specification as a whole giving a new function. The rule set defining the transformations is designed to produce a function optimised for the target architecture. This optimising tool will be the means of achieving efficiency without sacrificing portability.

- The EPIC software environment is C++ based, for conformance with effective industry standards. Users program in C++ but make use of EPIC tools and class objects. The initial target architecture is based around a nètwork of Texas Instruments C40 processors.

The first level of structure in the programming model requires viewing the parallel processing engine as an image processing coprocessor (attached to a host workstation). For efficient realisation of new (compound) functions though, the instruction optimiser is required. The overall model for program compilation and execution consists of five main stages and is illustrated in figure 1 below. The first three stages comprise the normal *edit, compile* and *execute* processes of a normal sequential program. Stages four and five deal with optimisation of the user program.

On the host, complete sequential programming freedom is allowed (in C++), should operations be required which cannot be readily expressed in terms of the basic operations. Thus code which manipulates images without using basic opertions is allowed but will not be parallelised. Objects for parallel processing (such as images) are normally resident on the coprocessor, but objects can be transferred between the host and the coprocessor for seamless sequential/parallel processing. In the simplest form a user writes an application program in C++ using the EPIC classes and methods provided. This program is then compiled and linked (with a standard C++ compiler) and subsequently executed on the host workstation and co-processor network (stages 1-3) with any results being returned to the user/programmer. In the more complex (and more useful) case where combinations of basic EPIC operations occur in an expression 'expression graphs' are generated during program execution and used to generate optimised instructions which will be called by the user program on subsequent executions. The five stages are outlined briefly as follows:

1. A user program is written in standard C++ using the object classes provided by the EPIC model. In effect the program is simply considered as sequential in nature - the data structures and operations provided by EPIC are automatically parallelised.

2. The program is compiled and linked with the EPIC object class library and an executable program created.

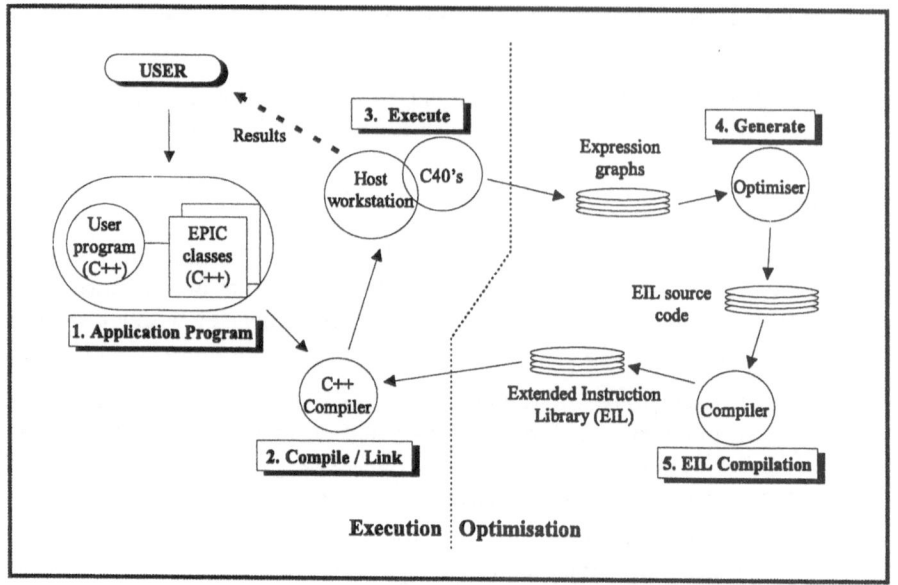

Figure 1: EPIC Model Overview

3. The program is executed on the host workstation. When calls are made to EPIC operations, they are passed to the coprocessor if they can be executed in parallel. Those which are sequential in nature are executed on the host workstation itself. In addition *expression graphs* are also generated for use in the optimisation stages.

4. The expression graphs generated in 3 above are read by the optimiser which generates optimised source code in the form of extended instructions.

5. The source code for the extended instructions is compiled and an *Extended Instruction Library* is created. This library of extended instructions is linked with the EPIC object library and the new instructions are therefore available on subsequent executions of the user program.

Stages 4&5 effectively comprise the optimisation phase and are described in more detail later. The following section provides a brief overview of the data structures and operations provided within the EPIC programming model.

3 EPIC Language Abstractions

In this section we give an overview of the language abstractions provided by the EPIC system. These are dealt with under data structures (classes) and operations (methods).

3.1 Data structures

The data structures provided by EPIC are implemented as a set of object classes in an EPIC class library. These provide abstractions and methods for accessing and using data which is processed by the co-processor. Class objects are provided for images, templates (a 2D neighbourhood) and vectors.

The library consists of a simple C++ master class (called EPIC) from which the others can be derived. For example the image class consists of three types of image, namely boolean, integer and real. The data held in an image object consists of not only the pixel data but information concerning the image size, any region-of-interest information, a unique numeric id, an image name etc. During program execution on a parallel machine information concerning the portion of the image (the image segment) residing on each processor is also held as part of the image class (for example the segment size, border information for neighbourhood operations, distribution strategy for the image).

For each EPIC class a series of constructors and a destructor methods are provided. There can be many constructors for a class, allowing objects to be created using different arguments. For example, to define an integer image we could simple write:

```
intimage image (256, 256);
```

which would declare an image of size 256 rows by 256 columns with pixels of type integer. The remaining data items in the object can be set or modified later by using the accessor functions of the class. Similar declarations can be made which also set object parameters. For example:

```
intimage image ('rathlin.raw');
intimage image ('rathlin.raw', 256, 256);
```

Each of the constructors allocates a unique 'id' for the object so that the object can be tracked throughout its lifetime. The examples above relate to the image class - similar objects and constructors/destructors are provided for templates and vectors.

3.2 Operations

The underlying set of operations provided by EPIC covers low-level image processing and was initially based on Image Algebra [12]. The instruction set includes binary point-to-point operators, unary point operators, neighbourhood operators and reduction operators. Binary point-to-point operators consist of standard infix arithmetic and logical functions such as '+', '-', '>', '==' etc. for binary operand combinations of *images, templates, scalars,* or *vectors* where scalar types are *int, float* and *boolean*. For example an *image-to-image* operation which computed the difference in pixel values for each pixel position in two image A and B would simply be written as

```
A - B
```

Similarly unary prefix operators are defined for arithmetic and logical nega-
tion: '-' and '!'. Standard mathematical functions for point operations are also
provided for *sin, cos, tan, abs, sqrt,* etc. Reduction operators take a number
of values (e.g. an image) and return just one. For example, the operator *max*
applied to an image will return the maximum pixel value in the image; the
operator *sigma* will sum all pixel values in an image. Finally, neighbourhood
operators take an image and a template as their two operands and return an
image as the result of the operation. The convolution of an image I with a
template T giving result image R can be written as :

```
R = conv(I, T)
```

The built-in operator *conv* will perform the convolution and return an image
as its result - this image is then assigned to the image variable R.

3.3   Example.

As an example of the use of EPIC operators consider the following code fragment which simply declares two integer images, performs a point-to-point addition on the pixel data and assigns the results to a third image. (We are
assuming appropriate image data has been read into the image variables).

```
intimage A (256, 256), B (256, 256), C (256, 256);
...
C = A + B;
```

If we use a graph representation for the expression A + B we could depict
the above statement as shown in figure 2.

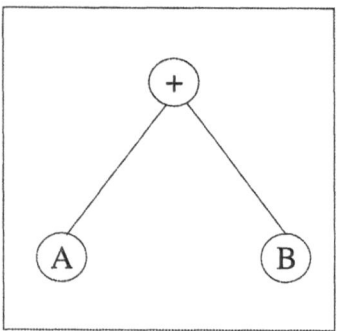

Figure 2: Graph for 'A+B'

Extending this example further, if we wish to perform a simple edge detection operation using two neighbourhood operations (convolutions) we would
write the following (given appropriate image declarations for input and result
images I and R and template declarations for Sh and Sv):

```
R = conv (I, Sh) + conv (I, Sv);
```

resulting in a graph of the form shown in figure 3 (the '@' represents convolution in this case).

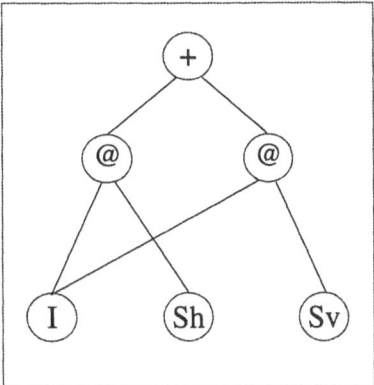

Figure 3: Graph for 'conv(I, Sh) + conv(I, Sv)'

It is obvious from the above that the two convolution operations are applied to the same image but use different templates. A traditional library operation for convolution would be *indivisible*, i.e. the convolution with 'Sh' must be completed first; then the convolution with 'Sv' and finally the addition would be performed. If a programmer were hand-coding the above he/she would combine the convolution operations within the same inner processing loops and thus save on computation time. In effect he/she would be providing a *new instruction* which performed a double convolution operation efficiently. The optimiser within EPIC automatically performs this type of optimisation - given a *syntax graph* for an expression it will attempt to create a new optimised instruction optimised for the whole expression which can subsequently be used in user programs.

4 Optimisation Via Delayed Evaluation

By using a graph representation for an expression, such as that shown above, we can construct a library of such expressions during a program's execution. Obviously, many of these expressions would be optimised if they were 'hand-coded' - e.g. the above example can be implemented by using one outer set of loops for the addition operation with both convolutions being performed inside this. If the normal EPIC instructions were used (as in the example) then the expression would be unwound and the convolutions performed separately. However, if we had an 'optimised' instruction for the expression

```
conv(I, Sh) + conv(I, Sv)
```

then if the same 'form' (i.e. the same expression graph shape) appeared again in a program we could use this optimised instruction rather than the EPIC primitive instructions.

In effect this is exactly what our approach to optimisation consists of. During a run of a user program not only does the program execute but a series of graphs are built with represent the expression / statements in the program. This is achieved by overloading many of the operators in C++ which, rather than implementing the (EPIC) operations required of them instead only create an expression graph or sub-graph. The evaluation of the operations is then delayed until an assignment operator is encountered. Hence, for a single statement no evaluation is actually performed until a complete expression graph is generated. For example, if an image-to-image addition operator occurred in a statement, the appropriate EPIC method (operator) is called which will add nodes to the current graph representing the expression. Once an assignment operator is encountered the appropriate overloaded function for assignment is called. This takes the current expression graph and determines if an optimised instruction is available for this particular graph and if so calls this instruction. Otherwise the basic operations comprising the expression graph are executed individually. As indicated earlier, subsequent to the user program terminating an optimiser is run which analyses the set of expression graphs created 'on the fly' and generates an optimised instruction for each expression where appropriate.

5   Conclusions

This paper has presented an overview of a novel approach to obtaining efficiency and portability in a high-level programming model for parallel architectures. In particular we have described a unique means of optimising programs without the need to either extend a language (and therefore extend the compiler) nor to write a 'pre-processor'. By making extensive use of the overloading feature of C++ we have been able to build and provide a high-level programming model (for image processing) which not only hides the underlying parallel architecture from a user but also retains efficiency of execution. The efficiency is retained through an optimisation stage which generates optimised instructions which can be subsequently included in a user program thus extending the programming model itself. Although the approach is currently domain specific future work will examine how it can be extended to other domains.

6   Acknowledgements

This research is supported through the Portable Software Tools for Parallel Architectures programme of the UK's Engineering and Physical Sciences Research Council.

References

[1] A.N. Choudhary and J.H. Patel, **Parallel architectures and parallel algorithms for integrated vision systems**, Kluwer Academic Publishers, 1990

[2] C.W. Swonger, Machine vision trends entering the '90s, **Machine Vision and Applications**, Vol. 4, pp124-126, 1991

[3] C. Jessope, The F-code abstract machine and its implementation, **Proc COMPEURO 1992**, IEEE Press, 1992

[4] L.G. Valiant, A bridging model for parallel computation, **CACM 33** (8), August 1990

[5] V.S. Sunderman, PVM: a framework for parallel distributed computing, **Concurrency 2** (4), pp315-339, December, 1990

[6] W. Gropp, et. al. **Using MPI: Portable parallel programming with the message-passing interface**, MIT Press, 1994.

[7] D. Crookes, P.J. Morrow and P.J. McParland, IAL: a parallel image processing programming language, **IEE Proceedings Part I**, Vol 137, No. 3, June 1990, pp176-182

[8] J. Brown and D. Crookes, A high level language for parallel image processing, **Image & Vision Computing**, Vol 12, No. 2, March 1994, pp67-79

[9] P.J. Morrow, Software tools for parallel image processing on transputers, PhD Thesis, 1993, The Queen's University of Belfast

[10] P.J. Morrow and D. Crookes, Using Prolog to implement a compiler for a parallel image processing language, **Proc. IEEE ICIP-95**, October 1995

[11] P.J. Morrow and D. Crookes, A Portable Abstract Machine Model for Image Processing: An Implementation Technique for Software Tools, **Proceedings EuroMicro Workshop on Parallel and Distributed Processing**, eds. P.Milligan and A.Nunez, IEEE Computer Society Press, pp466-473, 1993.

[12] G.X. Ritter, J.N. Wilson and J.L Davidson, Image algebra: an overview, **Computer Vision, Graphics and Image Processing**, 49, pp297-331, 1990

A FORTRAN 90 to F-code Compiler

Horia C. Sluşanschi

Department of Electronic & Electrical Engineering, University of Surrey
Guildford, United Kingdom

Chris R. Jesshope

Department of Electronic & Electrical Engineering, University of Surrey
Guildford, United Kingdom

Abstract

The recurring problem in supercomputer programming is the difficulty
of the software porting process, leading to high costs for software development. This paper outlines the benefits of using a portable software
platform, and details one such use.

The portable software platform we are concerned with is F-code,
which is specifically designed to support data-parallel languages. The
work described in this paper is part of a larger project, whose aim is to
provide a FORTRAN 90 compiler for the Cray T3D supercomputer.

1   Introduction

One of the major problems in the use of high performance computers is the lack
of suitable high-level and portable software tools. Most early and current use
of supercomputers relies on tools developed for the message passing paradigm
in which the user is responsible for explicitly partitioning and scheduling coarse
grain units of code.

The data-parallel abstraction on the other hand provides a paradigm based
on shared memory concepts, which gives a high level of abstraction in describing
algorithms and, if one ignores the intermediate attempts to promote this style,
as is exemplified by HPF [FOR93][FOR94], it offers an extremely good platform
on which to base portability. The problem with HPF is that it is based on an
abstract language, although it encourages the user to annotate the code with
explicit mapping information which by its nature is not machine-to-machine
portable.

It has been shown elsewhere [Sha95] that given a suitable typing hierarchy
the data-parallel or collective behaviour can be described by very few forms
annotated by abstract typing information and it is this goal that drives the
research reported here.

Unfortunately however, the language dimension changes very slowly, as can
be seen by observing the history of a rather long-in-the-tooth language such as
FORTRAN. Thus the most appropriate vehicle for investigating these theoretical projections is by controlling the compiled language, which in our case can
only be achieved at the intermediate level. Limitations in the user-level lan-

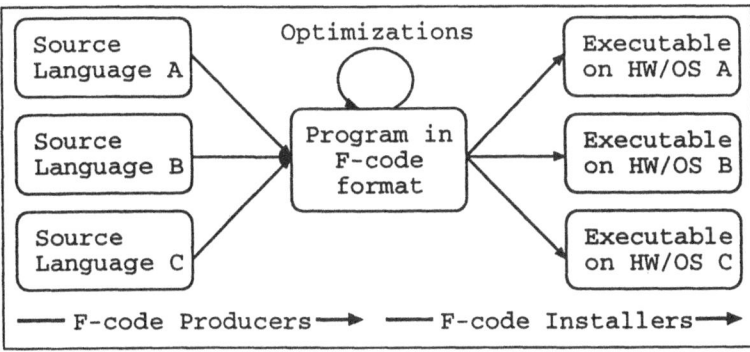

Figure 1: The F-code software development environment.

guage will always restrict the advances that can be made in compiler technology for practical applications.

However, if a solid platform based on theoretical principles is established then the benefits may be proved and higher level code-generation techniques, perhaps which bypass the user-level language may enable efficient applications to be developed from abstract specifications, which remain truly machine independent. It should be noted that with the increasing levels of concurrency found in today's' microprocessors the concurrency issues also benefit code generation for "sequential" uniprocessor machines.

This issue of concurrency in sequential processors is exacerbated by the slack required in instruction level scheduling in order to tolerate the latency of slow external memory, which is becoming more of an issue as the on-chip processor speed continues to increase. Thus the combination of multiple issue, pipeline depth and parallel slackness in memory fetch may require one or even two orders of magnitude more concurrency than the number of processors in the target system might suggest.

This paper describes a project that is funded by the EPSRC under its Portable Software Tools for Parallel Architectures programme—grant number GR/K40369. The eventual goal of this project, of which the work described here is a part, is to produce a prototype FORTRAN 90 [FOR91] compiler for the Cray T3D supercomputer, using F-code as an intermediate representation [BMS93].

Throughout the scientific world, FORTRAN is the most widely used programming language. FORTRAN 90 is now the latest standardised version of this language. It is specifically designed to provide data-parallel constructs to ease the scientific programs' development and to aide the generation of code for parallel machines.

In order to understand why we chose compilation via an intermediate representation, it must be remembered that one of the major problems encountered in the supercomputer industry is the lack of software portability. Let us suppose that we wish to build n compilers for m machines. In the straightforward

approach, we would need $n * m$ compilers. This is evidently extremely inefficient, leading to a huge development cost. If, on the other hand, we use some
form of intermediate language, we are able to write n compilers that generate
intermediate language programs, m code generators that produce real machine
code, and we have solved the problem using only $m + n$ programs instead of
$m * n$. Figure 1 illustrates this process.

The benefits derived from the use of this approach are obvious, with a
publicly defined intermediate representation [BMS93], parts of compilers may
be produced by the most appropriate suppliers, including third parties who
can provide reflexive optimisation modules without reference to either source
language or target machine.

2 F-code as an intermediate representation

The work reported in this paper concerns the generation of F-code from a
FORTRAN 90 front end. Previous work has already shown that F-code can be
compiled efficiently [Sut93] and indeed work continues in making the mapping
of data and computation an automatically generated process. The question we
will be asking here concerns the design of F-code and its ability to transmit
sufficient information from the original source code to the back end of the
compiler without loss of generality.

F-code was designed to be a portable software platform for data-parallel programming languages. As illustrated in [Bel90], the data-parallel programming
paradigm gives clear advantages in terms of simple and clean specifications of
applications, algorithms and languages, and makes the data-parallel programming model desirable for any kind of tightly coupled parallel or vector machine,
including multiple-instruction multiple-data (MIMD) machines.

Also, the range of applications and algorithms that can be described using data-parallel programming is extremely broad, much broader than is often
expected. Furthermore, in most applications there is significantly more data-
parallelism available than control parallelism.

In the past, F-code has been primarily used as a target for the EVAL data-
parallel programming language [MS96] which contains a number of unusual
but beneficial design decisions. However, if F-code is to be demonstrated as a
suitable platform for portability then it must provide all the necessary building blocks that will allow the compilation from a whole range of alternative
languages.

From a structural point of view, the work on F-code is very similar to the
ANDF [AND] project. The major difference rests in the fact that ANDF is
targeted to traditional processor architectures, whereas F-code supports data-
parallel constructs.

Otherwise, the goals of ANDF apply to F-code as well:

- Simplify compiler construction by creating language-specific front-ends
  and hardware specific back-ends independently.

- Provide a portable distribution format.

- Provide improved portability testing tools.

Using ANDF terminology, one might say that our project's aim is to develop a FORTRAN 90 F-code producer that will be interfaced with a Cray T3D F-code installer. In the mean time, we are also developing an F-code interpreter, similar to the ANDF GAI—General ANDF Interpreter, which interprets ANDF code in an architecture neutral way.

Perhaps in the not so distant future these two efforts will be unified, and provide the benefits of this software design and development approach on the widest scale ever.

It has already been shown [JS95] that the design of F-code makes it possible to infer all the necessary information needed to generate efficient code. This is made possible by using an architecture-neutral typing lattice, and a special approach to handling data. Special care has been devoted to insure that all F-code constructs are context independent, in order to simplify code generation. This is under no circumstances a drawback of F-code, as it is not intended to be used by humans. Its declared purpose is to serve only as an intermediate platform for all the major high-level programming languages, providing highly efficient support for the languages that use data-parallel operations.

The architecture-neutral typing lattice is designed to provide the necessary freedom for the code-generators to use the most efficient implementation of a given target computer. However, because in languages like C and C++ programmers are used to reason in terms of bytes and words, the correct program behaviour can be insured by using specific coercion constructs. It should be noted that this does not necessarily induce a performance penalty in the native code generated by the F-code compiler.

It is interesting to observe that in FORTRAN 90, one can specify the actual precision required for a number, be it integer or real. Although the standard declares that these precisions are to be mapped on a set of data kinds supported by the actual processor, we can postpone this mapping until the actual code generation by passing the precision information into the F-code intermediate representation—the neutral typing lattice permits us to do so. This simplifies portability, while ensuring that we retain the most efficient native code for each particular target machine. The mapping can then be chosen inside the F-code to native code generator, according to the specific architecture of the machine on which the program is to run, giving us all possible opportunities to make the right choices in producing the most efficient code.

An additional benefit of using F-code is that it lends itself readily to reflexive optimisations, making a fine performance tuning possible. As an example, consider the ability of F-code to express assignments with compound objects on the left hand side as well as on the right hand side. This fact can be utilised in an analysis of dependencies between adjacent data-parallel assignments in order to specify the maximum data-parallelism at the intermediate code level and hence enable more efficient code generation from the code generators for massively parallel computers. Such optimisations are independent of both source

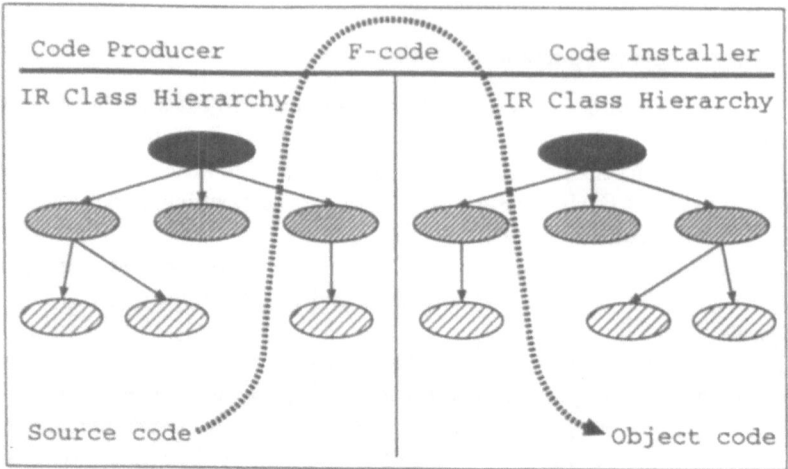

Figure 2: The class hierarchies that define the internal representations within F-code producers and installers written in C++ can be similar.

language and target computer. Without this ability at the intermediate code level we would have otherwise lost parallelism by performing the individual components' assignments sequentially rather than in parallel. On the other hand, if the target supports only a very limited amount of parallelism, the code can be serialised without incurring any performance loss due to the F-code representation.

An important source of input for the further refinement and development of the F-code specification is provided by other projects that aim to use F-code. One of them involves the development of a C++ F-code producer, as well as a DSP F-code installer. Both of these programs are to be written in C++. As one can imagine by looking at Figure 2, the class hierarchies that define the intermediate representations should be fairly similar, giving great scope for code reuse. Using this approach, one can significantly reduce the effort required to implement new F-code producers and installers.

3 The refinement of F-code

What was lacking though in the original specification of F-code [BMS93], and even in the revised definition presented in [MS96] in order to make it suitable as a practical target for compiling all the major high-level programming languages was support for program structure and project development and maintenance, and also the lexical structure of F-code could have been improved, to ease the scanner and parser development and maintenance for F-code installers.

As a consequence, the F-code specification has undergone a series of changes, most of which will be illustrated in this section.

The lexical conventions used are a variation of BNF. Bold text represents itself. Plain text comprises operators and terms which are defined hierarchically. The := operator separates a production from its definition, | separates alternatives, [] groups one or more alternatives that may appear zero or one time, {} groups a set of alternatives which may occur arbitrarily many times in arbitrary order, and ... signifies lots of other text which is omitted for brevity. Whitespace is not significant, except where a syntax ambiguity might arise from its complete elimination.

- Lexical and syntactic issues

  - F-code source files have to comply to a certain structure now. This clarifies parsing, and eases the management of projects that span over multiple source files—which will probably be the most frequent case by far. Support for development and debugging has been tremendously improved:

line	:=	# number
expr	:=	[line] expr-op
expr-op	:=	... | file-op | ...
directive	:=	... | file-dir | ...
file-op	:=	(file string { directive } $expr_{return}$)
file-dir	:=	(file string { directive } $expr_{return}$)
author	:=	(author string)
program	:=	(program string [version])
version	:=	(version string)
timestamp	:=	(timestamp number number number number number number)

  - Several directives have been added, as well as providing a directive version for some constructs, in order to provide a more flexible interface and ease development and debugging. Here are some of the more interesting ones:

include	:=	(include string)
static	:=	(static object-id [$expr_{init}$])
mark	:=	(mark)

  - Support for function declaration and definition, along with parameter and return value specifications.

function	:=	(function function-id { parameter } [result] [$expr_{body}$])
parameter	:=	(parameter object-id [parameter-sort] [where] [type])
result	:=	(result object-id [result-sort] [where] [type])
where	:=	stack | reg-reg

- A pointer type and indirection have been added. Also, an `addr` access specifier is in use.

built-in	:=	... | `pointer` | ...
star	:=	(`star` expr type)

- The templates have been redesigned for a greater flexibility.

template	:=	(`template` template-id { field })
field	:=	(`field` field-id mode { expr$_{extent}$ } [position] [width])
position	:=	(`position` number)
width	:=	(`width` number)
select-var	:=	(`select-var` template-id field-id expr$_{arg}$)

  ...

- The syntax for masks has been unified with that of integers, thus simplifying parsing.

mask	:=	number

- Provision for support of big numbers has been made in the language specification.

- The constructs which used an access specifier—e.g. (`var value x`)—have been spawned into different constructs for each specifier in order to reduce parser complexity—i.e. (`var-value x`). This approach was adopted readily since F-code is not intended as a language in which humans should write programs, and F-code producer structure has nothing to lose.

var-value	:=	(`var-value` function-id | object-id)
var-target	:=	(`var-target` function-id | object-id)
var-name	:=	(`var-name` function-id | object-id)
var-addr	:=	(`var-addr` function-id | object-id)

  ...

- Semantic issues

  - A more flexible strategy has been adopted for defining data types, by introducing "modes". A mode may hold information on alignment, bit width, byte width, numeric limits, huge and epsilon values, and overflow and rounding information. Here is the relevant syntax:

mode	:=	mode-id | template-id | (built-in { mode-attr })
mode-attr	:=	alignment | bits | bytes | epsilon | huge | max | min | overflow | round
alignment	:=	(`alignment` number)
bits	:=	(`bits` number)
bytes	:=	(`bytes` number)

```
epsilon       :=  ( epsilon number | unsigned )
huge          :=  ( huge number | unsigned )
max           :=  ( max number )
min           :=  ( min number )
overflow      :=  ( overflow overflow-attr )
round         :=  ( round round-attr )
overflow-attr:=  clip | never | throw | wrap
round-attr    :=  convergent | larger | nearest | smaller
                  | state | zero
directive     :=  ...| mode-def | ...
expr-op       :=  ...| mode-ref | ...
mode-def      :=  (mode-def mode-id mode )
mode-ref      :=  (mode-ref expr [mode-attr] )
```

- The completion statuses have been redesigned to be more consistent and provide basic support for exception handling facilities. The completion status is now a triple with three fields:
  * arithmetic/pointer value
  * break count
  * exception pointer
- Exception handling facilities have been added to the language.

```
break         :=  ( break expr )
throw         :=  ( throw expr )
catch         :=  ( catch expr_{try} object-id expr_{handler} )
```

- The seq construct has been redefined due to the new form of completion statuses, and the comma construct became redundant, so it was eliminated.

```
seq           :=  ( seq { expr } )
```

- A program start-up strategy has been defined. According to the current specification, a F-code program starts by executing the return expression of the first F-code module. Any return expressions of other F-code modules are ignored. In order to use a conventional linker, the F-code module comprising the main program should constitute the first linked object module. There are also some other finer issues related to the support of the start-up strategy of particular languages such as C++ which can be left implementation-dependent, rather than brought into the language definition.

Although the definition of F-code may yet suffer some minor additions or changes, the modifications outlined above have quite exhausted our unsatisfied requirements from the language.

4   The FORTRAN 90 to F-code compiler

For the implementation of this particular front end to F-code, we have obtained a copy of the source-code of the commercial FORTRAN 90 compiler from Numerical Algorithms Group Ltd., a collaborative partner in this project, and are modifying this it in order to enable it to generate F-code. The NAG compiler currently generates native code for most of the current workstation systems. It does this by effectively generating C code and then using the local C compiler to generate native code.

It is interesting to note that this approach is somewhat similar to our approach, with one major difference: F-code can accommodate data-parallel constructs, whereas the NAG compiler has to serialise all the data-parallel constructs, that may have appeared in the FORTRAN 90 source code, in its front end, rather than propagating these via its intermediate language.

Figure 3 illustrates the overall structure of this project and its interaction with the NAG Intermediate Representation and the Cray T3D F-code installer.

The NAG compiler uses a number of stages to generate code:

Scanner/Lexer This phase splits the source text into lexical tokens.

Parser This step is designed around a yacc grammar and builds a parse tree, a coarse symbol table and a scope table.

Static semantic analyser This stage scans the symbol table filling in information that requires multi-pass analysis and walks the parse tree annotating expression nodes with their data-type, rank, flags and, for constant subexpressions, value.

These are the passes that we can use from the NAG compiler. The next one, the code generation, serialises the data-parallel instructions, and so it is of no further interest to us.

Just as the NAG compiler is able to output not only native code, but also the intermediate C source programs that it's using as an intermediate language, we have decided to make a special effort in fitting the F-code generator in the NAG compiler in such a way as to make it accessible through a simple flag, just as the C generator.

This makes it possible to test the F-code compiler during development by using the same application. It is easy to imagine compiling to native code both through C and F-code in the development process, and insure that both versions exhibit the same behaviour.

The NAG compiler's internal representation offers enough information to generate an equivalent F-code program that captures all the information from the original FORTRAN 90 source code. It is important to note that nothing of the expressive power of FORTRAN 90 is lost in the translation to F-code.

Figure 3 illustrates the overall structure of this project and its interaction with the NAG Intermediate Representation and the Cray T3D F-code installer.

The only major unpleasantness in translating the FORTRAN 90 syntax to F-code comes from the renowned GOTO statement. The standard's definition

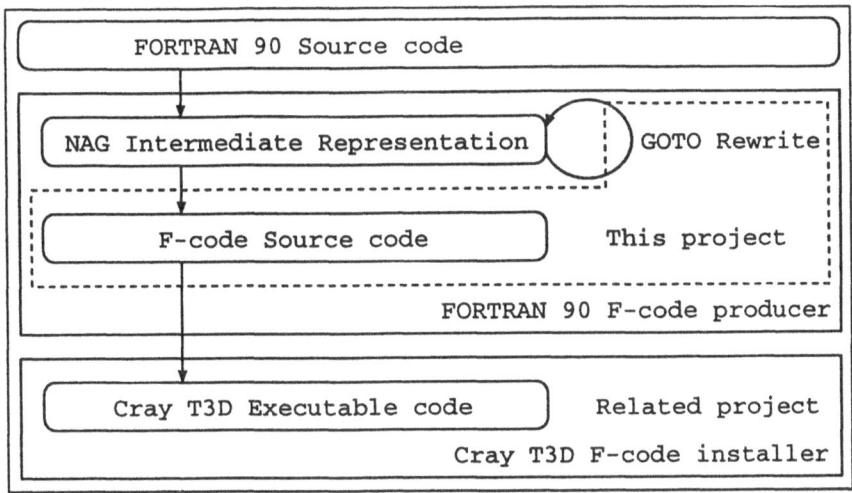

Figure 3: Global structure of the FORTRAN 90 to Cray T3D project.

for the unconditional GOTO can be implemented though in F-code by using a set of rather intricate, but possible transformations.

The definition specifies that an unconditional GOTO cannot branch inside a block. This means that it can specify a branch only:

- From within a block to another statement in the block.

- To the terminal statement of its enclosing construct.

- To a statement outside its enclosing construct.

It is easy to see that a branch to a terminal statement is nothing else but a branch in the same block, which means we can implement the second case using a solution for the first case.

Also, one can combine the second case—recursively if necessary—and the first one to implement the third one. This means that we can implement a branch to a statement outside the enclosing construct of the GOTO by combining branches to the terminal statements of all nested constructs up to the level of the target statement, with a final branch to the target statement.

Consequently, all that's left is to find a solution to the first case. We are now faced with an alternative. The branch might be:

- To a statement following the GOTO.

- To a statement prior to the GOTO.

The first alternative may lead to:

- A chunk of dead code, if there is no labelled statement between the GOTO and its target statement or if there is no GOTO to a labeled statement in that region. The dead code may be eliminated altogether.

- If there is a branch somewhere between the GOTO and its target statement, this will induce a replication in the F-code tree.

The second one may give rise to three situations which are not reducible to others:

- A backward branch with no branches in or out of the region between the GOTO and its target statement. This can be readily translated into F-code using a loop construct.

- A backward branch with an outward and forward branch out of the region between the GOTO and its target statement. If the GOTO is on a branch of a conditional, then this can be translated into F-code using again a loop construct, with the conditional inducing a termination of the loop combined with an external forward jump implemented again using a conditional. If not, then we are back to the first alternative.

- A backward branch with an inward and backward branch inside of the region between the GOTO and its target statement. The loop construct helps us again, this time the outer loop generated by the inward branch being complemented by a conditional which places us just where the branch was targeted to.

It is quite obvious that most unconditional branches are very expensive to implement in F-code, and this is due to the structure of the language, which was designed to support mainly data-parallel computation patterns rather than purely sequential patterns.

As such, if a translation unit contains GOTO's, the NAG IR tree is rewritten in terms of structured constructs, which in turn can be translated into F-code in a quite straightforward manner.

We have not yet added support for the computed GOTO or assigned GOTO statements, as they are already deprecated and obsolescent features respectively.

For a single source file, some analysis of the program structure is needed in order to generate the proper F-code program structure. This is done by the procedure handling the parse tree root node. The F-code program is then gradually generated by a set of mutually recursive procedures associated to the tree node types that gradually transform all the parse tree.

In the instances in which nodes derived from context-dependent constructs are encountered, localised versions of the node-type procedures are used for the nodes in these particular subtrees, where necessary.

Project management and compilation spanning multiple files can be readily supported using the facilities provided by the new definition of F-code.

5 Conclusion

There are two major benefits that this project can illustrate:

- Unification of software development can be achieved easily by using a common software platform. Different vendors and developers can provide pieces of code that may be integrated seamlessly. This may provide for a greater code reusability factor in the data-parallel arena, if one adopts a disciplined approach.

- Highly efficient code, on the other hand, is to be obtained by customised compilation of F-code. This means that the compilation process takes into account machine-specific information. Thus, one can efficiently compile F-code for anything from custom supercomputer processors to DSP's.

  Also, in most cases, using the F-code representation, efficient data mapping information can be inferred, and an approach based on the ideas outlined in [Sha95] can be used to provide high performance computation capabilities.

  For highly performance-sensitive applications, an even better design of the data-mapping structure can be achieved by using a more in-depth approach.

  The compilation process of F-code can be fine-tuned by gathering profiling information. Insight into the most adequate data-mapping and code structure for that particular architecture can be gained this way. This can be now used to generate an enhanced version of the code.

To conclude, it is the authors' opinion that this project may prove of significant importance in the unification of the supercomputing software development for data-parallel applications. As can easily be noted, it has all the necessary ingredients to become widely accepted: it can offer standard high level programming language compilers that produce highly efficient code on a wide range of supercomputers or workstations, all at a lower development cost than currently possible, and at the same time provide an easy path for further developments.

References

[AND]   ANDF web page. http://www.osf.org/andf/index.html.

[Bel90] Guy E. Belloch. *Vector Models for Data-Parallel Computing.* MIT Press, Cambridge, Massachusetts, 1990.

[BMS93] A.B. Bolychevsky, V.B. Muchnick, and A.V. Shafarenko. F-code: A portable software platform for data-parallel languages. CSRG report Version 2.1, Dept. of Electronic & Electrical Engineering, University of Surrey, March 1993.

[FOR91] *FORTRAN 90 International Standard, ISO/IEC 1539*, second edition, 1991.

[FOR93] High Performance FORTRAN Forum. *High Performance FORTRAN Language Specification*, May 1993. Version 1.0.

[FOR94] High Performance FORTRAN Forum. *HPF Scope of Activities and Motivating Applications*, November 1994. Version 0.8.

[JS95] C.R. Jesshope and C.D. Sutton. Compiling data-parallel languages for distributed memory multi-processors. In *Proceedings of the 5th Workshop on Compilers for Parallel Computers*, Malaga, 1995.

[MS96] V.B. Muchnick and A.V. Shafarenko. Data-parallel computing: the language dimension, 1996.

[Sha95] A.V. Shafarenko. Symmetries in data parallelism. In *The Computer Journal*, number 38 in 5, pages 365–378, 1995.

[Sut93] C.D. Sutton. *The implementation of a Portable Software Platform*. PhD thesis, University of Surrey, 1993.

A Strict occam Design Tool

Dave Beckett
Peter Welch
Computing Laboratory, University of Kent
Canterbury, Kent, CT2 7NF, England

Abstract

This paper presents a graphical design tool for the construction of multi-process systems that are guaranteed free from deadlock, livelock and starvation. The tool is strictly targeted to implementations based upon the CSP/occam synchronised message passing model, which includes systems programmed in occam itself, various parallel extensions to C (originally developed for the transputer), SuperPascal and a subset of MPI. The tool implements a mix of design paradigms whose synchronisation properties are well-behaved and easy to analyse, allowing only safe process networks to be built. The occam binding of the tool provides further guarantees against 'thread-unsafe' designs that are derived directly from the language. This paper gives the background to the work[1], the design tool methodology and an example of its use.

1   Introduction

Engineers who develop safe High Performance Computing (HPC) applications require the adoption of techniques that offer both performance and security. Performance is addressed by employing parallel processing – for supercomputing applications via a massive, but regular, physical network of processors and for embedded systems via application-specific, and often irregular, topologies. In either case, once we go beyond the 'embarrassingly parallel' or regular data-parallel arena, the special problems introduced by parallel computing – deadlock, livelock, starvation and uncontrolled non-determinism (caused by 'race-hazards') – need to be addressed.

A good start is to use the concurrency and synchronised message passing algebra defined by CSP[1], formalised through its traces/failures/divergences semantics and refined into the practical real-time multi-processing language occam[2][2, 3]. Note that this language is no longer tied to the INMOS transputer. Portable and efficient implementations of occam for any Unix[3] system (e.g. SPoC[4] and KRoC[5, 6]) already exist; multi-processor versions are in development[7] along with targetings to raw processors (e.g. DEC Alpha, PowerPC, AMD SHARC, M680x0, M68HC11) for embedded application.

Parallel designs conforming to this model are by default deterministic. Non-determinism, which is necessary to deal with certain real-world events, has to be

---

[1]Some of the methodology underlying the work reported in this paper was developed within a project for Defence Research Agency, Farnborough, UK

[2]occam is a Trademark of SGS-Thomson Microelectronics Ltd.

[3]Unix is a Trademark of X/Open

introduced explicitly and can therefore be kept under control. Undetected data-corruption, due to race-hazards resulting from asynchronous communication or incorrectly programmed shared-memory, cannot happen with this model – the rules of occam ensure that all parallel usage of procedures and functions are automatically 'thread-safe'. This is achieved through the maintenance of strict aliasing rules: the only data-structures that can have multiple names are constant ones; updatable data-structures and channel-structures can only have one name at a time. This enables the compiler to check all parallel usage of data, ensuring that data updates cannot occur concurrently either with reads from or other updates to that same data. Static checks are also enabled to ensure correct parallel channel usage – forbidding concurrent writes to a channel, along with concurrent reads, that would otherwise introduce non-determinism.

Note: occam is the *only* procedural language currently available (of which we are aware) that provides these thread-safe guarantees. Brinch-Hansen's SuperPascal[8] comes closest. It is described as a "secure programming language for the publication of parallel scientific algorithms" and implements a subset of the occam multi-processing model. It imposes the same anti-aliasing rules for data-structures and can, therefore, ensure secure parallel access to data. However, channels are implemented via pointers and their correct usage is not statically checked. The various parallel and message-passing extensions to C (e.g. [9, 10, 11]), including the synchronised subset of MPI[12], have nothing to offer in this context.

However, deadlock, livelock or starvation conditions can still arise from erroneous design and these are especially likely to be unfortunate in embedded systems that are safety critical. Furthermore, these conditions can arise intermittently and rarely so that they can easily be missed, no matter how thorough the testing regime, and show up in service. It is these problems to which the tool is primarily addressed.

The theory of deadlock has been the subject of much study (e.g. [1, 13, 14, 15]). From this work and long-term practical experience of designing parallel systems, we have identified in [16], and others have extended in [17], two particular design paradigms that guarantee deadlock-freedom – *I/O-PAR* and *Client-Server* – and cover a broad, but not necessarily total, range of application requirements. Rules for the safe construction of hybrid-algorithms containing a mixture of paradigms have also been developed[18]. The trick is to find the right mix of paradigms that will allow deadlock/livelock/starvation properties to be analysed and yet will be sufficiently free to allow us to build whatever needs to be built.

The rules enforcing these paradigms operate at a higher level than those defined by the current occam language and cannot therefore be checked by its compiler. In a sense, the occam primitives for processes and communication, in whatever language they may be expressed, provide an *assembler-level* language for the construction of parallel systems: fairly arbitrary ways of applying them are currently allowed and they are *not* all safe. In due course, higher-level languages may be built on top of these occam primitives that will only allow deadlock-free systems to be expressed.

Meanwhile, the rules have to be enforced rigorously by the engineer when designing a system architecture, and this is difficult to do reliably for a large application. For this reason, a design tool for working within these paradigms for parallel systems, that incrementally checks conformance to the safety rules as the design progresses, would greatly relieve this engineering burden from the designer. This paper describes such a tool.

2 Design paradigms

Deadlock occurs when, and only when, a network gets into a state where there exists a closed cycle of processes with each one committed to communicating with its neighbour (all commitments going clockwise or all going anticlockwise). The simple rule of forbidding closed cycles of data-flow in a design is insufficient (because a closed cycle of commitments can still be created – the direction of attempted communications do not all have to be aligned) and undesirable (we need to be able to build systems with closed data-flows).

Livelock occurs when a network gets into a state where an uninterruptable sequence of internal communications can take place that provides nothing to the external environment.

Starvation occurs when a process can get blocked indefinitely, trying to communicate with the rest of the network.

These conditions are, of course, interrelated. Deadlock is just global starvation and, from the point of view of their use to external environments, deadlocked and livelocked systems are equally useless.

Our tool currently supports two design paradigms for synchronised communication regimes (described in [16, 17]) that address these problems. They allow the construction of parallel systems that contain both regular data-flows (e.g. for continuous system simulation) and event-driven processes (e.g. for real-time control or complex user-interfaces).

2.1 I/O-PAR and I/O-SEQ

An *I/O-PAR* process is one that has a serial loop (main cycle) in which computation can occur at any time, but in which communications must take place in parallel – i.e. if one item is to be input from one channel, then one item must be input from all input channels *and* one item must be output to all output channels. For example:

```
WHILE running
  SEQ
    ...  computation
    ...  communications (parallel input/output all channels)
```

An *I/O-SEQ* process is similar to I/O-PAR, but in which the inputs and outputs take place in strict alternating sequence. When one input fires, all inputs must fire in parallel. Similarly, when one output fires, all outputs must fire in parallel. For example:

```
WHILE running
  SEQ
    ...  all input communications (in parallel)
    ...  computation
    ...  all output communications (in parallel)
    ...  computation
```

A *composite I/O-SEQ* process is recursively defined as *either* an I/O-SEQ process *or* a network of composite I/O-SEQ processes that has no cycle of data-flow.

A *composite I/O-PAR* process is recursively defined as *either* an I/O-PAR process *or* a network of composite I/O-PAR and composite I/O-SEQ processes such that:

1. there is no closed loop consisting of just composite I/O-SEQ processes;
2. there is no path consisting of just composite I/O-SEQ processes from an external input to an external output.

The relevant theorems resulting from [16, 17] can be summarised:

> *Composite I/O-PAR and composite I/O-SEQ processes are deadlock-free, livelock-free and starvation-free.*

The recursive definition of composite processes allow the hierarchical construction of parallel systems, with the design rules checked independently during each level of construction.

2.2 Client-Server

Client-Server networks are constructed from processes that communicate in two fashions – either as a *server*, in which the process guarantees to accept any request and service it in a finite time, or as a *client*, which makes a request and promises to complete any transaction that this generates (e.g. accept an answer).

A pure server for an array of clients may be visualised:

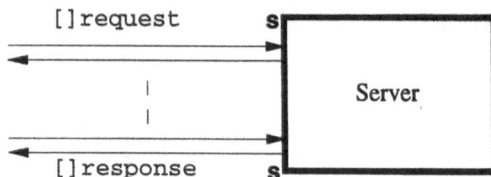

A pure client may be visualised:

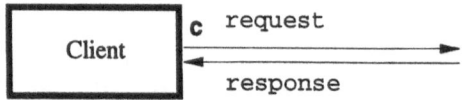

Note that a client-server connection usually consists of a pair of channels, enabling bi-directional communication during a transaction. Sometimes the return channel (from the server back to the client) is not needed. Client-server connections between processes define a *client-server ordering* between them.

In general, client-server processes will have both server connections and client connections. The rule is that if there is *any* server connection, service to that connection must not be indefinitely delayed. To analyse a process to check this constraint, only local inspection of the process code is necessary. Client transactions made by the process may be ignored in this analysis – i.e. we may assume they complete within a finite time. Global safety is assured by an induction argument on the network hierarchy of such processes.

A *basic client-server* is a serial process having only client connections and server connections. On any such connection, communication proceeds as a sequence of *transactions* initiated by a request (*to* the server or *from* the client). For a client transaction, the process must complete that transaction performing no other synchronisations. For a server transaction, the process may perform a finite number of other client transactions whilst servicing the initial request. Service on a server connection must be *fair* – i.e. clients must never be indefinitely waiting (starved).

A *composite client-server* process is recursively defined as *either* a basic client-server process *or* a network of composite client-server processes in which there is no closed cycle of client-server orderings.

The relevant theorem resulting from [16, 17] can be summarised:

> *Composite client-server processes are deadlock-free, livelock-free and starvation-free.*

As before, the recursive definition of composite processes allow the hierarchical construction of parallel systems, with the design rules checked independently during each level of construction.

2.3 Variations

The above rule for parallel composition of client-server processes is too strong in the case where those processes are not basic. What has to be ensured is that no client-server cycle exists when the network is expanded all the way down to its basic processes. This is formalised in [18], along with some extra rules for describing how server and client connections depend on each other in composite processes. This extra information enables the weakened composition rules to be checked locally – i.e. *without* having to know the implementation details of the processes being composed.

The application of these design paradigms is greatly liberated by allowing hybrid use. Computationally intensive components (at the heart of physical system models or control-law calculations) typically interact through I/O-PAR mechanisms. User, including sensor/actuator, interactions are irregular and are well-modelled through client-server notions. Rules that allow secure hybridisation are given in [18].

These variations are beyond the scope of this paper.

3 Design tool

The design tool is based on the rules outlined in Section 2 above. These rules describe how networks of processes (of various paradigms) can be constructed whilst preserving freedom from deadlock, livelock and starvation. The current tool is an experiment from which we hope to learn – it is not an integrated CAD system for parallel systems (but may become a useful component of one).

The tool allows the hierarchical design of a parallel system – *top-down*, *bottom-up* or anything in between. All parallel code defining the networks are generated automatically, the user supplying any application-specific channel protocols.

The lowest level processes in the hierarchy are basic I/O-PAR, I/O-SEQ or client-server. *Skeleton* code is generated for these processes to which the user needs to add application-specific data structures and serial code. The skeleton code handles all external communications for I/O-PAR and I/O-SEQ processes, apart from specifying the actual data communicated. It generates fair (starvation-free) servicing to the opening transaction requests on server connections, but leaves the application-specific processing of the transaction to the user. All client transactions, including their initiation, are application-specific and have to be the responsibility of the user. Warning: if the user alters any of the communication patterns generated in the skeleton, all safety guarantees are lost.

There are several parts of the tool, which correspond to natural software engineering elements that are used in designing parallel systems, promoting reuse and clarity in the system. These are **Interfaces**, **Implementations** and **Components**. The first are designed in the *Interface Editor* part of the tool, the latter two in the *Network* area of the tool.

3.1 Interfaces

Each process must have a defined **Interface** to its external environment – a description of the communication channels, message structures and paradigms used. This corresponds to an occam PROC header plus some extra information. The user designs this interface graphically. Figure 1 shows an example hybrid interface containing two bi-directional I/O-PAR connections, one bi-directional server and one uni-directional client.

INTERFACE X

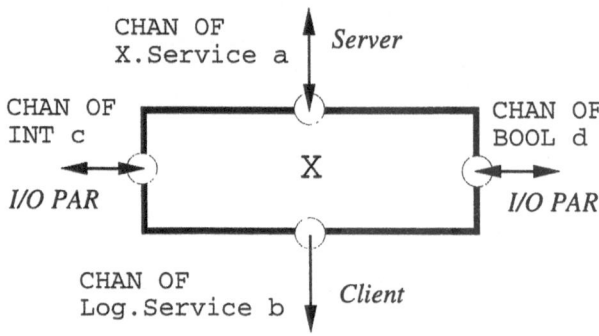

Figure 1: A graphical representation of a process interface

The tool can now generate an occam representation. Figure 1 contains four connections and corresponds to the following occam:

```
PROC X (CHAN OF X.Service    a.request, a.reply,  -- Server
          CHAN OF Log.Service b.request,            -- Client
          CHAN OF INT         c.in, c.out,          -- I/O PAR
          CHAN OF BOOL        d.in, d.out)          -- I/O PAR
  ...
  :
```

Note that only synchronising communications parameters are currently supported in these interfaces. The tool will be extended to allow VAL or reference data parameters, timers and ports to be included, but these have no impact on the deadlock, livelock or starvation issues addressed in this experiment. Meanwhile, the user may add them by hand and rely on the standard compiler checks to validate them.

3.2 Implementations

An interface just describes the *signature* of the process; it gives enough information about how the process synchronises with its environment to enable the deadlock analysis of its application to proceed, but says nothing about how it is implemented.

Once an interface has been designed, **Implementations** of the interface can be created. These allow the designer to pick a particular method for the implementation. For *basic* processes, this is through the editing of the skeleton source code generated by the tool *or* through legacy source code (if you trust it). For *composite* processes, this is through the graphical editing of a network of **Components**, with the relevant rules for each type of parallel composition (outlined in Section 2) enforced incrementally – an attempted connection that breaks the rule will simply be rejected.

Each implementation may be optimised for a different use. For example, a sorting process may be designed with a single interface, but with multiple implementations having different characteristics (e.g. being better for mostly-sorted data, using B-trees for random data, being cast into silicon). Each implementation must have a new name.

3.3 Components

A **Component** is an instance of an interface tied to a particular implementation (possibly null or skeletal). The main Network window allows components to be chosen, placed within an interface that is being implemented as a network and connected both to each other and to the external links defined by the interface. Several instances of the same interface/implementation can be used in a single network.

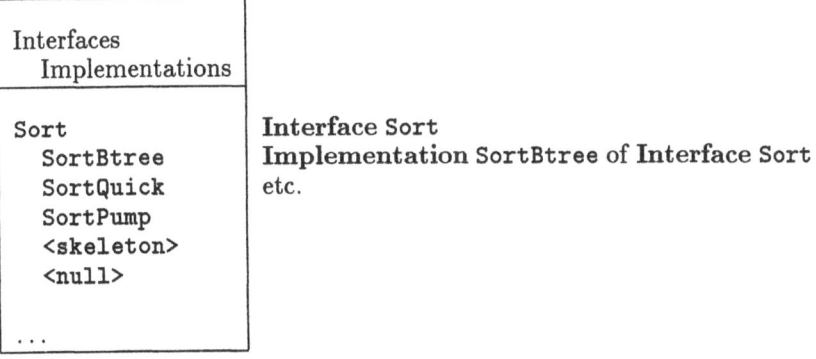

Figure 2: Menu of interfaces and implementations

To select a component, the user will be able to pick from multiple libraries of interfaces and implementations to allow code reuse. Each interface and implementation has a version number that must match – if the interface is edited, any implementations of it must be altered to match the new interface. This prevents any behind the scenes problems due to version mismatches. By default, the user is presented with a list of interfaces and implementations as shown in Figure 2.

When a component is first placed in the Network window, its links are shown as stubs waiting to be connected. The designer must make these connections by hand and mouse. When two components are connected, the tool checks that the link is legal: the direction, protocol and paradigm type of the end points must all be compatible and the link must be one-to-one (for standard **occam2** communications). If an illegal action is attempted, the tool refuses to perform the operation and reports the reason to the user. Network-wide checks are performed incrementally as connections are added. For example, the tool must ensure that no cycles of Client-Server dependencies or I/O-SEQ data-flow are created.

In a completed design, the main project consists of a network hierarchy of parallel components, each of which has a full implementation. Each level in the hierarchy is a network of parallel components whose construction has been forced to conform to the closure rules for the relevant synchronisation paradigms declared by the component interfaces. The lowest level components will be instances of interfaces that have (mainly serial) implementations that correctly support the declared paradigms. The resulting system is checked against deadlock, livelock, starvation, protocol violation, loose ends, version mismatch and (once it has been through the **occam** compiler) thread hazards. At any time in the project lifecycle, the particular implementation chosen for any interface can be changed without affecting the safety guarantees.

4 Example - Motif Widgets

4.1 Introduction

A final year student project at UKC has been interfacing the KRoC **occam** system, which runs on Unix workstations, to work with Motif[4] widgets. Each widget (or collection of widgets) is driven through a pair of **occam** channel interfaces – an update channel to perform actions on the widget and a callback channel to receive events such as button presses, slider movements, etc. The widget is managed by an application-specific **occam** client-server process that provides service on the callback channel and uses the update channel as a client. This process may be composite – i.e. there may be a separate process for each channel.

Any number of widgets may be managed. The student project has provided a generic server process to receive all application update commands and make the necessary calls out to the Motif C libraries. There is also a generic client process to receive callbacks from Motif and pass them on to the application widget servers.

---

[4]Motif is a Trademark of Open Software Foundation Inc.

The only documentation needed by the application engineer is the definition of the Motif widget protocols, a simplified fragment of which is:

```
PROTOCOL WIDGET.UPDATE IS
  CASE
    create.widget; INT; ...          -- to create a widget
    set.button.label; BYTE::[]BYTE   -- for a button
    move.slider; INT                 -- for a slider
    ...
  :

PROTOCOL WIDGET.CALLBACK IS
  CASE
    button.pressed                   -- for a button
    slider.moved; INT                -- for a slider
    ...
  :
```

The application GUI interface would be open arrays of channels carrying these protocols:

```
PROC gui (CHAN OF BYTE stdin, stdout, stderr,   -- Unix
          []CHAN OF WIDGET.UPDATE update,        -- Client
          []CHAN OF WIDGET.CALLBACK callback)    -- Server
  ... main body
  :
```

with the update channels declared as client connections and the callbacks as servers.

The user can now build complex widget systems that interact with each other and with the main computation being instumented/controlled. The design is very natural – it is event driven, object-oriented and highly parallel – and there is no fear of introducing deadlock, livelock or starvation.

4.2 Example application GUI

Figure 3 shows a window constructed of 11 elements: 8 horizontal sliders, buttons marked "Start", "Reset" and a vertical slider labelled "Speed". When the "Start" button is pressed, the horizontal sliders start moving from side-to-side and the button changes to say "Stop". The "Speed" slider controls how fast they move. The user may reset any of the horizontal sliders to any position and they will continue to move from that point. When "Reset" is pressed, all horizontal sliders return to their start position.

4.3 First design

This interaction between the 11 active Widgets requires coordination and must be checked for deadlock freedom. One design of the system is shown in Figure 4.

The individual widgets each have a process to handle the Widget server and client connections. The slider processes also have a widget group process that handles interactions for the slider Widget group. When buttons are

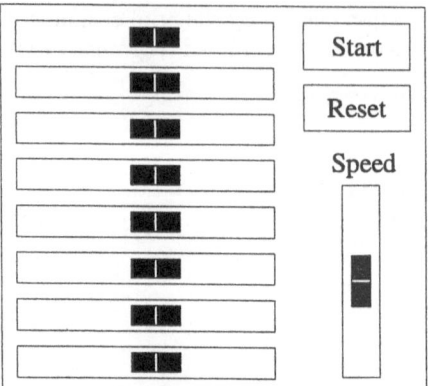

Figure 3: An example set of widgets

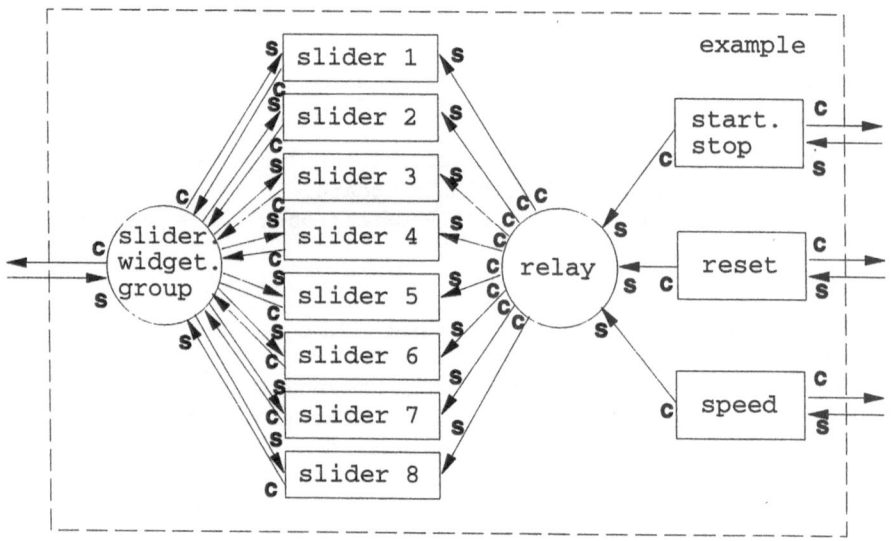

Figure 4: Incorrect implementation of the **example** GUI interface

pressed or sliders are moved by the GUI user, **WIDGET.CALLBACK** messages are sent along the relevant channels to the widget processes in the application. The **start.stop**, **reset** and **speed** processes respond by forwarding a simple protocol (**RELAY**) to the **slider** processes, via the **relay** server to save the sliders from having to service too many events. The **start.stop** process also updates Motif to display its changed label.

Each **slider** process is driven by an internal time-out (to update its slider position), by external start/stop, reset and speed (**RELAY**) messages and by external direct slider movements made by the user. All these processes are interfaced to Motif by the **slider.widget.group** process that multiplexes/demultiplexes Motif updates and callbacks.

This last part of the design would be rejected by the tool as creating a client-server loop (between the group plexer and each slider). If it were implemented, deadlock would occur if ever a **slider** process decided to update its position

63

at around the same time as the user tried to move it. This deadlock may not show up in testing because user slider movements are relatively rare.

4.4 Second design

The correct way to design this problem is to split the `slider.widget.group` process into two processes – one for servicing callbacks and de-multiplexing them to the sliders, and the second for multiplexing the slider updates to the Motif world. This is shown in Figure 5.

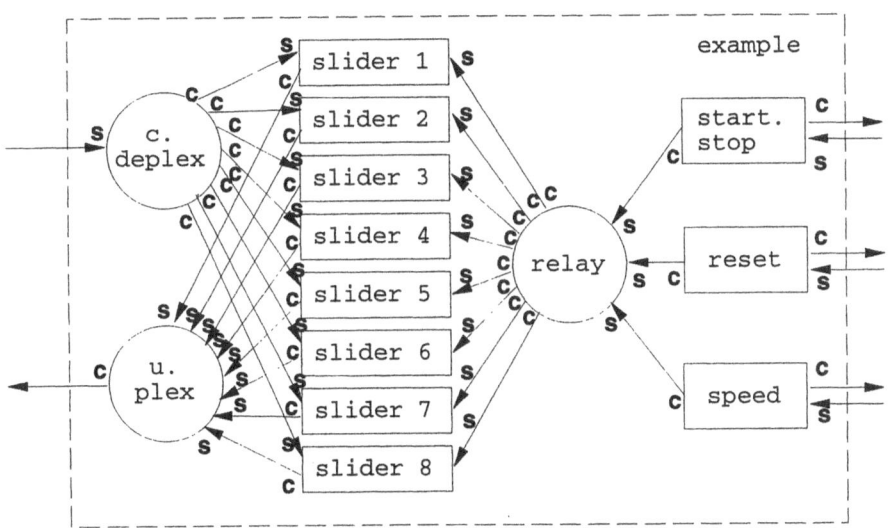

Figure 5: Correct implementation of the **example** GUI interface

In this figure, there are two new processes replacing the one in the original design – `u.plex` and `c.deplex`. This design is passed by the tool since there are now no client-server dependency cycles.

4.5 Tool output

The tool can generate several different things from the information entered during the design phase in the form of **occam** source codes and header files.

4.5.1 Interfaces

The **occam** PROC headers generated by the tool for each of the interfaces constructed during the design are as follows:

```
PROC example ([4]CHAN OF WIDGET.UPDATE update,        -- Client
              [4]CHAN OF WIDGET.CALLBACK callback)    -- Server

PROC start.stop (CHAN OF WIDGET.UPDATE update,        -- Client
                 CHAN OF WIDGET.CALLBACK callback,    -- Server
                 CHAN OF RELAY out)                   -- Client
```

```
PROC reset (CHAN OF WIDGET.UPDATE update,              -- Client
            CHAN OF WIDGET.CALLBACK callback,          -- Server
            CHAN OF RELAY out)                         -- Client

PROC speed (CHAN OF WIDGET.UPDATE update,              -- Client
            CHAN OF WIDGET.CALLBACK callback,          -- Server
            CHAN OF RELAY out)                         -- Client

PROC relay ([3]CHAN OF RELAY in,                       -- Server
            [8]CHAN OF RELAY out)                      -- Client

PROC slider (CHAN OF RELAY in,                         -- Server
             CHAN OF WIDGET.UPDATE update,             -- Client
             CHAN OF WIDGET.CALLBACK callback)         -- Server

PROC c.deplex ([8]CHAN OF WIDGET.CALLBACK app.callback, -- Client
               CHAN OF WIDGET.CALLBACK callback)         -- Server

PROC u.plex ([8]CHAN OF WIDGET.UPDATE app.update,      -- Server
             CHAN OF WIDGET.UPDATE update)             -- Client
```

If any user-defined PROTOCOLs are used in the system, and they are in this case, the #INCLUDE file in which they are defined must be given at design-time. This information will be generated before the relevant PROC headers.

4.5.2   Composite process implementation

The top-level example process is a composite client-server for which the tool generates the following code:

```
#INCLUDE "widget.inc"    -- definitions of the WIDGET protocols

PROC example ([4]CHAN OF WIDGET.UPDATE update,         -- Client
              [4]CHAN OF WIDGET.CALLBACK callback)     -- Server
  #INCLUDE "relay.inc"   -- definition of the RELAY protocol
  [8]CHAN OF WIDGET.CALLBACK deplex.to.slider:
  [8]CHAN OF WIDGET.UPDATE slider.to.plex:
  [8]CHAN OF RELAY relay.to.slider:
  [3]CHAN OF RELAY buttons.to.relay:
  PAR
    start.stop (update[0], callback[0], buttons.to.relay[0])
    reset (update[1], callback[1], buttons.to.relay[1])
    speed (update[2], callback[2], buttons.to.relay[2])
    relay (buttons.to.relay, relay.to.slider)
    PAR i = 0 FOR 8
      slider (relay.to.slider[i], slider.to.plex[i],
              deplex.to.slider[i])
    c.deplex (deplex.to.slider, callback[3])
    u.plex (slider.to.plex, update[3])
:
```

In practice, the tool would not bother to generate meaningful names for the internal channels – this code is not for human consumption or modification.

4.5.3 Low-level process skeletons

All the basic processes in this example use the Client-Server paradigm. Skeleton
code for these have two forms: one for when multiple channels are being served
and a much simplified version if only a single channel is being served In the
latter case, we have:

```
...  declare local data structures
SEQ
  ...  initialise (may make client calls)
  WHILE TRUE
    SEQ
      server.channel ? ...
      ...  computation on message (may make client calls)
```

For starvation-free servicing of an array of server channels, one of the standard
occam idioms for "fair" ALTs (see [19]) may be employed:

```
...  declare local data structures
INT favourite:
SEQ
  ...  initialise (may make client calls)
  favourite := 0
  WHILE TRUE
    ALT i = favourite FOR SIZE server.channel
      VAL INT j IS i REM (SIZE server.channel):
      server.channel[j] ? ...
        SEQ
          ...  computation on message (may make client calls)
          favourite := j + 1
```

4.6 Filling in the skeletons

The code for the bodies of the lowest-level processes can now be expanded from
skeletons. For example:

```
PROC start.stop (CHAN OF WIDGET.UPDATE update,
                 CHAN OF WIDGET.CALLBACK callback,
                 CHAN OF RELAY out)
  ...  declare state variables (BOOL running)
  SEQ
    ...  initialise state and draw widget (running := FALSE)
    WHILE TRUE
      callback ? CASE
        button.pressed
          IF
            running
              ...  (out ! stop)  || change state & widget label
            TRUE
              ...  (out ! start)  || change state & widget label
        ...  ignore other events
  :
```

The code for **reset** and **speed** is even simpler – no local state information needs to be maintained and no update to the button or slider display is needed when an event occurs.

The **relay** process is a server running a *fair* ALT over the its incoming RELAY channels, broadcasting all messages to the slider processes:

```
PROC relay ([3]CHAN OF RELAY in, [8]CHAN OF RELAY out)
  INT favourite:
  SEQ
    favourite := 0
    WHILE TRUE
      ALT favourite = 0 FOR SIZE in
        VAL INT j IS i REM (SIZE in):
        in[j] ? CASE
          start
            SEQ
              PAR k = 0 FOR SIZE out
                out[k] ! start
              favourite := j + 1
          ... similarly for the other message types
  :
```

The **slider** processes are servers waiting on three things: messages from the buttons, callbacks from Motif (via **u.plex** and **c.deplex**) and timeouts from an occam TIMER that mean that the slider must be moved. The latter results in a call to Motif to update the slider image.

```
PROC slider (CHAN OF WIDGET.UPDATE update,
             CHAN OF WIDGET.CALLBACK callback,
             CHAN OF RELAY in)
  TIMER time:
  ... other state variables
  SEQ
    ... initialise state, draw widget and set timeout
    WHILE TRUE
      PRI ALT
        running & time ? AFTER timeout
          ... move slider onwards and set next timeout
        in ? CASE
          ... handle application messages (start, stop, ...)
        callback ? CASE
          ... handle callback messages (change slider value)
  :
```

5 Conclusions

We have taken the approach of constraining the way parallel systems are designed to those with well-behaved patterns of synchronisation that can be guaranteed free from deadlock, livelock and starvation. This is in contrast to allowing arbitrary patterns of process synchronisation (through the free application of communication primitives) and the retrospective analysis of the resulting design.

The supported design paradigms, I/O-PAR and client-server, are the (recursive) closure of basic synchronisation behaviours under particular rules for parallel composition. This allows structured system design with only local verification necessary for each level of structure. This means that the tool supporting the design is computationally light and that the methodology is practical.

The theorems and proofs concerning the paradigms are rooted in the traces, failures, divergences model of CSP, as are the formal (denotational) semantics of occam2 [20, 21]. The initial binding of the tool is, therefore, strictly bound to this language. Bindings can be made to other languages that support (or have been extended to support through, for example, MPI) the CSP communication primitives (!, ?) and constructors (parallel and choice). However, we are not aware of *any* formal semantics for these extensions (or even for the underlying languages) and so would view such bindings with caution – especially in a safety-critical context. Bindings to asynchronous communication mechanisms (such as exist in PVM and MPI) are certainly not in order.

Other design paradigms will be supported in the future. In particular, the rules governing data-sharing in occam2 – that automatically ensure thread-safety in all designs – can be relaxed to allow much more concurrency to take place *without* removing that thread-safe guarantee. Correct exploitation of the proposed data-sharing mechanisms require their guarding with appropriate synchronisation patterns. A tool that is aware of the rules can guarantee correct usage. These data-sharing rules will be especially important for future parallel architectures incorporating virtual shared-memory, where they will enable dynamic process allocation, greatly reduce the need for run-time cache-coherency hardware, increase physical concurrency and yield proper parallel scaling of performance [22, 23].

Ultimately, once these paradigms have been proved useful, they should be bound into the programming language. Code-generation can be made much more efficient if the code-generator can see the high-level paradigms rather than just low-level primitives. In principle, it is possible to merge the graphical design tool with the programming language compiler and eliminate the 'programming' stage entirely.

The current version of the tool is implemented using Tcl/Tk [24] and is, therefore, portable across Unix and Windows platforms. It targets occam2.1 [3], which is now a widely available portable multi-processing language. Context-switching is extremely fast with KRoC (around 250 nanoseconds on a 133 MHz DEC Alpha running OSF/1 and with no limit on the number of processes [5]), so that performance is not degraded by all the (software) concurrency.

We are especially grateful for feedback and advice from: our sponsors at the DRA Farnborough; our colleagues in the *occam-for-all* project (which is part of the EPSRC Portable Software Tools for Parallel Architectures programme); Jeremy Martin (Oxford) and Ian East (Buckingham) who formalised the safety rules underlying this paper; and Tom Locke, Steve Neal and Mark Joslyn, whose undergraduate project at UKC on occam/Motif inter-operation provided the example outlined in this paper.

References

[1] C.A.R. Hoare. *Communicating Sequential Processes*. Prentice Hall, 1985.

[2] INMOS Ltd. occam2 *Reference Manual*. Prentice Hall, 1988.

[3] SGS-Thomson Microelectronics Ltd. occam2.1 *reference manual*. SGS-Thomson Microelectronics Ltd., <URL:http://www.hensa.ac.uk/ parallel/ occam/documents/>, 1995.

[4] M. Debbage, M. Hill, S. Wykes, and D. Nicole. Southampton's portable occam compiler (SPOC). In Roger Miles and Alan Chalmers, editors, *Proceedings of WoTUG-17: Progress in Transputer and occam Research*, volume 38 of *Transputer and occam Engineering*, pages 40–55, IOS Press, Amsterdam, April 1994.

[5] P.H. Welch and D.C. Wood. KRoC – the Kent Retargetable occam Compiler. In B. O'Neill, editor, *Proceedings of WoTUG 19*, IOS Press, Amsterdam, March 1996. <URL:http://www.hensa.ac.uk/parallel/ occam/ projects/occam-for-all/kroc/>.

[6] M.D. Poole. occam *for all*: Two approaches to retargeting the INMOS occam compiler. In B. O'Neill, editor, *Proceedings of WoTUG 19*, IOS Press, Amsterdam, March 1996. ISBN 90 5199 261 0.

[7] K.J. Vella. CSP/occam on networks of workstations. In A. Shafarenko et al., editors, *Proceedings of UKPAR96*. Springer-Verlag, July 1996.

[8] P. Brinch Hansen. The programming language superpascal. *Software Practice and Experience*, 24(5):467–483, May 1994.

[9] PACT, Foulkeslaan 87, 2625 RB Delft, The Netherlands. *The PACT Parallel C Reference Manual*, February 1992.

[10] Computer System Architects, 100 Library Plaza, 15 North 100 East, Provo, UT 84606-3100, USA. *Logical Systems C for the Transputer: Version 89.1 Manual Set*.

[11] INMOS. *ANSI C Manual Set D0314-DOCA*.

[12] MPI Forum. *MPI: A message-passing interface*. Technical Report CS/E 94-013, Department of Computer Science, Oregon Graduate Institute, March 94.

[13] E.W. Dijkstra. *A Class of Simple Communication Patterns, Selected Writings on Computing: A Personal Perspective*. Springer-Verlag, 1982.

[14] P. Brinch Hansen. *Operating System Principles*. Prentice-Hall, 1973.

[15] A.W. Roscoe and N. Dathi. *The pursuit of deadlock freedom*. Technical Monograph PRG-57, Oxford University Computing Laboratory, 1986.

[16] P.H. Welch, G.R.R. Justo, and C. Willcock. High-level paradigms for deadlock-free high-performance systems. In Grebe et al., editors, *Transputer Applications and Systems '93*, pages 981–1004, IOS Press, Amsterdam, 1993

[17] J. Martin, I. East, and S. Jassim. Design rules for deadlock freedom. *Transputer Communications*, 2(3):121–133, John Wiley & Sons Ltd, September 1994.

[18] J.M.R. Martin and P.H. Welch. A design strategy for deadlock-free concurrent systems. *Transputer Communications*. John Wiley & Sons Ltd, (submitted September 1995).

[19] G. Jones. Carefully scheduled selection with ALT. occam *User Group (OUG) Newsletter*, 10, 1989.

[20] M.H. Goldsmith, A.W. Roscoe, and B.G.O. Scott. Denotational semantics for occam2 (part 1). *Transputer Communications*, 1(2):65–91, John Wiley & Sons Ltd, November 1993.

[21] M.H. Goldsmith, A.W. Roscoe, and B.G.O. Scott. Denotational semantics for occam2 (part 2). *Transputer Communications*, 2(1):25–67, John Wiley & Sons Ltd, March 1994.

[22] P.H. Welch. Parallel hardware and parallel software: a reconciliation. In *Proceedings of the ZEUS'95 and NTUG'95 Conference, Linkoping, Sweden*, pages 287–301, IOS Press, Amsterdam, May 1995. ISBN 90-5199-22-7.

[23] B. Cook and R. Peel. The para-pc, an analysis. In B. O'Neill, editor, *Proceedings of WoTUG 19*, pages 89–102, IOS Press, Amsterdam, March 1996. ISBN 90 5199 261 0.

[24] J. K. Outsterhout. *Tcl and the Tk Toolkit*. Addison-Wesley, 1994.

CSP/Occam on Networks of Workstations

Kevin J. Vella

Computing Laboratory, University of Kent at Canterbury
Canterbury, Kent, U.K.
Department of Computer Science and A.I., University of Malta
Msida, Malta

Abstract

This paper introduces oc-net, a software communications system which implements the CSP/occam model of communication and synchronisation across networks of workstations. The spotlight is initially directed towards the design of oc-net, the finer grain parallelism it accommodates, and its careful integration into the operating environment, which distinguishes itself, if mishandled, in being hostile to oc-net's objectives. The second part of the paper describes a preliminary empirical measurement of oc-net's raw message passing performance *vis à vis* popular parallel computing software for networks of workstations. Parallels are drawn between the latters' unrestrained models of parallelism, and occam's carefully controlled communication topologies, to which various advantages can be attributed.

1   Introduction

oc-net is a software communications system which implements the CSP/occam model [13, 15] of communication and synchronisation across interconnected UNIX [24] based computers, communicating through a variety of suitable underlying transport layers. Initially, this system targets TCP/IP-driven [27] workstation networks. No strings are attached to this particular configuration, however, as the system is sufficiently flexible to allow third parties to include support for multiple coexisting transport mechanisms. The communications system integrates tightly with run-time environments which schedule user level processes, representing occam processes, within a single operating systém process (see [32, 5]). The design of the run-time environment itself is not an integral part of this project.

oc-net communicates with the run-time environment through a clean, simple interface, which makes it possible to extend a whole range of CSP- and occam-like environments to handle external communication alongside their inbuilt internal communication support in a uniform manner. Nonblocking primitives which initiate external communication and return immediately allow the user level scheduler to overlap external communication with further computation by executing other runnable processes, while presenting individual processes with a synchronous outlook on communication. The processes themselves are not able to distinguish between internal and external communication, and use the same operation to perform both; it is the run-time environment that distinguishes between the two and acts accordingly.

Since the weight of operating system communication calls is ultimately borne by the same processor as that which performs computation, their impact cannot be hidden completely. Nonetheless, experiments with oc-net have the motivation of cutting back on further overheads by reducing the number of operating system context switches it induces, and minimising the fraction of allocated time-slices wasted in a blocked state and in performing system functions. Reaping the benefits of such efforts, oc-net will be used to promote and examine the extent to which fine grain parallelism can be exploited in a hostile operating environment such as UNIX.

To date, the KRoC [32] kernel for occam programs has been adapted for use with oc-net with success. This kernel achieves context switch and internal interprocess communication times well under a microsecond on current microprocessors, and represents the class of run-time environment which oc-net readily accommodates. The overhead thus incurred on oc-net operation is negligible, and the speed of internal communication is not affected at all. Integrating similar run-time environments with oc-net should present no ulterior difficulties or overheads.

After explaining how oc-net relates with other work in the same vein, and briefly reviewing the occam philosophy, we deal with the central issue of the communications system design. Subsequent sections give details pertaining to the operating environment of oc-net, and mention the problem of network configuration and program initialisation. Finally, the raw message passing performance of one oc-net configuration on an Ethernet-based network of UNIX workstations is briefly analysed and compared with that of other message passing systems. The performance of real occam applications distributed using oc-net and exploiting fine grain parallelism will be discussed in a separate report.

2 Related research

An environment for executing parallel programs expressed in a safe, pure parallel language on a wide variety of architectures is a desirable tool. Various parallel programming environments exist in the form of libraries used in conjunction with a sequential language such as C or FORTRAN. PVM [9], P4 [3] and MPI [7] are instances of this approach. MPI only specifies a standard programming interface: current implementations such as MPICH build a layer on top of existing message passing systems. It is our belief that such combinations make both formal and intuitive reasoning about a parallel program as a single entity rather difficult, since the semantics of parallelism are not part and parcel of the language, but are stuck on as an afterthought. Consequently communicating processes cannot readily be thought of as part of the *same* program [31]. On the other hand, the occam language [15, 1] offers parallelism as an integral part of the language, and a stable formal basis for reasoning about parallel algorithms [10, 11, 4], based on CSP [13], or related process algebræ [22].

Furthermore, the coarse grain parallelism which such libraries impose limits the amount of readily identifiable fine grain parallelism which can be exploited on architectural platforms with low communication overheads. In less favourable situations, these libraries depend on this coarseness to hide high communication overheads. Instead, the occam approach [2] aims to hide such overheads by allocating several small processes to a processor and exploiting the parallel slackness [28] thus made available. On architectures with low communication overheads, occam programs expose the fine grain parallelism which can now be exploited to improve execution speed.

3 The CSP/Occam paradigm

The occam language is based on the CSP model of concurrency. Three primitive processes are defined, analogous to statements in a sequential imperative language: assignment, input and output. Both parallel and sequential composition are presented as first class constructs to be used at the same level of granularity. The parallel construct PAR contains an implicit barrier synchronisation between its components at their termination. Message passing is through unidirectional, point-to-point, synchronous channels connecting pairs of processes. Consequently, normal communication is deterministic, since contention does not occur on occam channels. Strict usage rules which can be statically checked are enforced for variables and channels in parallel processes, excluding the possibility of any form of contention, and consequently nondeterminism which could be casually overlooked by programmers.

occam programmers can willingly introduce nondeterminism using the ALT choice construct, which creates contention on a process residing on the receiving end of multiple channels, rather than contention on a channel. No fairness is guaranteed by this construct. By allowing the introduction of nondeterminism only explicitly, groups of processes can be guaranteed to be safe from nondeterminism, and the points which act as a source of nondeterministic execution can be pinpointed statically, thus allowing the partitioning of a program into deterministic groups of processes with nondeterminism at the boundaries. Priority choice can be expressed using the PRI ALT construct which can be used to promote any kind of fairness desired for resolving contention.

4 System design

In this section the major design decisions taken during the development of oc-net will be exposed and justified, while describing the present system structure. Details relating specifically to UNIX and TCP/IP are covered separately in Section 5.

4.1 Interfacing with the run-time environment

An occam run-time environment must provide a set of operations which processes use to perform communication and synchronisation. Differing implementations of these mechanisms may influence the choice of operations offered to the processes. The predominant implementation is that incorporated in the Inmos Transputer [16, 18], since reproduced in other known occam implementations such as [32, 5]. The following is a subset of these operations, which will be referred to in this paper:

in(c, a, l) initiates an input on channel c, to receive l bytes of data into local memory starting at location a. The process issuing this operation blocks until the input is completed.

out(c, a, l) initiates an output on channel c, to send l bytes of data starting at location a in local memory. The process issuing this operation blocks until the output is completed.

altstart indicates the start of a guarded alternative section.

enable(c) includes channel c in the set of channels to take part in the current alternative.

altwt blocks the process until an enabled channel is ready for communication.

disable(c) removes channel c from the set of enabled channels, checking whether the channel is ready for communication. In the affirmative case, the channel identification is stored for later use.

altend indicates the end of a guarded alternative section. Subsequent to this operation, an in is typically performed across the selected channel, which is now guaranteed to be ready for communication.

oc-net presents a corresponding set of operations which implement the distributed version. The oc-net counterparts to these operations, though, do not block, as other occam processes must be executed while the communication proceeds. The process calling the operations through the run-time environment is not aware whether the process on the other side of the channel lies within the same environment (i.e. the channel is an internal channel) or not. Logic within the run-time environment identifies the nature of the channel, and processes are descheduled and rescheduled as necessary. The run-time system handles communication on an internal channel without outside involvement. This way, the introduction of oc-net has practically no adverse effect on internal communication cost. If, however, the channel is external, the run-time system simply invokes the analogous — non-blocking — operation in oc-net after performing the necessary descheduling. Figure 1 depicts this interface.

The run-time system is notified of input and output completion asynchronously by oc-net, which calls specially written routines within the extended

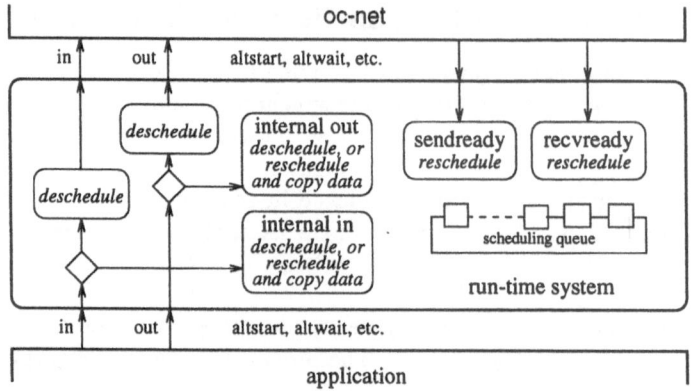

Figure 1: The interface between the run-time system and oc-net.

run-time environment to reschedule the appropriate occam processes. For instance, **recvready**(c) and **sendready**(c) are called when **in** and **out** operations respectively are completed on the external channel c. Care must be taken to control concurrent access of shared scheduler structures between the normal run-time environment execution flow, and the interrupting completion notification routine. This problem is handled within the extended run-time environment and not occam as it involves run-time environment specific details.

4.2   System organisation

Having defined a clean interface between oc-net and the run-time environment, the organisation of oc-net will be described in some detail. Figure 2 illustrates the context in which oc-net operates.

The preliminary design report for oc-net [29] argues in favour of housing oc-net in a separate operating system process from the run-time environment where applicable, using an inexpensive mechanism such as shared memory for coordination. This design is currently, possibly temporarily, shelved in favour of cohabitation, due to limitations in shared memory facilities in current UNIX implementations, increased communications startup latency, and the envisaged high cost of frequently switching between the two processes. The current arrangement, whereby both oc-net and the occam processes reside within a single UNIX process, enables incoming data to be written directly into its final destination, and similarly, outgoing data to be read directly from source.

After the run-time system initiates an external communication, oc-net proceeds mainly in the background in an interrupt-driven manner, stealing application execution time. Whenever the host process receives a packet or a message, oc-net takes over in the form of a signal handler (or an interrupt handler, if appropriate in the operating environment). Depending on whether the relevant communication operation is completed or not, oc-net either sends a response

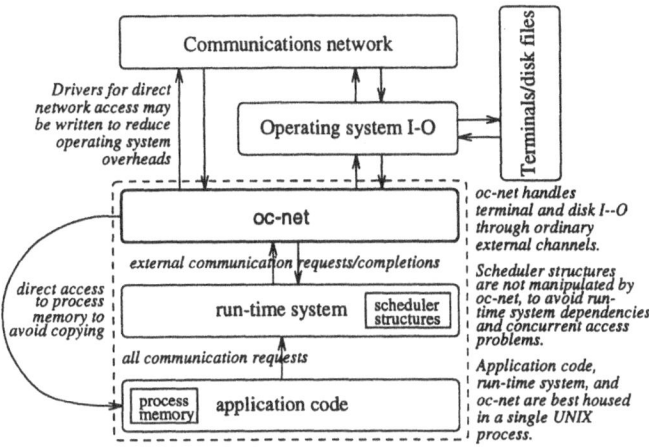

Figure 2: oc-net in context

to the other end and immediately relinquishes control, or calls the completion
routine supplied by the run-time environment.

4.3 Implementation of message passing

The oc-net design for message passing was heavily influenced by the Inmos
T9000's Virtual Channel Processor (VCP) [21]. The VCP creates a 'virtual
channel' abstraction to multiplex channels over a physical serial link by pack-
etising messages, and operates independently of the T9000's computational
engine. In a network of C104 routers, which implement a full crossbar switch
in VLSI, a large number of external channels can extend between processes on
remote T9000s. oc-net can be thought of as a 'refittable VCP'. Here too, the
network fabric is not visible: in the case of TCP/IP networks, IP routing will
replace the C104 functionality.

Prior to application execution, a series of connections is set up on the workstation network, to be maintained throughout (unless a communications driver
chooses to establish connections dynamically, which can be inefficient). These
connections link pairs of processors together. Each link can either be set up
as a *stream link* which holds one or two unmultiplexed channels in opposite
directions, or a *packet link* over which multiple *virtual links* each holding a pair
of *virtual channels* can be multiplexed. These resemble Inmos T800 stream
links [16] and Inmos T9000 links [17] respectively. Unlike T9000 links, packet
links often connect the same pair of processors, as many packet link transport mechanisms, for example TCP, form point-to-point connections (on the
other hand, UDP, being connectionless, can send and receive packets from several other hosts). The internal organisation of oc-net, depicting the message
passing mechanisms, is shown in Figure 3.

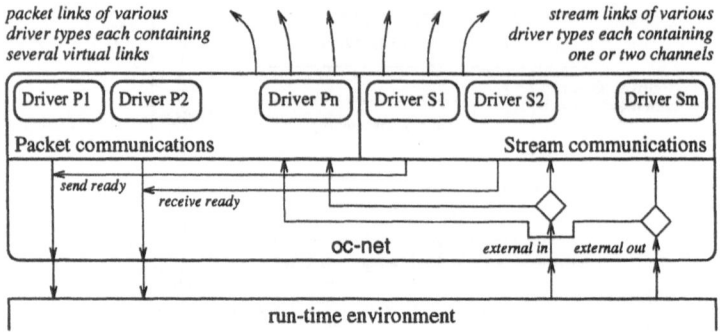

Figure 3: The anatomy of oc-net.

One reason for introducing packet links into oc-net is to overcome limitations imposed by the underlying operating environment. The number of network connections pertaining to a process in various operating systems is severely limited. Though dedicating a connection to a stream link can lead to better performance, wasteful use will limit application scalability. Through careful use of packet links, each pair of processors holding several mutually communicating processes uses up only one connection on either side. This does raise the threshold of this limitation, but does not remove it; complementary solutions will be suggested in Section 5.2. It is hoped that packet links can also be put to use in multiplexing channels over other communications devices, such as serial ports. Only one buffer of fixed length is held by each virtual link on a packet link.

Stream links in general involve less overhead than packet links. Packet links can introduce extra memory copying in order to construct packets to be sent, or to separate packet headers from data in received packets. Moreover message passing using stream links involves oc-net less often than using packet links, as in the latter case, every packet received invokes oc-net to send a response packet.

4.4 Communications drivers

A projected use for oc-net is in comparing the effectiveness of different underlying communication mechanisms. It will be relatively straightforward for third parties to compile in new packet and stream drivers to the active suite. Drivers are isolated in modules with a simple interface to the oc-net communications logic. Besides the initialisation, connection setup, and shutdown functions, which are not called during actual program execution, a driver has few points of contact with oc-net. A packet driver must provide a **sendpkt** function, while a stream driver must provide the analogous **sendmsg** function. Whenever a packet or message is received, an interrupt is raised by the operating environment and handled by oc-net. It identifies the link which holds the pending packet or message, looks up the driver handling the link, and calls the driver's **recvpkt** or **recvmsg** function.

Currently, packet drivers which take advantage of TCP/IP protocols, such as TCP and UDP, in various ways are being experimented with. Stream drivers can be developed for terminal I-O, and for general file I-O in a UNIX environment. oc-net should be able to serve all application I-O requirements in a CSP/occam style. To achieve higher performance, it should be possible to write drivers which bypass operating system I-O and manipulate hardware devices directly.

As an added bonus, occam programs need not be aware of changes in the link structure, or link types, which carry their channels: occam does not even indicate which channels in a program are external. Program modules do not have to be recompiled, as the instruction sequence for external communication across any link type is identical to that for internal communication. All that needs to be done is to change initialisation data which defines the process-to-processor and channel-to-link mapping. Tools for defining the components of the parallel computer within the workstation network, and for specifying the program mapping, are not an integral part of oc-net; the concept will be discussed briefly in Section 6.

5 The operating environment

oc-net presently operates under the UNIX operating system [24], though future adaptations may target other environments, possibly even bare microprocessors. Large operating systems in common use, of which UNIX is a prime example, typically provide mechanisms for interprocess communication and synchronisation, networking, and more recently, support for lightweight processes. However, some of these features are too expensive for realistic use in an occam environment.

5.1 Process scheduling and interprocess communications

It is generally agreed that UNIX process scheduling is too expensive for efficiently supporting fine grain parallelism. This cost arises partly from managing protected memory areas belonging to each UNIX process. Various lightweight process, or thread, implementations aim to rectify this deficiency by forsaking memory protection for faster scheduling of lightweight processes within a single UNIX process. Still, few or none at all manage to achieve context switch times under a few tens of microseconds, which is too costly for effective exploitation of occam parallelism. The principal means of interprocess communication (IPC) in current UNIX systems suffer from similar ailments: message queue and semaphore operations both consume milliseconds of processor time [26]. Their lightweight process counterparts achieve better results, but remain too expensive for the sub-microsecond times desired for occam interprocess communication within the same environment.

Consequently, existing implementations of occam on UNIX [32, 5] implement their own user level process mechanism, achieving faster operation by context switching only at predetermined points in the processes, where a minimum of state has to be stored, and, in the case of KRoC, keeping scheduler data such as queue pointers in machine registers. oc-net integrates easily with such implementations.

5.2 TCP/IP sockets, asynchronous I–O and signals

The *de facto* standard for UNIX networking is the TCP/IP protocol suite [27, 6], predominantly accessed through the sockets programming interface [25]. The sockets interface enables connections, once established, to be used as ordinary files identified by file descriptors. Hence oc-net can handle different connection types in a uniform manner through file descriptors. Adding on support for a new transport medium is more straightforward if the device is accessible through the file system interface. This unified interface allows oc-net to concurrently handle various link types based on TCP, UDP, disk files, terminal I–O, and serial ports.

UNIX imposes limitations on the number of file descriptors, and consequently on links, which individual UNIX processes can own. This can severely limit interprocessor connectivity through TCP/IP which is envisaged to be the main medium for oc-net on workstation networks. Various ways of overcoming this limitation have been identified. A single, connection-less, UDP socket (with appropriate reliability enforcement added on) can be used to multiplex connections between multiple hosts at the cost of one socket per environment. This is the method used by PVM unless specifically instructed to do otherwise. Alternatively a special multiplexing process on one host can act as a crossbar to push the connectivity limit up — though the store-and-forward technique employed will probably be much more expensive than simply using UDP (which, incidentally, completely does away with the limit). The third method, which will be employed in oc-net, involves multiplexing a TCP connection stream between multiple channels. This technique has the advantage of integrating easily with the other methods just mentioned: the same multiplexing logic can be used for both TCP and UDP connections, and the multiplexing process described earlier can likewise be used to carry data from such connections.

Normally input and output operations on file descriptors can block the calling UNIX process until they are completed. Nonetheless, it is possible to make a file descriptor non-blocking, causing send and receive operations to return with an error condition if the operation could not be completed immediately. An additional setting instructs UNIX to notify arrival of any data on the descriptor by sending a signal to the process (this is often referred to as asynchronous notification, and should not be confused with asynchronous I–O which will be discussed next). Furthermore, in the case of TCP, the size of the send buffer can be increased, thus enabling larger amounts of outgoing data to be accommodated without blocking. In such an environment, it is possible for oc-net to send amounts of data without blocking, and be notified asynchronously of incoming data, effectively removing the need for polling.

Some UNIX implementations, such as SunOS and Solaris, provide a form of asynchronous I-O [14], which allows the programmer to initiate an input or an output without blocking the process, and be notified only when the operation has finished. This feature can facilitate the operation of oc-net significantly. However, it seems that Sun's implementation up to Solaris 2.4 operates at a user level, using Sun's lightweight processes, and preliminary tests indicate that startup time is not insubstantial. As from Solaris 2.5 a more efficient kernel level implementation has been introduced. On a brighter (and more portable) note, the POSIX.1b specification [8], also known as POSIX.4, includes asynchronous I-O amongst other features, and more operating systems (such as SGI IRIX, DEC OSF/1 and IBM AIX) are beginning to provide some extent of POSIX.1b functionality. Such implementations are at the kernel level, and will therefore operate efficiently.

The main aim being performance, one cannot help noticing that TCP/IP carries substantial baggage for our purposes. In its favour are ubiquity, portability across platforms, medium independence, and transparent routing. To improve performance it is necessary to tune some settings. The greatest impact is achieved by disabling the Nagle algorithm [23], which normally delays the flushing of a near-empty TCP send buffer by a few hundreds of milliseconds. While the Nagle algorithm can help increase overall network capacity by decreasing the number of small packets in transit, it wreaks havoc with small message latency in parallel programs.

6 Configuration and initialisation

A vital issue which has not yet been tackled is how to initialise and run application programs on the resulting 'parallel computer' in an elegant and transparent manner; currently, much of the initialisation is performed through manually coded low level setup routines. The requirements will now be discussed, and a preliminary solution sketched, drawing from the T9000 Transputer Development System (TDS) [19, 20] approach. The initialisation process involves:

1. distributing a base system across processors which will form part of the parallel computer. Once loaded, these dæmons may be retained for subsequent execution of different programs;

2. setting up links between processors to form a virtual topology of processors. At this point, a parallel computer configuration is fully formed, and different applications may execute on it without reconfiguration;

3. loading the processors with executable application code, and setting up external channels across the links. The link setup between processors, in (2), may be automatically decided on the basis of the external channel requirements for the particular application;

4. starting execution of the application across the parallel computer.

To the extent that is technically possible, these tasks should be performed by a module which is detached from both the run-time system and oc-net. The information required to perform the above four steps is conveyed in two specifications in addition to the occam program. The first, termed the *network description* specifies the hosts on the network to act as components of the parallel computer and their interconnection structure in terms of packet and stream links of various driver types; the second specification maps occam processes and channels onto the processors and links defined in the network description language. The programmer can be equipped with a simple language to convey these specifications. In order to avoid unnecessary repetition of all the initialisation steps, which may take a nontrivial proportion of the overall execution time for small applications, the module should make it possible to skip initialisation steps and reuse existing configurations. This is by no means the final formulation of the initialisation process, and some rethinking may be necessary at a later stage.

7 Performance of a TCP-based packet driver

Preliminary tests were performed comparing oc-net with other popular message passing software for networks of workstations. An experimental packet driver based on TCP was constructed using only portable UNIX features, and all tests were carried out using this driver. The tests only measure raw message passing performance, and should not be considered a definitive measure of the adequacy of a particular system, since real application performance also depends on other factors.

One important distinction must be made between oc-net and the other systems being considered. Whereas in other systems, the invocation of a communication operation suspends the entire UNIX process, oc-net attempts to minimise the time spent in a blocked state. This does incur some overheads, mainly due to time spent in asynchronous completion notification. However, the overall effect is not overwhelming, and has the significant advantage of allowing computation to continue within the *same* UNIX process. In the other systems, when the communicating process is blocked, the UNIX scheduler is used to activate other processes in the parallel program as heavyweight UNIX processes; oc-netattempts to avoid this scheduling overhead.

The unpredictable communication paths allowed in both PVM and P4 prevents these systems from establishing connections prior to application execution. Consequently, the first communication between any two processes over a TCP connection is burdened with the cost of establishing the connection. The static nature of occam parallelism allows the channel topology of the application to be determined prior to run-time and ensures that no such unpleasant events occur during application execution.

7.1 A non-blocking I–O TCP packet driver

As the tests were carried out using a packet driver, overheads were incurred mainly through two activities: constructing and dismantling packets in memory, and having to communicate acknowledgment for the current data packet before the next data packet is sent. This packet driver sends and receives packets over TCP, through the standard sockets interface. The driver increases the TCP send buffer size sufficiently in order to accommodate outgoing packets without blocking the send system call. The system asynchronously notifies the driver of any data received on the socket. During setup time, the Nagle algorithm is disabled on the socket, so as to prevent delays when sending small amounts of data. The send buffer size is set to accommodate the maximum amount of data that can be issued at any one time by all the channels multiplexed over the link: the more channels are multiplexed over the link, the smaller the packet size allowable. Since the TCP stream abstraction does not care for message boundaries, the driver is notified of received data as it arrives and not necessarily at packet boundaries, so provision must be made for the reception and reassembly of a fragmented packet. The driver takes advantage of the fact that the fragments of a packet arrive in order and not interleaved with fragments from other packets. For the purposes of the test, a 50000 byte packet size was set up.

7.2 The other message passing software

The systems whose message passing performance is analysed, PVM and P4 (a descendent of PARMACS), are arguably the commonest systems in use on networks of workstations. The popular MPICH [12] implementation of MPI interfaces with either of the two above systems.

7.2.1 PVM – Parallel Virtual Machine

PVM houses processes within the same host in separate UNIX processes. A PVM dæmon on each host launches user programs and performs various other tasks. PVM has various send and receive operations, none of which implement synchronisation between the communicating processes. The programmer can choose to pack data using XDR (external data representation), essential for heterogeneous operation, though rather expensive in terms of processor time. Two communication techniques are used by PVM. The default method passes messages through the PVM dæmon, which subsequently communicates the message using UDP to the dæmon at the far end. The other, more efficient method can be specified by the programmer, and involves the setting up of a direct TCP connection between the two communicating processes. Since PVM cannot predict at compile-time which processes will eventually communicate, connections are established at run-time, when two processes first communicate between themselves, at substantial cost. PVM version 3.3 was used for testing.

7.2.2 P4 – Portable Programs for Parallel Processors

P4 processes are also housed in separate UNIX processes, and inter-host communication is carried out through TCP connections directly between processes. P4 features a *rendezvous* mode for sending and receiving messages in a synchronous manner. The programmer can opt to preallocate message buffers and use this memory to work in, in order to avoid copying messages between buffers and program variables. Again, TCP connections are established at run-time at the instance when two processes first decide to communicate. P4 version 1.4 was used for the tests.

7.3 The test environment and procedure

Tests were carried out on a pair of Sun SPARCstation 4 computers each with 32 Megabytes of main memory. The two hosts were connected through a dedicated Ethernet, guaranteeing that no extraneous traffic affected measurements. Both hosts were running standard Solaris 2.4, with a reduced setup eliminating NFS clients and servers, system log processes, and most other services, excepting the bare essentials: the Internet 'super-server' (inetd) and a handful of system processes. Hence no other processes could compete with the test processes for processor time.

All test programs, prior to entering the timed portion, executed a number of 'warming up' communication operations to eliminate start up costs which may otherwise have manifested themselves during testing. The execution time for 100 repetitions of the operation under examination was measured, and divided by 100 to obtain a mean timing for a single operation, be it a round trip, or otherwise. Each such test was performed four times on different occasions, and the four timings thus obtained were used to derive the quoted value for a single operation. The gettimeofday() call was used for timing. Generally, the sterile testing environment succeeded in keeping deviation from the average very low.

All test programs were written in C. External data representation options for heterogeneous computing in PVM were disabled, as these unfairly add up to communication cost. User managed buffers were used in P4 to reduce the amount of memory copying. For PVM, which does not offer synchronous communication, synchronisation was implemented by having the receiver return an empty acknowledgment message to the sender, which in turn blocks until this acknowledgment is received. On the other hand, P4's *rendezvous* option implements this mechanism internally. Both PVM's default dæmon mediated UDP mode, and the faster direct TCP mode were tested. The rationale behind forcing synchronous communication in all systems was to compare the efficiency of similar operations. It is true that while programming models promoted by these other systems use asynchronicity to increase efficiency, oc-net relies on parallel slackness to a much greater extent. However, for the scope of testing raw message passing performance, such a normalisation was seen as reasonable.

The oc-net tests consisted of a simple C program which interfaced with oc-net in a similar manner to KRoC. Two variants were used, the first of which

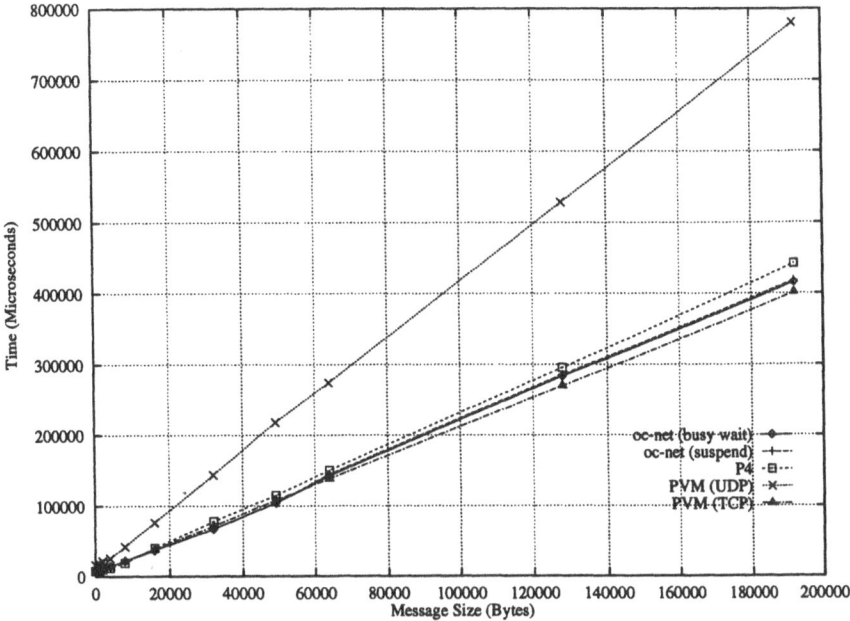

Figure 4: Round Trip Time comparisons for large message sizes.

entered a tight busy waiting loop until a flag was set from within the completion routine. This was used to emulate continued occam processes executing within the same UNIX process. The second variant instead suspended the whole UNIX process, emulating the scenario where no more occam processes can execute.

7.4   Performance evaluation

Round trip times (RTTs) for various message sizes, plotted in Figure 4, were gathered for the systems being tested, and the data transfer rate was calculated as $2 \times message\ size/RTT$. As the data transfer rates in Figure 5 demonstrate, the packet driver's performance is reasonable, growing at a faster rate than PVM or P4 for messages below the packet size of 50000 bytes (Figure 7 shows round trip times for messages fitting in a single packet). At around 50000 bytes, oc-net packet driver performance decreases to just over 7 megabits/second due to packetisation costs, and improves slowly with message size.

Figure 6 indicates that for small messages, the signal driven manner in which oc-net performs in order to avoid blocking shows up as an increase in latency. This is inevitable, since where other systems engage in a blocking operation and are reawakened with the data transfer completed, oc-net has to enter a signal handler which then completes the operation. When measuring from within a real occam environment, this latency may appear to increase slightly further,

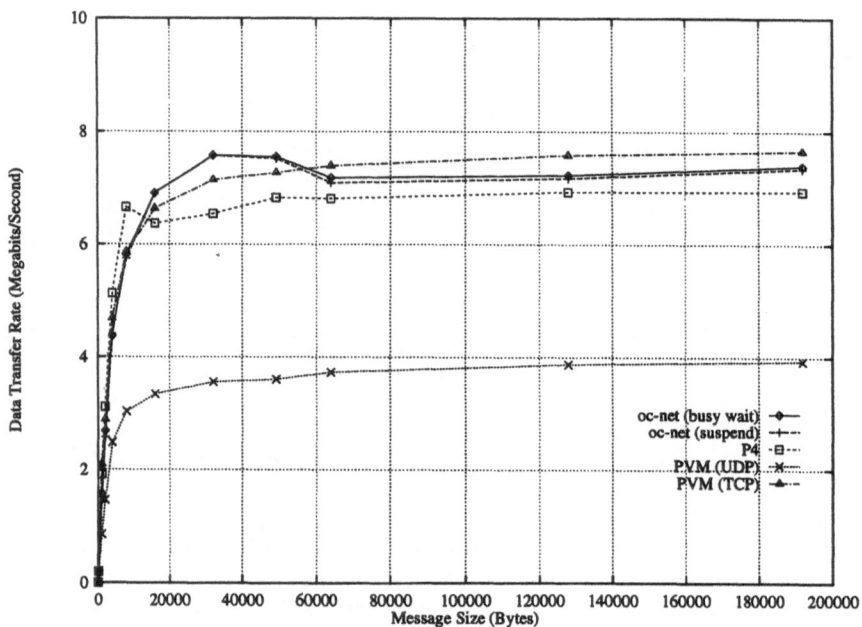

Figure 5: Comparative data transfer rates for large message sizes.

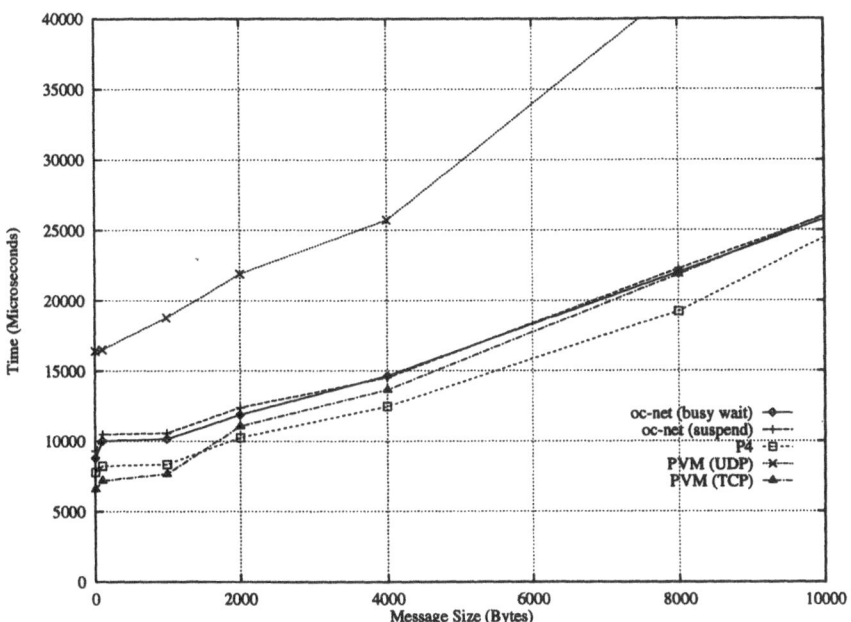

Figure 6: Round Trip Time comparisons for small message sizes.

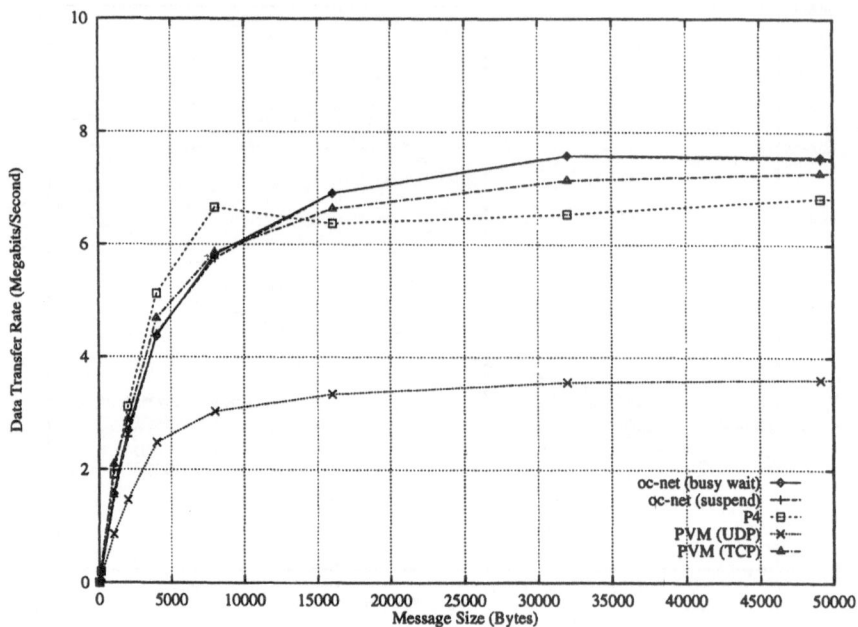

Figure 7: Comparative data transfer rates without oc-net packetisation.

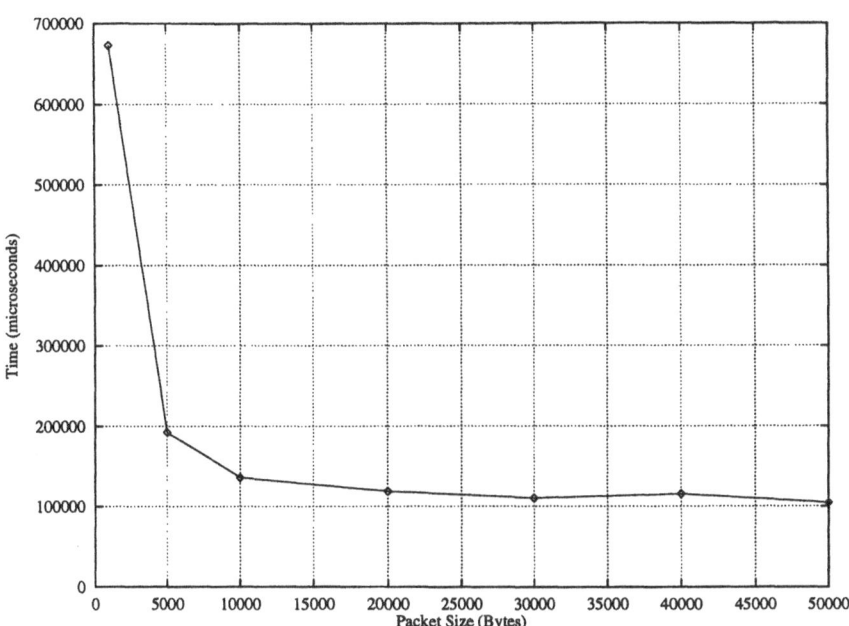

Figure 8: Effect of packet size on Round Trip Time for a 49152 byte message.

as the process for which communication has completed may not be rescheduled immediately if other occam processes are runnable at the time. The PVM UDP mode round trip time is elevated at small message sizes because of the extra overhead involved in conversation between the communicating process and the PVM dæmon.

The effect of packet size on round trip time is illustrated in Figure 8, which times a round trip for a 49152 byte message using the same packet driver with packet sizes ranging from 1000 bytes to 50000 bytes. It is immediately clear that small packet sizes are infeasible, and that packetisation does result in an overall performance degradation for messages larger than the packet size. Still, this cost is small when compared to the time required to re-establish connections at run-time as the process runs out of file descriptors, or the overheads incurred by building on UDP.

As yet, no definitive figures for time spent in initiating input and output operations and in signal handlers have been obtained. It is desirable that the amount of time spent in this regard is minimal, leaving more processor time to program execution. Ideally, the UNIX process would not be suspended at all by socket operations during the lifetime of a communication. Preliminary results indicate that the non-blocking I–O which this packet driver uses, while not as expensive as Sun's own asynchronous I–O seems, can still incur delays in milliseconds during the course of a communication. A closer investigation is warranted into the exact amount of time spent, and how: busily performing related tasks, or suspending the entire UNIX process on the way? If the latter is true, this must be rectified in some way within the packet driver.

8 Future directions

At present, a version of oc-net has been attached to the KRoC kernel, through which occam processes running on a number of workstations can communicate in an rudimentary manner using TCP/IP protocols. Work is in progress to complete stream communications logic, and various packet and stream drivers for TCP, UDP and file/terminal I–O. The performance of various oc-net drivers is still being evaluated and compared with that of other popular message passing implementations on networks of workstations.

The initialisation issue has been briefly mentioned in this paper. Initialising an exclusively TCP/IP network can be done in a uniform manner. If, however, the network contains some processors which are not interconnected through TCP/IP in any way, a method has to be devised to initialise these processors consistently with the remainder of the network. Moreover, heterogeneous processor architectures with differing word lengths and byte ordering present a challenge which should not be underestimated, since expensive conversion between complex external data formats can degrade overall system performance.

9 Conclusion

This paper outlines the design of a software communications system which implements CSP/occam communications across a network unobtrusively. A principal reason for advocating the use of large numbers of small processes in program design is the increased portability enjoyed across a variety of architectures. If an occam program can be shown to run as efficiently as coarse grain implementations on the same network of workstations, the winning argument follows from the fact that the occam program, unaltered, can also exploit the better communications performance of a dedicated parallel computer to a much greater extent than the coarse grain implementations. Another belief underlying this work is that a simple model of concurrency leads to an efficient implementation which avoids the excessive execution overheads caused by unrestrained dynamicity. This advantage can be carried over to workstations hosting large operating systems which tend to cause substantial performance deterioration unless handled with care. oc-net was designed to fit in a larger framework, with the motivation of investigating these ideals.

To conclude, we observe that prevalent network technologies such as Ethernet are often considered to be the bottleneck in current networks of workstations. With the adoption of newer, faster, and scalable technologies such as ATM [30], the computation–communication ratio will shift, revealing the weight of current operating systems. The use of light and simple techniques for communication and synchronisation will therefore continue to increase in importance in this domain.

Acknowledgments

I am grateful to Juanito Camilleri, Alex Mifsud, Mike Rizzo and Peter Welch for their comments on the content and structure of this paper. Thanks go to the entire occam For All team at the Universities of Kent and Keele for their assistance, and in particular, to David Wood and Barry Cook for help in understanding and modifying the KRoC kernel. Finally, I would like to acknowledge Peter Welch's guidance, and his role in inciting me to work in this area.

References

[1] G. Barrett. occam3 reference manual. Technical report, INMOS Limited, Bristol, BS12 4SQ, England, March 1992.

[2] G. Barrett. How to write a highly parallel program. In J.M. Kerridge, editor, *Transputer and* occam *Research : New Directions*, pages 209–217, 1993.

[3] R. M. Butler and E. L. Lusk. Monitors, messages, and clusters: the P4 parallel programming system. *Parallel Computing*, April 1994.

[4] J. A. Camilleri. An operational semantics for occam. *International Journal of Parallel Programming*, 18(5), October 1989.

[5] M. Debbage, M. Hill, S. Wykes, and D. Nicole. Southampton's portable occam compiler (SPOC). In Roger Miles and Alan Chalmers, editors, *Proceedings of WoTUG-17: Progress in Transputer and occam Research*, volume 38 of *Transputer and occam Engineering*, pages 40–55, Amsterdam, April 1994. IOS Press.

[6] S. Feit. *TCP/IP – Architecture, Protocols and Implementation*. McGraw Hill Series on Computer Communication. McGraw Hill, 1993.

[7] Message Passing Interface Forum. MPI: A message-passing interface standard. Technical report, University of Tennessee, Knoxville, May 1994.

[8] B. O. Gallmeister. *POSIX.4 – Programming for the real world*. O'Reilly & Associates, 1995.

[9] A. Geist, A. Beguelin, J. Dongarra, and W. Jiang. PVM3 user's guide and reference manual. Technical Report ORNL/TM-12187, Oak Ridge National Laboratory, May 1993.

[10] M. H. Goldsmith, A. W. Roscoe, and B. G. O. Scott. Denotational semantics for occam2 (Part 1). *Transputer Communications*, 1(2):65–91, November 1993.

[11] M. H. Goldsmith, A. W. Roscoe, and B. G. O. Scott. Denotational semantics for occam2 (Part 2). *Transputer Communications*, 2(1):25–67, March 1994.

[12] B. Gropp, R. Lusk, T. Skjellum, and N. Doss. Portable MPI model implementation. Technical report, Argonne National Laboratory, July 1994.

[13] C. A. R. Hoare. *Communicating Sequential Processes*. Prentice Hall, 1985.

[14] S. Leung. Programming asynchronous I–O in Solaris 2. *SunWorld Online*, March 1996. <URL: http://www.sunworld.com/sunworldonline/swol-03-1996/swol-03-aio.html>.

[15] INMOS Limited. occam2 *Reference Manual*. Prentice Hall, 1988.

[16] INMOS Limited. *The Transputer Databook (2nd Edition)*. INMOS Limited, 1989.

[17] INMOS Limited. *T9000 Transputer Hardware Reference Manual*. SGS-Thomson Microelectronics, 1993.

[18] INMOS Limited. *T9000 Transputer Instruction Set Manual*. SGS-Thomson Microelectronics, 1993.

[19] INMOS Limited. *T9000 Transputer Development Systems Manuals: Hardware Configuration Manual*, May 1994.

[20] INMOS Limited. *T9000 Transputer Development Systems Manuals: Toolset Reference Manual*, May 1994.

[21] M.D. May, R.M. Shepherd, and P.W. Thompson. The T9000 communications architecture. In M.D. May, P.W. Thompson, and P.H. Welch, editors, *Networks, Routers and Transputers*, chapter 2, pages 15–38. IOS Press, Amsterdam, 1993.

[22] R. Milner. *Communication and Concurrency*. Prentice Hall, 1989.

[23] J. Nagle. Congestion control in IP/TCP. RFC 896, Internet Engineering Task Force, January 1984.

[24] D. M. Ritchie and K. Thompson. The UNIX timesharing system. *Communications of the ACM*, 17(7):365–375, July 1974.

[25] W. R. Stevens. *UNIX Network Programming*. Prentice-Hall, 1990.

[26] W. R. Stevens. *Advanced programming in the UNIX environment*. Addison-Wesley Publishing Company, 1992.

[27] W. R. Stevens. *TCP/IP Illustrated, Volume 1: The protocols*. Addison-Wesley Publishing Company, 1994.

[28] L. G. Valiant. A bridging model for parallel computation. *Communications of the ACM*, 33(8), August 1990.

[29] K. J. Vella. An occam style communications system for UNIX networks. Technical Report 13-95, Computing Laboratory, University of Kent at Canterbury, November 1995.

[30] R. J. Vetter. ATM concepts, architectures, and protocols. *Communications of the ACM*, 38(2):30–38, February 1995.

[31] P. H. Welch. An occam approach to Transputer engineering. In *Proceedings of the 3rd Conference on Hypercube Concurrent Computers and Applications*, Pasadena, California, U.S., January 1988.

[32] P. H. Welch and D. C. Wood. KRoC – the Kent Retargetable occam Compiler. In B. O'Neill, editor, *Proceedings of WoTUG 19*, Amsterdam, March 1996. WoTUG, IOS Press. <URL: http://www.hensa.ac.uk /parallel/occam/projects/occam-for-all/kroc/>.

Model Generation Using Genetic Programming

A.Salhi

Dept of Electronics and Computer Science, University of Southampton
Southampton, UK

H.Glaser

Dept of Electronics and Computer Science, University of Southampton
Southampton, UK

D.De Roure

Dept of Electronics and Computer Science, University of Southampton
Southampton, UK

17th April 1996

Abstract

In search, optimisation and simulation applications, model building is largely manual. However, it may be automated if a complete enough body of data is available. The objective of the present work is to generate models for use in decision support.

In the following we shall concentrate on the method, namely genetic programming, suitable for our problem. A review of genetic programming and a description of an implementation of a tool for symbolic regression is given. Limited experimental results are reported and future improvements to the tool are also discussed.

1 Introduction

An important step in the process of generating applications in the search, optimisation and simulation domains is the generation of a requisite model. The task of building such a model is tedious, time consuming and prone to errors. It requires an accurate representation of the different entities involved (variable definition), and the pinning down of relationships between them, usually in an algebraic form. One or more of these relationships form the objective; others, the constraints. The constraints define the search space.

Some relationships are obvious and easily derived from the problem definition. Others, however, can be difficult if at all possible to find, since their existence is uncertain. One way of looking for them is to consider the accumulated data about the application. There is no guarantee that relationships will be discovered at all, and it is not even clear what relationships or models are looked for. However, 'something' may be found if the data is complete enough. Moreover, it is an automatic process and hence by extension, one hopes to generate whole requisite models in a similar way. Note that these relationships can also be used on their own as regression models and it is in this respect that they are considered here for the time being. The process is computationally intensive which points to the use of novel algorithms and hardware architectures.

In the following we shall introduce the context of our problem, i.e. data mining, give a detailed review of genetic programming (GP), and discuss the particular aspect of GP which is of interest to us, i.e. symbolic regression (SR), [20]. A simple implementation of a SR-based tool for data mining is also discussed.

2 Context

Recently, businesses have come to realise the potential of the large amounts of data they keep gathering. Although a lot of it is in databases easily accessible through specialised query languages, less organised data is common. The trend now is to put all business data in data warehouses aimed at providing decision support. The aim is to be able to extract manageable chunks of information (*Data Summarisation*, see [15]) from the organised as well as the nonorganised, ever growing volume of data and make sure that it is understandable to humans, or more precisely to the decision maker.

Decision support systems already achieve this in many ways such as cluster analysis, trend spotting, visualisation of large data, induction and pattern recognition and behavioural modelling. However, we are here concerned with data mining in its narrow and specific sense as matched by the need to extract computer models that may be used for simulation and other applications, [27].

2.1 Data Mining

Data mining is frequently attached to databases, data warehousing, image processing, pattern recognition and much more. Because of the various contexts in which it has been used, it is slightly debased. This calls for refocusing the term to what it normally means, and to what it means in our context.

Data mining is three fold:

1. There is the statistical approach, *hypothesis testing*. Here the system is presented with a hypothesis such as 'Those who buy coal have toddlers. Is that so?' More precisely it can be formulated as: 'Is there a positive correlation between coal and baby food?' The system is restricted to a certain type of data, which may still be vast, but, nevertheless, is well specified.

2. There is *directed data mining* where the system is steered towards what to look for as in 'Is there a link between spending at a supermarket and residence area or address of customer?' Here the problem is an induction one. The steering however is not as strong as in hypothesis testing. The problem is commonly solved using decision analysis approaches as well as classification neural nets, clustering methods and perhaps regression.

3. There is *pure data mining* where no steering and no constraints are imposed on the system. In this situation, the user does not know what to look for. The problem is in the same spirit as that contained in the question: 'Is there anything interesting in my data?' It is then hoped that the system will unravel interesting facts about the data that will assist the decision maker.

3 Search and Optimisation: Stochastic Approaches

In search/optimisation problems [28, 43, 31] the aim is to find the best plan to configure a system. This plan is usually in the form of a vector. Here, however, we are looking for an expression, a model which best represents a given set of data. Ultimately, this expression may be used as a simulation model in its own right or as a building block in the construction of the objective functioni(s) and constraints of a search/optimisation problem itself.

All expressions form a search space. To proceed with the search we need a criterion function, or objective function, and a description of the space itself, using limitations or constraints. The objective function provides us with a handle for choice between different members of the search space, and the constraints tell us what is a valid member. Note that constraints may be implicit. For instance, expressions are restricted to those returning values that can be found in the mined data, up to a tolerance.

Even though we have a selection criterion, the objective function, except in special cases where assumptions on it (Convexity, Continuity,...) are made, it may not be possible to guarantee that the global optimum (global optima) is found. Instead, it is practical to settle for the 'best so far' as the candidate solution, usually only a local optimum. The reason is in limitations on the computational expenses allowed, or simply the chosen stopping criteria. Behind it all, still, is the fact that global optimisation problems are notoriously difficult to solve, i.e. it is virtually impossible to construct search algorithms which will guarantee that a global optimum is found. Exhaustive search techniques are especially doomed to failure except when the search space is very small.

Stochastic methods begin with a given candidate, known beforehand or randomly generated in the search space. A move in a random direction is taken from the candidate. If it leads to a better one, then the current point is superseeded by the new, else another random move is operated. Such techniques belong to the hill-climbing, or gradient, family of techniques. Hill-climbing, of course, as just sketched will unlikely lead to the global optimum unless the function is unimodal, although, on some problems such as *Boolean Circuit Synthesis*, [18], a debate is going on at present as to which approach, hill-climbing or genetic search is more effective, cite95:Lang. Devices which help escape from local optima have been extensively studied as in Simulated Annealing, Multistart, Tabu Search, Clustering algorithms [35].

If the search space is disconnected, some random moves may not be valid.

Bearing this in mind, connectivity or connectedness may be assumed and the notion of neighbourhood of a point can be defined. It is technically the set of points falling within a distance δ of a given point. When a point returns the best value for the objective function in its neighbourhood, it is called a local optimum. These points are relatively easy to find as opposed to global optima. Note that a global optimum is also a local one.

3.1 Genetic Algorithms

Genetic algorithms (GA's), [14], are stochastic search methods modelled upon natural selection. They rely on the concept of fitness which measures the success of an individual in reproducing, i.e. passing on its genes to future generations. GA's are an attempt to capture aspects of natural selection essential to their problem-solving capacity. This capacity of GA's has been observed in many areas as will be seen later.

GA's differ from traditional search techniques in that, inherently, they work on discrete spaces; binary encoding being the main reason. The basic move, unlike hill-climbing, depends on more than one point or individual. In fact a population of individuals is first drawn from the search space, and maintained generation after genaration to be of some size larger than one, although constituents may change.

The move from one generation to another or from one population to the next is effected by the use of appropriate operators, such as reproduction, crossover and mutation. Note that mutation, as well as reproduction, work from one individual, a single parent, to obtain a new individual. Mutation especially is similar to the move in the hill-climbing approach but is not typical in GA's.

In GA's, there is a flurry of selection/replacement procedures and operators. Selection pressure is exercised through the careful design of these selection procedures and operators. It is important to note that if good individuals are favoured *a outrance*, early convergence may result into a poor local optimum. This is because the variety in the population which allows the natural selection process to thoroughly cover the search space is fatally reduced by acute selection pressure. On the other hand, no selection pressure at all will result in a very slow convergence which may not be acceptable in practice. It is essential to strike a balance between the number of fit elements in every population and the variety of its pool of genes.

GA's belong to the larger class of Evolutionary Algorithms. Their kin are the so called *Evolutionary Strategy Algorithms* first introduced in Germany in the 60's, [30, 36, 24], where mutation is the typical means of evolution as opposed to crossover in GA's.

Note that the distinction is now so blurred after the modifications brought into boths types of algorithms that it should not be ambiguous to refer to all of them as Evolutionary Algorithms.

4 Genetic Programming: A Review

Genetic Programming (GP) pioneered by J.Koza [6, 18, 21, 19], is an extension of GA's to operate over spaces whose elements are programs. It is a randomized, adaptive search method which represents programs by their parse trees, [32]. It allows computers to find solution programs to some problems without being explicitly programmed to deal with those problems.

A distinguishing element between GA and GP, commonly found in the literature, is that GA's work on constant length *chromosomes* while GP works on variable length chromosomes. The tree structures processed by GP are of variable length.

A model GP algorithm can be described as follows:

1. Define the set of terminals, i.e. the variables and constants that will form the leaves of the tree structure;

2. Define the set of functions, i.e. the operators, logical expressions, and all the functions which are required by the program. They form the inner nodes.

3. Construct a fitness function to measure the problem-solving capacity of valid programs;

4. Choose control parameters;

5. Choose stopping criteria or ways for recognising a solution;

6. Generate a population of programs;

7. Find the fitness value of each program in the population. If stopping criteria satisfied go to 10, else continue.

8. Generate a new population by applying some genetic operator and a breeding policy to the elements of the current population.

9. Repeat from 7.

10. Solution is the program with best fitness. Stop.

Some of the terms used in this algorithm will be explained later.

4.1 Theory

To those familiar with search and optimisation techniques and their theoretical basis, there is little theory in the case of GA's. Where GP is concerned, theoretical results are even scarcer, however, understanding is developing of why these algorithms work and where they might not work.

4.1.1 Fitness Landscapes

GA's usually work on populations of individuals represented by fixed length bitstrings, (chromosomes). If n is the length of a string, the cardinal of the search space is 2^n. If the elements of this space are represented as dots on a plane with distance between every two dots equal to the Hamming distance, i.e. the number of bit changes to transform one string to the other, and if each dot is now raised above the plane by the fitness value of the individual it represents, then hills and valleys will show. This is a *fitness landscape.*

A fitness landscape gives a pointer to how difficult a problem might be to GA's. If it is mainly flat and featureless then the search for a hill top would be very difficult. If it looks like a hedgehog's back, again guaranteeing that a global optimum is found will be almost a lost cause, if on the other hand one or very few hills are apparent then the search may produce a 'good' optimum.

Fitness landscapes are useful when GA's are concerned. They are not so useful however when GP is concerned because there is no equivalent of Hamming distance when the strings are not bitstrings and are of different lengths to represent the adjacency of individuals. In GP, programs are represented as trees and genes can be any predefined operand or operator. The adjacency of programs is rather difficult to catch.

4.1.2 Schemata, the Schema Theorem and BBH

In his ground breaking work [14] Holland introduced the notion of a *schema* which is no more than a hyperplane. But the insight was that while explicitly the GA operates on a finite population of individuals, implicitly it processes, in parallel, a very large number of schemata which crisscross the search space. Also, an average estimate of their fitness is recomputed for each generation. Why are they so important? Because they represent building blocks of fit individuals in the search space, as long as they are short, of low-order and highly fit themselves. In addition the Schema Theorem stipulates that the schemata with high fitness are perpetuated more often in the new generations, making GA's probably the only class of algorithms which exploit exponential explosion. This theorem is the basis to the now notorious Building Block Hypothesis (BBH) [11, 10], which is the assumption that simple GA's combine, short, low-order, above-average shemata (Building Blocks) to form near-optimal strings.

What about GP? The equivalent of a schema in GP is a set of subtrees with common features. This set is infinite but can be made finite if a limit is imposed on the size of acceptable trees [18], which is the case in practice. There is a difficulty with this notion of schema in GP due to the definition of a schema which is a string built over an extended alphabet with a wild card. This means that if the alphabet is, say, {0,1}, schemata are built over alphabet {0,1,*} where '*', a wild character, can be '0' or '1'. In the case of GP, the alphabet is made up of higher order entities, such as functions, so a schema is unlikely to be a valid program in the general case. The notion will be viable only under tight restrictions. Attempts to build a GP BBH on the GA equivalent of the schema theorem have not been satisfactory, although O'Reilly's thesis is a very good attempt, [26, 25]. A GP-hill-climbing hybrid algorithm has also been developed and the results point to the superiority of such an algorithm over simple GP or simple hill-climbing algorithms.

4.1.3 Minimal Deception

In order to understand what makes a problem difficult to GA's and also due to the shortcomings of the shemata approach and BBH, attempts have been made to construct problems which 'fool' the algorithm so as convergence is never achieved or only at great costs. The work of Goldberg, [11, 10], is the starting point. It is possible to build such problems, but not for all variants of the GA, i.e. given the opportunity, an algorithm may be tuned to deal with problems. The *minimal deception* idea does not seem to apply to GP.

This lack of satisfactory theoretical tools to make predictions, measure performance and analyse GP as well as GA's is a stumbling block to newcomers to evolutionary approaches. However, efforts are being made to overcome it, such as those of Altenberg for instance, [1], who considered evolvability as the main ingredient in the success of GP.

4.2 Practical Aspects of Genetic Programming

4.2.1 Measuring Fitness

The fitness measure is the criterion used to distinguish between programs. A measure whose sink is of very low cardinality (≤ 5, say) will not be suitable as a large proportion of individuals in the population will be of the same fitness; progress towards a fit individual will be very slow. The ideal fitness measure is the one which reveals all differences between any two individuals. If a population is ordered according to it, then every number between 1 and the population size should be allocated. In other words, no clusters of individuals with the same score should show. Such a fitness measure will be hard to find, but it should be the target when designing such a measure.

A simple measure of fitness in GP is the error measure [18]. It computes the difference between the output of a given program and the target output, when it is known. This is usually the case in regression type problems.

Other fitness measures can be the computation time of programs in the population, or their memory requirements, or the number of hits scored given the input to all programs. This is termed *absolute fitness*. When it is the score of an individual in a subset of the population, which is itself evolving, then *relative fitness* is the term. When program runtime gives the fitness, some programs with infinite loops may cause the break down of the whole entreprise. Measure, such as maximum number of loops, or maximum CPU time allowed may be introduced.

A mixture of measures may also be used. *Pareto scoring* for instance uses multiple criteria such as functionality and efficiency to compare programs [23].

4.2.2   Genetic Operators

Reproduction:
Reproduction is an asexual genetic operation. It promotes fitness in the population by selecting individuals using a fitness measure and copying them into the next generation unaltered, [18, 14]. The positive aspect of the reproduction operator is that it is not expensive: no fitness is recomputed for the individuals copied into the new population as their fitness is already known. However, it is only best if applied to a low percentage of the population, say 10%.

Crossover:
Crossover is a sexual operation in that it operates on two individuals chosen by some means based on fitness. These two individuals exchange parts, such as branches in the case of tree structures. The result is two children which will join the new population. Unlike reproduction, here the fitness of the offspring has to be computed. This is expensive since the computation of fitness absorbs most of the CPU time for any non-trivial problem.

Self-crossover:
Self-crossover operates on a single program as both parents. The selection of the individual can be done through any selection approach.

Cassette-crossover:
Cassette-crossover allows subexpressions in the middle of two parent programs to be swapped. It relaxes the standard crossover which permits only subtrees to be swapped. It is however difficult to implement so that offspring are valid programs. This operator appears to make gains in the standard GP, i.e. without ADF's, [23], (see below).

Hoist:
Hoist is an asexual operation which randomly chooses a subtree from an existing program structure to be included in the new generation. This operator promotes parsimony, [23].

Mutation:
Mutation operates on single individuals and thus is asexual. It alters randomly chosen nodes in the tree structure representing a program. Terminal nodes can be changed into any other terminals but function nodes can only be changed into functions which accept the same arguments.

Mutation promotes diversity in the population: terminals and functions that have been driven out of the pool of the programs in the current population may be brought back.

A useful variant is *shrink mutation* which takes the subtree with root the node to alter and replaces with it the whole parent. That keeps the size of programs in check, [38].

Mutation is considered a secondary operation compared with reproduction and crossover. Other secondary genetic operators are *permutation, editing, encapsulation and decimation*, [18].

4.2.3 Re-usability and Abstraction

Re-usability of modules is important to the success of any high level programming language. The concept is embodied in the notions of *subroutine* and *function*. In GP, it is easy to see how beneficial re-usability can be: simply, sequences of code that are useful need not be rediscovered in different parts of the tree representation [19, 23]. Moreover, recursivity can be harnessed and generalisation of the concepts of hierarchical problem solving may be possible.

Automatically Defined Functions (ADF's):
In [19] ADF's are extensively studied. They are evolvable modules of an evolving genetic program. They can be called by the main GP program itself and used as functional building blocks or by another evolving program. To illustrate this last point, let π be a module that is recognised to be reoccuring in some other parts of an evolving program. π is then isolated and put in the form of a function with its dummy arguments the arguments π requires for evaluation. They are the leaves of the subtree containing π. π is then included in the extended functions set Φ^*, (see Section 4.3.2). If, for instance, mutation is carried out, a node of a tree corresponding to a function is randomly selected for swapping. As long as it has the same number and type of arguments as π, the latter may replace it.

To allow these modules to carry on evolving, operators such as crossover are difficult to implement. However, results show that problems not satisfactorily solved with standard GP, have been satisfactorily solved when ADF's were used. These problems are rich in regularity. ADF's help reduce the effort spent in rediscovering expressions already known.

Concepts Reuse:
In [37], Seront attempts to introduce libraries of *concepts* which are then used by GP based systems to inject into the population of programs they are evolving. It is a different view, from ADF's in that it's internal as well as external as subtrees which form a valid 'concept' may be used in a totally different problem. With ADF's subtrees are only used in the course of solving a given problem; ADF's are only for internal use. Moreover an ADF may not be a valid 'concept' in Seront's definition. It is rather akin to system libraries which are familiar.

Adaptive Representation:
Adaptive representation is another attempt to introducing reusability. In [33] it has been reported that by analysing the evolutionary trace of GP's, subtrees which increase the fitness of programs are isolated and added to the set of

functions of the main GP program. Enrichment of the latest generation with newly generated programs using the extended function set seem to have a positive effect on the overall performance of GP on some prblems.

Other attempts, [23], were made in *abstracting data types, ADT's* and, [2], in *genetically building libraries, GLiB's*. Results are not conclusive, but it is the direction for fruitful research, [16].

4.2.4   Breeding Approaches

Breeding approaches go hand-in-hand with fitness measure. They concern ways by which a new generation is obtained from the current one, i.e. how parents are chosen, which individuals may be replaced and so on. Their ultimate aim, common to GA's and GP, is to ensure a good cover of the search space and avoid premature convergence to poor local optima.

fitness-proportionate selection:
In this approach, selection depends on fitness and chance. A roulette wheel is used, but a bias in favour of individuals proportional to their fitness is enforced [11], so that the 'survival of the fittest' concept is implemented. That is to say that if a program has fitness which is 50% of the total fitness of all programs in a population, then this program will be represented on the wheel to occupy half of it, 180°. This means it will be selected more often and its genes have a higher probability of passing to the next generation.

Tournament selection:
Two individuals are picked at random, the one with higher fitness is the candidate to replace an unfit element previously selected or to mate with it. Tournament selection tries to simulate what happens between animals during the mating season. Usually bouts between two individuals are fought to serve a female [18].

Rank selection:
Here selection pressure is introduced so that among comparatively fit programs, those which are dominant are selected. Rank selection exaggerates the difference between losely clusterd fitness values so that the better ones are sampled more. [18, 45].

Generational and Steady State Genetic Programming:
Generational GP (GGP) occurs when, population size kept constant, the entire population changes from generation to generation. No elements are spared on any basis. In Steady state GP, however (SSGP), only a small number of elements are replaced from generation to the next.

Demes and Locality:
Demes or islands, are semi-disjoint populations which are allowed to evolve

locally, but migratory agents probabilistically selected are allowed to cross the boundaries to mate. This helps avoid early convergence and promotes diversity. Results [22, 13, 8, 40] show benefits of the demetic approach. In [40] explicite islands of different sizes were used, while in [8] the islands are defined using a form of geographic neighbourhood. Parents are selected from a neighbourhood and the offspring are placed in that area. It is reported that the notion of demes increases the generality of the whole population and the overall efficiency.

The advantage of the demetic approach is its inherent parallelism. In [17] linear speed-up has been achieved when this approach is adopted in the implementation of GP on a network of transputers for some problems.

In [22] it has been suggested that the selection of similar parents from the demes, and crossover points which minimise the difference between the parents and the offspring also result in improvements.

Elitism:

It is a breeding policy which favours the fittest individuals in the population. Its draw back is that some elements never get replaced as in SSGP. Because of that elitist approaches may cause premature convergence.

There are numerous breeding policies on top of the ones discussed here. Notable ones are *Brood Selection*, [41], *Population Enrichment*, [29] and *Disassortative Mating*, [34]. They all seem to have positive effect on GP implementation results on some problems according to the reports. It remains however to try them on other problems and perhaps carry out a one-to-one comparison to see their individiual merits.

4.3 Applications: Symbolic Regression

Given the wide scope for applying GP, an exhaustive list will be very long. Among the areas in which it has been successfully applied, to name a few, are: *optimal control, robotic planning,* [21], *game playing strategies,* [3, 4], *market strategies,* [42, 12, 7], and *evolution of emergent behaviour.* A longer list may be found in [18]. Here, our main interest is in *Symbolic Regression.*

Symbolic regression, SR, already attempted in the 50's and 60's, [44, 5], is an important applications of GP, [18]. It is an attempt to automatically generate models (whose structure is unknown beforehand or unspecified, unlike classical regression) to fit data comprising two distinct groups, input data and output data, [20, 42]. In more precise terms, the symbolic expression looked for is the one which, given as argument a subset of the accumulated data input, will produce, after evaluation, a result within a tolerance ϵ of a subset of the accumulated data output. In noisy data environments, it is customery to talk of *empirical discovery* and when sequences are involved where the aim is to find a sequence element of a certain index given some previous elements, then *sequence induction* is concerned. They are special cases of SR.

Just as in the model algorithm for GP given earlier, here SR requires the six key steps for the system to be initiated, namely:

1. Determine the set of terminals;

2. Determine the set of functions;

3. Devise a fitness measure;

4. Determine the control parameters;

5. Determine the stopping criteria;

6. Generate an initial population of programs.

In the following we develop each of these steps and

4.3.1 Set of Terminals

If Θ is the set of terminals, then Θ consists of dependent and independent variables, as well as all constants relevant to the problem in hand, (see *sufficiency* of Θ in [18]). Terminals form the leaves of the tree structure containing the evolved programs.

Constants:
Constants are particularly difficult to guess. Ways of evolving them have been devised. In [18], ephemeral random constants are used to introduce constants into evolving GP expressions. In [39] a genetic operator is described which affects only these ephemeral random constants of Koza in [18]. The operator is called a *Constant Perturbation Operator*. It serves fine-tuning coefficients in evolving expressions and introduces new terminals in Θ. This is achieved by multiplying all these ephemeral constants by a random number in the range $[0.9, 1.1]$, which is a perturbation of 10%. This seems to be particularly useful in SR.

4.3.2 Set of Functions

Let Φ represent the set of functions. Φ consists of the standard operators $(+, -, \div, \times)$ and other functions such as sin, cos, exp, logical expressions, recursion and other, which may be relevant to the problem in hand, (see *sufficiency* of Φ in [18]).

Closure:
This property is required from all evolved programs. It means that expressions and the different arrangements of them must be valid programs. All functions in Φ should be handled with attention in all expressions using them. For instance the division operator '$\div$', as it cannot be given '0' as divisor, must be written so that it can handle it if it occurs without causing a crash in the evolved program.

4.3.3   Fitness measure

As explained earlier, the fitness measure should tell us how good the expression generated is with respect to the set of data we have in hand. Let this expression be $\phi(x)$ and the working data the real values (float) stored in arrays x[] and y[]. The fitness function can be the discrepancy between the values in array y[] and the values returned by $\phi()$ when it takes as arguments values from array x[], or the number of values returned within ϵ of those in y[], or some average over differences between values returned and those in array y[]. It can be a combination of these ideas.

4.3.4   Control parameters

These parameters control the process of GP. In [18], 19 parameters are listed. Obviously, not all of them are required in an application. They depend very much on the breeding policy adopted and the genetic operators. Parameters which are most common and used here are the population size PopSz, the proportion of this to be generated, after initialisation, by the genetic operator crossover, XRate, the rate of mutation MuRate, the maximum size of any program to be generated , i.e. the maximum size of the tree which will hold it, MaxTreeSz.

4.3.5   Stopping criteria

One the most potent stopping criterion is the available CPU time. This is implemented by imposing a limit on the maximum number of populations the GP program may generate in the course of its run. The number of hits is an obvious stopping criterion as well, because it allows to recognise a very 'fit' expression which may be what we are looking for, it is a *success predicate*. It can be a great saver of CPU time. Other stopping conditions can be devised especially, if a lot of information is known about the data mined.

Here, the stopping criterion is either a generated program matches all y[] values when we pass to it as argument the values in x[], or the maximum number of generations allowed is exceeded, i.e. MaxNbGen.

4.3.6   Initial population

The random generation is the most popular and effective way of constructing an initial population. However, as in the previous section, advantage may be taken of the knowledge of the data to generate individuals likely to fit it. For instance, in market data there might be a periodicity element to it which may be exploited by making sure that expressions have trigonometric functions in them.

4.3.7   Basic SR Algorithm

In algorithmic form the steps described above will look like this:

Initialisation:
  set MaxNbGen the maximum number of generations;
  set PopSz the size of the population (constant);
  generate an initial population of random programs made up of the
  elements of the terminal and function sets of the problem;
  NbGen := 0;

Start:
  While (NbGen < MaxNbGen+1 and No Program is 100% fit) do:
        Assign a fitness value to each member of the population
        according to how well it solves the problem.
        Generate new population from a selected number of programs
        according to fitness using the following operators:
        1) Copy existing programs to new population;
        2)Mutate programs from old population and incorporate
           in new population to increase diversity of stock;
        3) Create new ones by crossing two randomly chosen programs;
  Endwhile
  Choose from resulting population the program with best fitness as a
  candidate solution to problem.
End:

4.4   Implementation of a SR-based Tool

GP-SR is the symbolic regression tool being developed. It is a general purpose
tool for generating models to be used in search/optimisation applications, data
mining, forcasting and simulation areas. It is based on the algorithm of Section
4.3.7.

The tree structure is the adopted data structure for GP-SR. This is due to
the fact that unlike the standard GA algorithm, in GP the chromosome has a
variable length. GP-SR, is stack based. Programmes are stored in prefix tree
structures.

The fitness function used is as follows. Let Π be the evolved expression. If
n is the size of x[] and η the cumulative error of Π over all entries of x, i.e.
$\eta = \sum_i (y_i - \Pi(x_i))$, then $\phi(\Pi)$, the fitness of Π is: $\phi(\Pi) = \frac{n}{\eta+n}$. Note that a
100% fit element has fitness 1.0.

Three genetic operators are used: reproduction, crossover and mutation
with rates 39%, 60% and 1% respectively. A random number is generated
between 0.0 and 1.0. If random() $\leq$ 0.01 mutation takes place. If random()
$\leq$ 0.6 crossover takes place. If random() > 0.6 reproduction takes place. These
operators are as explained earlier.

The breeding policy implemented in GP-SR is the fitness-proportionate selection given in Section 4.2.4. This means the parents responsible for the creation of succeeding generations are chosen in proportion to their fitness in the
current population.

Problem	No-of-Pnts	Mean-fitness	Mean-CPU(s)	Mean-Hits
$x^4 + x^3 + x^2 + x$	10	0.6840	2.53	5.80
$x^4 - x^3 + x^2 - x$	10	0.6888	2.91	3.90
$x^4 + x^3 - x^2 + x$	10	0.3724	3.32	2.60
$x/\pi + x^2/\pi^2 + 2\pi x$	10	0.2228	3.21	1.30
$R_i = \frac{P_i}{(d_{ki})^2}$	10	0.2726	2.70	2.50

Table 1: Summary of results

Termination is decided upon the number of hits scored by any evolved expression or when the maximum number of generations is reached.

4.4.1 Experiments

At the moment, GP-SR is tested on simple problems such as found in textbooks. Polynomials fitting the data are evolved, but the tool remains to be refined and tested on larger sets.

Following are some problems on which GP-SR is being tested.

Problem 1 is that in [18] page 163. It is concerned with discovering the polynomial $x^4 + x^3 + x^2 + x$ from a set of pairs of values (x[i],y[i]). Problems 2 and 3 are variants on it; their y[] values are more clustered than the first. For these examples $\Theta = \{x\}$ and $\Phi = \{+, -, \div, \times\}$.

Problem 4 is from [19] page 146. It is concerned with the discovery of the polynomial $x/\pi + x^2/\pi^2 + 2\pi x$. This problem is interesting because of the presence of the constant π. The terminal set is $\Theta = \{x, \pi\}$ and Φ is the same as for Examples 1, 2, and 3.

Problem 5 concerns the discovery of the well known gravity model in Locational Analysis, due to W.J. Reilly, [9]. This model states that 'A city will attract retail trade from a town in its surrounding territory, in proportion to the population size of the city and in inverse proportion to the square of the distance from the city.'

Let R_i be the attraction of city$_i$ with population P_i, exerted upon the inhabitants of town$_k$ which is at distance d_{ki}, then $R_i = \frac{P_i}{(d_{ki})^2}$. Here the constant is P_i for a given city and the cardinality of Θ is 2, as in Problem 4.

50 runs of 50 generations each were carried out with GP-SR on each problem on a Pentium 90, with 16 Mbytes RAM, running Linux and gcc, the C compiler. The library function time() was used to time each run. The 'Problem' column refers to the model we try to discover. Column 'No-of-Pnts' refers to the number of points over which the regression is carried out. 'Mean-fitness' is the average fitness of best candidate in each run.'Mean-CPU(s)' refers to the average time in seconds for the 50 runs, and 'Mean-Hits' refers to the average number of times the model is found in 50 runs. A summary of the results is in Table 1.

Comments:

GP-SR does relatively well on the polynomials with $\Theta = \{x\}$. It does discover the models few times in 50 runs and fast due to speed of the Pentium based machine used. On the models with constants, it does not seem to perform well. The way the constants are handled is probably not appropriate.

5   Conclusion and current work

We have considered model generation in the context of data mining and looked at the most promising approach to tackle it with. This approach, namely genetic programming has been reviewd. The basic components of a tool for symbolic regression have been presented. The tool is still under development and no major experiments have been carried out on real world data yet. In due course the tool will be tested on data from the financial and other markets. Improvements under consideration are as follows:

Cropping:
In the process of evolving expressions, extraneous subexpressions are likely to appear. These will be evaluated for fitness despite them being redundant, for instance. They can also propagate in successive populations. If they can be recognised, then removing them prior to fitness evaluation will be beneficial, and make the final model more transparent. Subtle approaches are required in order to recognise an extraneous subtree. It may be just as expensive to find it, or costly if wrongly removed as it may be best to leave the process of evolution deal with it, and crop the final solution if necessary.

Note that the idea of cropping is not too different from the notion of ADF's of section 4.2.3. Also, as cropping is concerned as well with keeping the size of tree structures in check, shrink mutation is relevant, (see Section 4.2.2).

Parallel implementation:
It is already apparent that the computational demands of GP-SR can be substantial, as is the case with most genetic processing based software. These demands may be met by an algorithmic approach such as cropping, but exploiting parallel/distributed platforms may also be valuable. The parallelisation of GP-SR is underway.

Acknowledgements
The work reported in this paper was supported by UK Engineering and Physical Sciences Research Council grant GR/K40475. Our thanks to John Putney of National Power for his useful comments.

References

[1] L. Altenberg. The evolution of evolvability in genetic programming. In

K.E. Kinnear, editor, *Advances in Genetic Programming*. MIT Press, MA., USA, 1994.

[2] P.J. Angeline. Genetic programming and emergent intelligence. In K.E. Kinnear, editor, *Advances in Genetic Programming*. MIT Press, 1994.

[3] R. Axelrod. *The Evolution of Cooperation*. Basic Books, New York, 1984.

[4] R. Axelrod. The evolution of strategies in the iterated prisoners' dilemma. In L. Davis, editor, *Genetic Algorithms and Simulated Annealing*, pages 32–42. Morgan Kaufmann, Los Altos, Calif., USA, 1987.

[5] J.S. Collins. A regression analysis program incorporating heuristic term selection. In E. Dale and D. Michie, editors, *Machine Intelligence 2*. Elsevier, 1968.

[6] K. De Jong. On using genetic algorithms to search program spaces. In J.J. Grefenstette, editor, *Genetic Algorithms and their Applications: Proceedings of the 2nd International Conference on Genetic Algorithms*. Lawrence Erlbaum Associates, 1987.

[7] G.J. Deboek, editor. *Trading on the Edge: Neural, Genetic, and Fuzzy Systems for Chaotic Financial Markets*. Wiley and Sons, 1994.

[8] P. D'Haeseleer and J. Bluming. Effects of locality on individual and population evolution. In K.E. Kinnear, editor, *Advances in Genetic Programming*. MIT Press, MA., USA, 1994.

[9] D. Foot. *Operational Urban Models*. Methuen and Co. Ltd, London, 1981.

[10] E.D. Goldberg. Simple genetic algorithms and the minimal, deceptive problem. In L. Davis, editor, *Genetic Algorithms and Simulated Annealing*, pages 75–88. Morgan Kaufmann, Los Altos, Calif., USA, 1987.

[11] E.D. Goldberg. *Genetic Algorithms in Search, Optimisation and Machine Learning*. Addison Wesley, 1989.

[12] S. Goonatilake and J.A. Campbell. Genetic-fuzzy hybrid systems for finacial decision making, 1995. Working Paper.

[13] I. Harvey. Species adaptation genetic algorithms: A basis for a continuing saga. In F.J. Varela and P. Bourgine, editors, *Proceedings of the first European Conference on Artificial Life, (ECAL)*. MIT Pess, 1992.

[14] J.H. Holland. *Adaptation in Natural and Artificial Systems*. University of Michigan Press, Ann Arbor, Michigan, USA, 1974.

[15] M. Holsheimer and A.P.J.M Siebes. Data mining: The search for knowledge in databases. Technical Report CS-R9406, Centrum voor Wiskunde en Informatica, CWI, P.O. Box 94079, 1090 GB Amsterdam, The Netherlands, 1994.

[16] K.E. Kinnear, editor. *Advances in Genetic Programming.* MIT Press, Mass., USA, 1994.

[17] J. Koza and D. Andre. Parallel genetic programming on a network of transputers. Technical Report CS-TR-95-1542, Dept. Comp. Science, University of Stanford, Jan. 1995.

[18] J.R. Koza. *Genetic programming: on the programming of computers by means of natural selection.* MIT Press, Cambridge, England, 1993.

[19] J.R. Koza. *Genetic Programming II: Automatic Discovery of Reusable Programs.* MIT Press, Cambridge, England, 1994.

[20] J.R. Koza. Genetic programming for economic modelling. In S. Goonatilake and P. Treleaven, editors, *Intelligent Systems for Finance and Business,* pages 251–269. John Wiley & Sons Ltd, 1995.

[21] J.R. Koza and J.P. Rice. Genetic programming: The movie, 1992.

[22] W.B. Langdon. Pareto, population partitioning, price and genetic programmimg, 1995. Research Notes.

[23] W.B Langdon and A. Qureshi. Genetic programming: Computers using "Natural Selection" to generate programs, 1995. Working Paper.

[24] Z. Michalewicz. *Genetic Algorithms + Data Structures = Evolution Algorithms.* Springer Verlag, London, second, extended edition edition, 1994.

[25] U.-M. O'Reilly. *An Analysis of Genetic Programmimg.* PhD thesis, School of Computer Studies, Carleton University, Ottawa, Ontario, 1995.

[26] U.-M. O'Reilly and F. Oppacher. The troubling aspects of a building block hypothesis for genetic programming, 1992. Working Paper.

[27] N.H. Packard. A genetic learning algorithm for the analysis of complex data. *Complex Systems,* 4:543–572, 1990.

[28] P.M. Pardalos and J.B. Rosen. *Constrained Global Optimization: Algorithms and Applications.* Springer Verlag, Berlin, 1987. Lecture Notes in Computer Science no.268.

[29] J.E. Perry. The effect of population enrichment in genetic programming. In *Proceedings of the 1994 IEEE World Congress on Computational Intelligence.* IEEE Press, 1994.

[30] I. Rechenberg. *Evolutionsstrategie: Optimierung technischer Systeme nach Prinzipien der biologischen Evolution.* Frommann-Holzboog Verlag, Stuttgart, 1973.

A Comparison of Developing Codes for Distributed and Parallel Architectures

Shirley A. Williams

Department of Computer Science, The University of Reading
Reading, UK

Graham E. Fagg

Department of Computer Science, University of Tenessee
Knoxville, USA

Abstract

There are a number of problems that can only be solved in a realistic time frame by using high performance computing environments. Large scale Monte Carlo simulations are an example of such problems. There are many different high performance environments ranging from massively parallel processors to clusters of distributed workstations. Here we present our experiences of developing a simulation code across the range of parallel environments, in some cases the transition from one architecture to another is virtually seamless, in others completely new algorithms have to be developed.

1 Introduction

Over the last few years we have collaborated with colleagues in other departments on the development of codes for a variety of architectures. The architectures have included: a massively parallel processor, a transputer based machine, a network of homogenous workstations and a network of heterogeneous workstations. Here we present our experience in developing codes for a chemistry problem to fit on to differing parallel architectures.

2 Particle Growth

The growth kinetics of a perfect crystal face with two dimensional nuclei can be modelled in terms of the time taken by a growing particle to cross a test point. Our aim was to develop a general method to simulate the growth particles in a multi-dimensional space.

Our starting point was work on Monte Carlo simulation of the growth of passivating films on electrode surfaces through a process of electrocrystallisation under potentiostatic conditions [1]. In the original model two-dimensional growth nuclei were allowed to grow at a constant rate into crystals modelled as flat circular discs. We subsequently extended this work to multi-dimensional, monitoring the growth of crystals by test points.

3 Simulation

The process of nucleation and growth can be simulated using a Monte Carlo approach. Within a grid a number of random nucleation sites and test points are set and the time to cover increasing fractions of the test points by the growth from the nucleation sites is calculated. By repeating this process many times and averaging the time taken to cover fractions of the surface accurate simulations can be achieved. The growth rate (g) can then be calculated from the simulated surface coverage.

$$g = \frac{dr}{dt}$$

Where r is the area covered and t is the time taken to cover that area.

To calculate the coverage of n nucleation sites we have developed the following algorithm:

1. Generate n randomly placed nucleation sites N.

2. Generate test points T.

3. Calculate the coverage rate of test points.

   This calculation is repeated many times and the results are averaged, until these averaged results are within what is deemed to be an acceptable deviation.

The number of nucleation points within a multi dimensional space, their growth function and the size of the space will vary according to the growth kinetics that are to be modelled. Similarly, edge effects may be dealt with in a variety of manners, including wrap around and windowing. None of these refinements however affect the basic algorithm described above.

4 Potential Parallelism

At the top most level if we were required to calculate the nucleation and growth process for M different numbers of nucleation sites n, we could perform the calculations on M independent computers. For example if we wished to simulate the effect of 100, 200, 400 and 1000 nucleation sites in a sample, we could use 4 computers, one to calculate each set. This would effectively give us a speed up of 4 times the performance of calculating the results on a single of machine. This is arguably not parallel processing as there is no need for communication between processors, the speed up is however real.

At the opposite level we could consider the growth of all nucleation sites simultaneously, across a number of simulation runs and sample sizes. For example if we wished to simulate the effect of 100, 200, 400 and 1000 nucleation sites in four samples, using 3000 simulation runs for 100 test points, for each calculation to be done independently we could use in excess of 500 million processors, i.e.

$$(100 + 200 + 400 + 1000) \times 100 \times 3000$$

Each processor calculating for a single nucleation point growth to a single test point.

5 Architectures

There is a number of different parallel architectures available. We were particularly interested in developing this application on available machines. Thus our choices were:

- a single workstation

- a massively parallel processor

- a network of workstations

- a multiprocessor.

5.1 Sequential Processing

A sequential processor is a conventional computer where instructions are executed one after another. Most current workstations and personal computers (PCs) are inherently sequential machines.

5.1.1 Sequential Solution

A sequential solution was developed to work on a single workstation. This approach required: the initialisation of both nucleation and test points to random locations, the calculation of the distance from each test point to its nearest nucleation point and hence the coverage calculated. The process is repeated many times, with different random number sets, to get the result of a Monte Carlo simulation for a given number of nucleation points. The sequential algorithm is essentially:

```
1. Generate n randomly placed nucleation sites N.

2. Generate test points T.

3. Calculate the shortest time to reach each T from all N.

4. Calculate how long before x % of Ts are covered.

   This calculation is repeated many times and the results
   from 4 are averaged, until these results are within what
   is deemed to be an acceptable deviation.
```

5.2 Massively Parallel Processor

A massively parallel processor consists of a large number of simple identical processors, each processor has its own data but the follows the instructions issued by a central controller. The processors are usually linked in some fashion to allow processors to exchange data.

An example of a massively parallel processor is the DAP (Distributed Array Processor), originally developed by ICL in the 1970's, then AMT and more recently Cambridge. The DAP is based on a 32 by 32 array of one-bit processing elements, linked in NEWS fashion (north, east, west, south), with wrap around at the edges (e.g. north of the top row is the bottom row). The DAP can be programmed in a dialect of Fortran or in assembler.

5.2.1 Massively Parallel Solution

The massively parallel processor implementation was developed such that each processor represented a test point. Nucleation points were randomly allocated. Then in lockstep the nucleation points grow and at each step the percentage of test points covered can be calculated. The algorithm used can be summarised as:

```
Generate nucleation points
REPEAT
     FOR ALL Nucleation Points
          Grow nucleation point
     END FOR ALL
     Calculate the coverage
UNTIL all covered

This calculation is repeated many times and the results
are averaged, until these results are within what is
deemed to be an acceptable deviation.
```

5.3 Network of Workstations

Within a shared, distributed network, the majority of computers are idle most of the time. A typical workstation is idle 60% of the time [2]. This spare capacity can be harnessed to provide a powerful computing resource at apparently no cost, other than making programs operate across the network. There are now available a number of toolkits that allow the writing of parallel programs that operate across a network of computers.

Examples of such toolkits are MPI [3] and PVM [4]. Both provide general support for constructing parallel and distributed programs. The support is in the form of library routines that can be added to C or Fortran. The library routines offer operations to support: synchronisation, communication and process control.

5.3.1   Cluster Computing Solution

With a network of computers communication is a considerable overhead, so it was decided to spread the work such that communication was reduced. This was achieved by making each of the distributed computers responsible for running one complete pass of the simulation. The results from all computers were collected and then averaged to give the result of a Monte Carlo Simulation. It was found we needed thousands of simulation runs for the results to be within acceptable error bounds. As we had less than one hundred workstations readily available in our cluster, each machine did over a hundred runs of the simulation, which were themselves the same as the approach used for the sequential algorithm. This approach has limited data communication. Initially each machine needs to receive a distinct seed for its random number generator. Final results have to be collected and averaged. This means that when using a cluster that is lightly loaded this approach will lead to almost linear speed up. The algorithm can be summarised in two parts:

Master Process

1. Calculate seeds.

2. Pass seeds to slaves.

3. Receive results from slaves.

4. Average and display.

Slaves

1. Receive seed.

2. Initialise random number generator.

3. Perform algorithm, as in the sequential version.

4. Pass results back to master.

We used PVM [4] for our cluster computing implementation. Initially the performance with this approach was variable depending on the loading of the workstations that created our cluster. Although 60% of our machines were lightly loaded at any one time, these were not necessarily the machines allocated by PVM for our work. We have developed approaches for avoiding allocating work to heavily loaded machines [2]. These approaches include:

User Monitoring The user can monitor the performance of individual machines within the cluster and delete the laggards.

Excess Slaves The program can be structured so that an excessive number of slaves are started and the program as a whole terminates when sufficient slaves have returned their results. The excess slaves approach has the advantage of improved performance, however it has the antisocial side effect of further loading already heavily loaded machines, and then not using their results.

Reading Method PVM can be adapted so that before tasks are spawned the load of machines are established and work is always allocated to the least loaded machines.

5.4 Multiprocessor Architectures

The INMOS transputer was developed as a single chip processor, with in-built memory and input/output links. The links enable any number of transputers to be joined together to form a network of processors communicating via message passing. A number of commercial machines based on the transputer are available including the Meiko Surface CS1. The same architectural model was used when the CS2, but not this time based on the transputer.

5.4.1 Multiprocessor Solution

Having developed the cluster computing solution using PVM we expected to be able to directly port our program on to the Meiko Surface CS1 and CS2 as both have PVM available.

Our initial attempt to port to the CS1 failed because the grid size used in the simulation meant that we had arrays that required more space than was available on individual processors. By reducing the sample size of the simulation we were able to succeed in running our PVM program developed for a cluster of workstations directly on the CS1.

The porting to the CS2 was easier. There was sufficient room for the arrays and the program ran on the first attempt. There was no need in either case to change the algorithm from the form presented above.

6 Random Numbers

When running Monte Carlo simulations large numbers of random numbers are consumed and it is important that the random number generator used has the following properties:

- a long cycle,

- the series of random numbers are repeatable,

- the sequence has good statistical properties.

Number of workstation	longest time seconds	shortest time seconds
2	671	276
4	498	204
8	206	105
10	265	90
16	293	95
20	123	115
25	194	93
32	125	75

Table 1: Elapsed time using Conventional PVM

One random number generation technique is not applicable to all architectures. With the sequential version we were able to use the random number generators available under UNIX. Initially we used RAND, but this had too short a cycle time and so was replaced by DRAND with a cycle of 2^{48}. We were able to take advantage of existing work on producing random numbers for the DAP [5]. Producing independent sequences of random numbers for the PVM implementations presented a number of problems [6]. We initially used RAND to generate seeds for DRAND, later we adapted the Modified Leapfrog Method presented by Foster [3] using the existing generator (DRAND) on each processor with a personalised seed that ensured the sets were disjoint [7].

7 Performance

The programs were benchmarked, for elasped execution time, for 3200 iterations on 50 nucleation points, with 100 test points. We chose to benchmark with respect to elasped time, so as to indicate how long the user had to wait for results to arrive.

Running on a single Sun workstation the sequential program took between 5 and 20 minutes depending on the load of the machine chosen. The user could almost always achieve the shorter time if many machines were available and a manual check of the loads were made. Occasionally the arrival of another person at a distant laboratory would make a machine that had appeared to be unloaded suddenly become very busy.

Using conventional PVM on the cluster gave diverse results, depending on the loading of individual workstations within the cluster. Although there appeared to be an improvement in performance as the number of workstation in the cluster were increased, there were peaks were the results from one machine had delayed the whole, see Table 1.

Performance was less erratic when we used our verion of PVM (the Reading method) that allocated work to the least loaded workstations, see Table 2.

When the code was ported to four processors on the Meiko CS2, the elasped execution time was 24 seconds.

Number of workstation	longest time seconds	shortest time seconds
2	375	353
4	189	181
8	114	98
10	107	83
16	76	71
20	65	59
25	60	59
32	54	54

Table 2: Elapsed time using the Reading Method

The massively parallel code took a different form, with its own random number generation and the use of all points on the grid as test points. The elasped time during execution was less than a second.

8 Conclusions

Our experience shows how some problems can be readily solved on a variety of sequential, distributed and parallel architectures. In this example the massively parallel processing solution was significantly different to the others that were fundamentally the same.

The use of a tool set such as PVM facilitates the porting of code developed on clusters of workstation onto parallel machines, however the transfer is not necessarily straight forward.

9 Acknowledgements

The successful implementation of these codes has been as a result of close collaboration between colleagues in the University of Reading. We particularly would like to thank: Paul Minchinton of Cybernetics, Philip Mitchell of Chemistry and Ken Williams of Computer Science.

Between 1991 and 1994 Graham Fagg was an SERC funded research student, at the University of Reading.

References

[1] S.A. Williams, P.C.H. Mitchell and G.E. Fagg, A Cluster Computing Implementation of a Monte Carlo Implementation of a Particle Growth Mechanism, Parallel Algorithms and Applications, 4, 1994, pp 275-280.

[2] G.E. Fagg and S.A. Williams, Improved Program Performance using a Cluster of Workstations, Parallel Algorithms and Applications, 7, 1995, pp 233-236.

[3] I. Foster, Designing and Building Parallel Programs, Addison Wesley,1995.

[4] P. Sunderam, Pvm: A Framework for Parallel Distributed Computing, Concurrency Practice and Experience,1990,2, pp.315-339.

[5] K.A. Smith, S.F. Reddaway, and D.M. Scott, Very High Performance Pseudo-random Number Generation on the DAP, Computational Physics Communications, 1985, 37 pp 239-244.

[6] N.M. Maclaren, The Generation of Multiple Independent Sequences of Pseudorandom Numbers, Applied Statistics, 1989, 38, pp 351-359.

[7] K.P. Williams and S.A. Williams, Implementation of an Efficient and Powerful Parallel Pseudo-random Number Generator, EuroPVM'95, J.Dongarra et al (eds), 1995, pp197-202.

Capturing Branch-and-Bound using Shared Abstract Data-types

Don Goodeve   Robert Briggs
John Davy
School of Computer Studies, University of Leeds
Leeds, UK

Abstract

To support the routine construction of large-scale parallel applications requires an effective mechanism of abstracting from the underlying machine. In this paper, abstraction using Shared Abstract Data-types is illustrated through a case-study of an irregular problem; the Travelling Salesman Problem. This design of a Branch and Bound algorithm to solve this problem is investigated, demonstrating the separation of algorithmic and implementation issues that the SADT approach offers. Issues in the composition of SADTs, and methods of exploiting the shared data weakness/performance tradeoff are discussed.

1   Introduction

Both message-passing and shared memory provide low-level models of process interaction for structuring parallel programs. A higher level programming model is provided by skeletons[6, 7], where entire computational structures are captured as higher-order functions with efficient parallel implementations. This paper presents another approach to abstraction involving the use of *Shared Abstract Data-types* to capture useful models of data sharing employed in parallel applications[9, 10].

A Shared Abstract Data-type (SADT) is an abstract data-type that is concurrently accessible by a number of client processes, hiding details of communication and synchronisation behind the abstraction boundary. To support scalable application performance, the operation throughput of an SADT is designed to scale well with the size of a computer system in which it is used. An example of such an SADT is the queue presented in [9].

Parallel applications may be constructed by composing several SADTs into useful computational structures. To ensure the correctness of these applications, the semantics of SADT operations, in particular, the compositional semantics should be well understood.

It has been proposed that the development of a suitable set of Shared Abstract Data-types (SADTs) will form a powerful basis for the development of efficient and scalable parallel and distributed applications[9, 10]. To investigate this thesis, demonstrations of the use of SADTs in a variety of applications are being sought. These demonstrations should help to resolve several issues surrounding the efficacy of a set of SADTs:

120

- The models of sharing that should be embodied in a set of SADTs.

- The compositional properties of the set of SADTs, required for reasoning about the correctness of applications.

- The performance issues and tradeoffs arising in different styles of SADT implementation.

In this paper, we present an example application composing two SADTs; an *Accumulator* and a *Stack*. The application is designed to solve the well-known Travelling Salesman Problem (TSP) using a branch-and-bound technique. The investigation of the possible solutions to this problem illustrates several issues in the design and usage of a set of SADTs in the construction of parallel applications; notably consistency, computational organisation and performance. In section 2, the case for using shared data abstractions for parallel programming is discussed, and the properties of Shared Abstract Data-types (SADTs) are introduced. The Branch-and-Bound application is introduced in section 3. An SADT-based solution to this programming problem is then developed in section 4, discussing both the application issues and the design issues this exposes in the set of SADTs used. Section 5 summarises the key points of this work and outlines the scope for future development.

2 Shared Data Abstractions

To provide effective support the construction of parallel applications, some means of abstraction from the details of communication and synchronisation is required. Shared Memory programmers are well aware of the complexities and costs of explicit concurrency control. Programming using message passing systems can rapidly become a problem of coping with the complex plumbing required and the co-ordination of control and message flows. By introducing Shared Data abstractions, the complexities of the underlying architecture and mechanisms can be effectively hidden. Through suitable design, this abstraction layer need not sacrifice performance.

We are interested in the properies of data abstractions that can fulfil this role, as a suitable basis for the production of efficient and effective parallel programs, controlling the complexity managed by the programmer.

2.1 Parallel Data-structures

A significant body of work has been developed that describes data structures that can be effectively accessed in parallel. This requires both the elimination of locking, and the distribution of the representation to remove serialising influences that limit scalability[1]. Parallel data structures and their operations have been presented for queues[9, 12, 13, 23], trees[8] and sets[18] amongst others. These developments have tended to focus on single structures, and has defined their semantics in an instance-dependent manner. There is the potential to develop a new parallel programming model, based on the use of these data structures. Before this can be achieved, the problems of composing these structures must be addressed.

2.2 Shared Abstract Data-types

A Shared Abstract Data-type (SADT) is an abstract data-type with the following additional characteristics:

- It may be accessed concurrently by many processes.
- It has the potential for distributed implementation, facilitating true parallel access.

An SADT may be viewed as a wrapper around a (potentially) parallel data structure, providing a well defined interface. We distinguish SADTs due to the emphasis in their design on compositional properties and system building. The aim is to produce an programming model based on SADTs with well defined compositional properties, as an appropriate basis for the construction of parallel applications targeted to a wide variety of parallel platforms. We also distinguish SADTs from Objects as it is not clear that inheritance has a clear role in defining the behaviour of concurrent data abstractions[15]. Also, the internal structure of an SADT is likely to be more complex than that of a simple object.

Similar work includes Concurrent Aggregates[5]. This work focussed on the integration of mechanisms for building *concurrent data abstractions* into a concurrent language. We are interested specifically in the design of these abstractions and facilitating their use in building parallel applications.

2.2.1 Concurrent Semantics

Defining the semantics of an SADT, such as a queue, from the perspective of a single process is straightforward as it collapses to the sequential operation semantics. The introduction of concurrency requires an extension to this semantics, defining how sharing between concurrent processes operates.

Sequential Consistency requires that the results of all operations on shared data are consistent with a total ordering of the operations of that data that does not violate program ordering (ie. ordering within one process). This permits sequential reasoning over the use of single shared items of data.

The composition of more than one data item can give rise to contradictory total orderings, as identified in [17]. Sequential Consistency is therefore an insufficiently strong condition on individual data items to permit the construction of sequentially consistent systems. System-wide sequential consistency can be maintained by forcing all operations on shared data to occur in a single sequential order, as in Symmetric Multi-Processing (shared-bus) systems and some Concurrent Object systems, such as Orca[2, 3]. The problem with these approaches is scalability.

A novel approach to the composition problem involves the use of the *Linearizability* correctness condition[12]. A data item is said to be linearizable if a sequential ordering of operations can be constructed, such that all observable ordering between operations at different processes is not violated. To formalise this notion, Herlihy[12] uses the notion of a *history* of operations extracted from a concurrent system, consisting of an interleaving of invocation (start of operation) and response (end of operation) events. The operations represented by a history are totally ordered if the history is *sequential*, that is the response event of an operation immediately follows the invocation event. If this is not the case, the operations of the history will be partially ordered. The ordering relation $<_H$ of operations represented in a history H is such that for two operations e_1 and e_2, $e_1 <_H e_2$ if the response of operation e_1 precedes the invocation of e_2 in the history H.

A formal definition of Linearizability, paraphrased from [12] is as follows:

Definition 1 (Linearizability) *A type is Linearizable if a history of operations H on the type can be re-ordered into a sequential history S such that:*

- *The ordering of operations in S does not violate program order.*

- $<_H \subseteq <_S$.

The first condition is equivalent to sequential consistency. The second condition ensures that orderings *between* concurrent processes are maintained, in turn ensuring that the composition of linearizable components is itself linearizable and hence sequentially consistent.

Linearizability offers the potential for scalability, as no central mechanism is required to enforce system sequencing. Several authors have identified linearizable implementations of data structures, notably queues and stacks[5, 9, 12, 23, 25]. These implementations are decentralised and have been demonstrated to be capable of providing scalable performance[9, 23]. As an aside, the solution to the correctness problem proposed in [17] appears to be an application of the principle of Linearizability[12, 25].

The semantics for concurrent operations are defined by using a sequential semantics for operations on the data item combined with the assertion that these operations are linearizable[25]. This provides a strong, and perhaps overly strict semantics. There is a well-known tradeoff between weakened consistency and performance. To exploit this tradeoff without abandoning the advantages of linearizability requires that the sequential semantics of operations are weakened. The non-determinism due to concurrency is translated therefore into non-determinism in the sequential semantics. This means that the system can be reasoned about in a sequential mode, considering concurrent non-determinism as an aspect of the sequential behaviour of types.

A well-developed set of SADTs may therefore offer a number of implementations of an SADT, such as a queue. These would offer different sequential semantics, from the strict (ie. strong FIFO) to the weak (ie. Fair heap). This would allow the programmer to make an choice in exploiting the weakness/performance tradeoff whilst ensuring that the correctness of the program is maintained.

3 Branch and Bound

Branch and Bound[19] is a style of algorithm applicable to a wide class of problems solvable through combinatorial search. Typically these problems lie in the complexity class $\mathcal{NP}$. Branch and Bound algorithms explore the search space of a problem by expanding a tree. The internal nodes of the tree represent intermediate steps towards possible solutions; the leaves of the tree represent fully expanded solutions, covering the search space. The optimal solution to the problem is selected through applying some quality function to the solutions at the leaves, permitting the best to be selected.

3.1 Pruning

Expanding the complete tree would lead to an execution time proportional to the size of the search space. The number of possible solutions in this space is factorial in the number of problem elements that may be combined to form a solution, ie. the problem size. To reduce the computational load, yielding a tractable execution, the search tree can be pruned. This pruning minimises the total space explored to some small fraction of the size of the total search space. Through pruning correctly, it will be known that the optimal solution lies in the part of the tree that is explored. Additional heuristic information may be used to direct the search towards promising areas of the tree first. This will in general have no effect on the asymptotic complexity of the algorithm, but will reduce the proportion of the tree explored, expanding the range of tractable problems.

A pruning decision results in a node of the tree not being expanded. This decision reflects the knowledge that this node cannot be the ancestor of a better solution than is currently known. To formulate this decision requires:

- A measure of the quality of the best solution found so far.

- A measure of the quality of the partial solution at this node. This measure must be *monotonic*, ie. it cannot be improved by further expansion from this node.

With these two measures, the pruning decision is formulated by comparing these two values; one global and one derived from the local node. Figure 1 shows this behaviour in the expansion of a search tree. Once the solution $l = 20$ has been found, there is no point in expanding any internal nodes with $l \geq 20$ as they cannot possibly lead to a better solution.

3.2 Parallelising Branch and Bound

To parallelise branch and bound, an opportunity for introducing concurrency is needed. This opportunity may be realised through the expansion of many nodes of the search tree in parallel. This expansion introduces a breadth-wise behaviour into the tree expansion. This technique combined with a depth-first

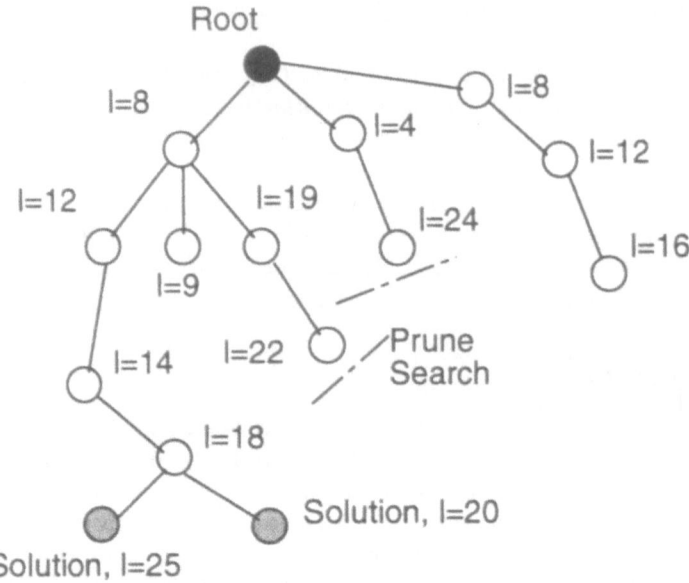

Figure 1: A partial expansion of a search tree, showing monotonic parameter increases down the tree and the effect of pruning.

sequential strategy for efficient pruning forms the basis of several concurrent branch-and-bound algorithms[14, 16, 20, 22].

The distinguishing features of the different algorithms for Branch and Bound problems are how they manage local (node) information, information local to a single processor, and global information. Techniques for this management have been suggested in the literature based on message-passing [14, 20, 22].

3.2.1 Anomalous Behaviour

The exact choice of expansion strategy, and the non-determinism due to concurrent execution can lead to significant differences in the amount of work that an algorithm performs in solving a problem. This can readily lead to anomalies such as super-linear speedup, and and slowdown, where a solution on n processors takes more time than on m processors, even though $n > m$[16]. The selection of expansion strategies and the effect of this on algorithm behaviour is therefore of concern to the designer.

3.3 The Travelling Salesman Problem

The Travelling Salesman Problem (TSP) is a combinatorial optimisation problem. The input for a TSP algorithm is a set of cities, and the distances between them. The output from an algorithm is an ordered list of all cities such that the distance travelled by visiting each of the cities on this list in turn and then returning to the initial city is the minimum over all possible such lists.

For a system of n cities, the computational complexity is $O(n!)$, placing the problem in the complexity class $\mathcal{NP}$. Deterministic algorithms, based upon variants of the branch-and-bound technique are generally used to solve this class of problems[14, 19, 22]. These guarantee the optimal solution, but retain an exponential asymptotic time complexity. These algorithms rely on pruning techniques and other heuristics to minimise the size of the solution space that is explored, thus yielding acceptable execution time.

4 Developing an SADT-based solution

In this section, a parallel implementation of a TSP solver, employing a Branch-and-Bound technique using SADTs is developed. The implementations presented rely on an *Accumulator* SADT[10] to maintain the global bound information. An Accumulator captures a common mode of sharing where many processes co-operate in producing and using a result. The interface to the accumulator is specified by the following (imperative) signatures:

$$
\begin{array}{rcl}
\text{Create} & : & \alpha \times (\alpha \times \alpha \to \alpha) \to \alpha Accumulator \\
\text{Destroy} & : & \alpha Accumulator \to \text{void} \\
\text{Update} & : & \alpha \times \alpha Accumulator \to \alpha \\
\text{Read} & : & \alpha Accumulator \to \alpha
\end{array}
$$

An accumulator is *specialised* with a type. On creation of an accumulator, an initial value of that type and a modification function are specified. In polymorphic systems such as ML, this can be expressed directly in the language. In other modern languages such as C++, the same effect can be achieved within the language by using templates.

The accumulator *Update* function passes in a value and applies the modification function to this value and the value stored in the accumulator. The value of the accumulator prior to this update is returned. The *Read* function simply returns the value in the accumulator. The strong sequential semantics of the accumulator state that all results are consistent with operations occuring in a single sequence. Weaker semantics, where a strong sequenced behaviour is not required are also useful.

4.1 Simple Accumulator-based solution

The Accumulator SADT captures a common mode of sharing, where a result is used by many co-operating processes to control the evolution of a computation. In the case of branch-and-bound, it is used to store the shortest tour found so far. The Accumulator type is created with an initial value, and a function specifying the manner in which the accumulator is updated. For example, parameterising an accumulator with the minimum function will store the minimum of all values written to it.

```
City Set all_cities; // Initial problem
City start;              // Arbitraty starting city
Length Accumulator min_tour(infinity, MIN);

void tourfind(City Set cities, Length so_far, City current) {
  if (Set_empty(cities))
    Acc_update(min_tour, so_far)          // Accumulate minimum
  else
    if (Acc_read(min_tour) > so_far)      // else prune...
      PAR for (i in cities)
        tourfind(Set_subtract(cities, i),
                 so_far + distance(current, i), i)
}
tourfind(Set_subtract(all_cities, start), 0, start);
```

Figure 2: Pseudo-code for an Accumulator SADT-based branch-and-bound solution to the Travelling Salesman Problem.

Processes expanding the search tree check their progress against the accumulator. If they have accumulated a distance above the bound represented by the value of the accumulator, then they terminate, pruning the search-tree.

4.1.1 Drawbacks

This implementation has several problems. Firstly, it will generate a large number of processes for even modest-sized problems. This will pose an unreasonable burden on any underlying operating system. Secondly, the branch-and-bound technique relies for its efficacy on quickly finding an approximation to the minimum value. Assuming fair scheduling, nearly the entire problem space will have been explored before any pruning will begin. A third problem concerns the use of the synchronous PAR construct, which is not generally available in programming systems.

4.2   Explicit task-management solution

The problems of the simple implementation are addressed by abstracting the set of *worker* processes from the implementation of figure 2. The implementation is changed so that it generates *tasks* that can be assigned to worker processes. This assignment is achieved through workers reading from a shared task store SADT. The number of workers is therefore abstracted from the implementation and can be dictated by parameters of the target system. This new solution is shown in figure 3. Removing the PAR construct exposes the problem of termination detection. This can be solved by using an accumulator parameterised with the addition operation. This is used to track the number of tasks currently in the shared task structure. When new work is generated, the accumulator

```
City Set all_cities;      // Initial problem
City start;               // Arbitraty starting city
(Length, City List) Accumulator min_tour(infinity, MIN_TOUR);
INT Accumulator tasks(1, +);
type Task = (City List, City Set, Length, City) | FINISHED;
Task Stack taskstack;

void tourfind() {                    // Worker task
 BOOL finished = FALSE

 WHILE (NOT finished) {
  task = Stack_pop(taskstack)
  task_count = Acc_update(tasks, -1)
  if (task != FINISHED) {       // Catch termination signal
   (visited, to_visit, so_far, current) = task;
   if (Set_empty(to_visit) ||
       Acc_read(min_tour) < so_far) { // prune
    Acc_update((visited, min_tour), so_far)
    if (task_count == 1)        // I am last active worker
     Stack_push(taskstack, FINISHED)
   } else {                            // Generate next level
    Acc_update(tasks, Set_size(to_visit))
    for (next in to_visit) {    // Note: Store is allocated
     newtask = (List_add(visited, current),
                Set_subtract(to_visit, next),
                so_far + distance(current, next), next)
     Stack_push(taskstack, newtask)
    }
   }
  } else {
   finished = TRUE                    // Note termination
   Stack_push(taskstack, FINISHED)   // Signal to other workers
  }
 }
}
Stack_push(taskstack,
           ([], Set_subtract(all_cities, start), 0, start));
start_workers(n, tourfind);   // Spawn 'n' worker processes
```

Figure 3: Pseudo-code for a refinement of the Accumulator SADT-based branch-and-bound TSP solver. The provision of worker processes executing tourfind is now orthogonal to the tourfind procedure itself.

is incremented. When work is removed, the accumulator is decremented. The last worker can detect when there are no more tasks and can signal all other workers to terminate, through the shared task structure.

To obtain depth-first behaviour, fair scheduling is not required. By exposing the tasks rather than hiding them in the scheduler, choices about task scheduling can be made. In this case, depth-first behaviour will be facilitated if the shared task structure is implemented by a *Stack* SADT. The stack supports push and pop operations. The type of tree-expansion expected when using the stack in the presence of concurrent workers is shown in figure 4.

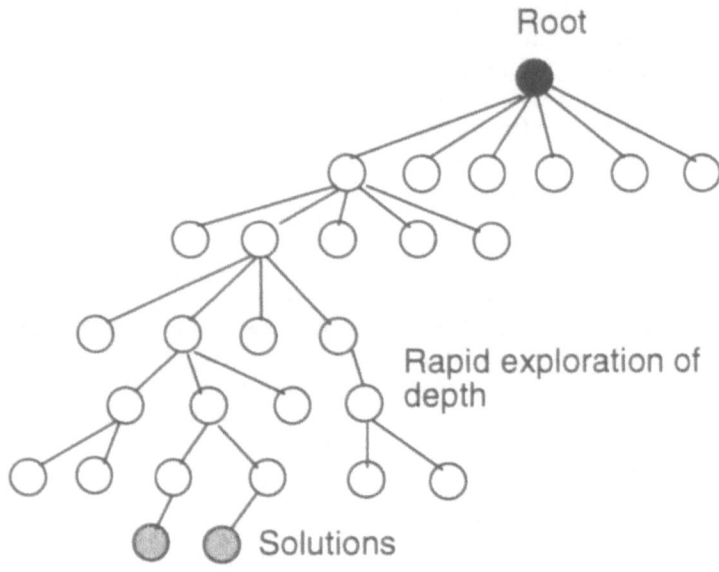

Figure 4: Snapshot of tree expansion due to the use of the stack for task storage in the presence of concurrent workers.

A final problem is that the first implementation does not return the minimal length tour. This is solved by storing the minimal length tour in the accumulator along with its length. The MIN_TOUR operator takes two items containing a tour and its length, yielding the tour and its length where that length is the minimum. Note that the accumulator is specialised with both a value type and an update function.

4.2.1 Modus Operandi

The implementation of figure3 relies on a set of three SADTs; an integer Accumulator specialised with the addition operation, a minimum-length tour Accumulator and a Stack. Initially the stack contains the task corresponding to the root node of the tree, where the starting city has been chosen. The integer accumulator tasks is initialised to 1.

A worker attempts to take a task from the stack, blocking until one is available. A worker removes a task, decrements the task counter Accumulator, and tests if the node the task represents can be expanded. If it can, and the length of tour that this node represents does not exceed the best known, then the node is expanded.

If the node is expanded, all the children are placed into the task pool (Stack) and the accumulator is incremented to reflect the additions. If the node cannot be expanded and the number of tasks that were left before this one was obtained is 1, then this worker has consumed the last task and is the last active worker. It therefore signals termination. On termination, the tour length Accumulator contains the best solution.

4.3   Accumulator Implementation

In the algorithm, there are two instances of the Accumulator SADT. The first of these keeps track of the number of tasks in the stack SADT. The second is used to control pruning, and contains both a tour length and the tour itself. In the following, the implementation styles for these accumulators and their semantics are discussed.

4.3.1   Integer Accumulator

The integer accumulator is used to detect termination, and thus its semantics are the basis of a correctness condition for the algorithm. In terms of its sequential semantics, a read on the accumulator must return a value consistent with all previous operations in the concurrent system having completed, ie. no sequential non-determinism is allowed. This is required so that the last worker process to remove a task from the stack can detect that it is the last, and so signal the other workers to terminate.

There is a well-known implementation structure for this type of data abstraction, based on dynamic combining[11]. The accumulator is specialised with a commutative operation, addition. The ability to arbitrarily re-order commutative operations permits the construction of a tree, distributed across the address spaces of a machine. This tree combines operation traffic through a number of stages to minimise the load on the root of the tree where the actual value is stored. This structure offers superiour throughput and latency under load to a value stored in a single location. This type of structure is shown in figure 5.

The semantics of this type of structure with regard to operation sequencing are well understood. In particular, a proof of linearizability for this form of accumulator, where a strong sequential semantics are assumed has been developed[4]. The proof relies on deriving the partial ordering for operations at successive levels in the tree, using a message-passing model of the accumulator implementation.

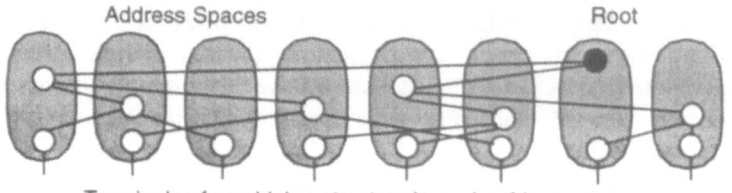

Terminals of combining structure in each address space.

Figure 5: An Accumulator SADT implemented by a binary combining tree structure, scattered across the address spaces in a parallel machine.

4.3.2 Tour and Length Accumulator

The second accumulator is used to maintain a record of the current best-known solution. Partial solutions are compared against the best known solution to formulate pruning decisions.

The semantics of this accumulator need not be as strong as the integer accumulator. The correctness of the algorithm does not rely on the properties of this accumulator; however there is a performance issue involved. If the information obtained from this accumulator is out of date, then more nodes may be expanded than necassary. This overhead computation can be avoided by using an accumulator with a stronger timeliness guarantee.

4.4 Stack Implementation

The stack is a key data structure from the point of view of performance. As with the tour accumulator, the exact sequencing semantics of the stack are not required for correctness. Due to the amount of traffic the stack handles, a very efficient implementation is required.

A stack with strong sequencing semantics has been proposed in [23], based on the use of an *Elimination Tree* structure to direct accesses across a set of stacks, distributed across a machine. This structure offers good performance, but requires a significant amount of copying. Also, the sequencing behaviour of this structure has been proven to be *Linearizable* with a small probability of encountering an out-of-sequence value.

An alternative stack SADT implementation can eliminate a great deal of data movement if the algorithm can tolerate a weaker stack-like semantics. A weak stack may be implemented as a set of stacks distributed across a machine. In this type of implementation, an access to the SADT always touches the local stack. Activity within the SADT is responsible for avoiding starvation by migrating contents between stacks. This implementation will cause the solver to behave in a similar manner to a local stack based message passing implementation, such as [20], where the application explicitly manages the communication between private work stacks.

It is clear that the SADT approach separates the correctness issues in algorithm design from those concerned with performance. There are also some additional issues of what should be available in the interface to an SADT. It would be possible, for example, to integrate a counter into the stack to keep track of the current depth, subsuming the role of the separate accumulator. This then gives rise to the problem that the stack can be weak, but the count must be strong for correctness reasons. To resolve these issues, a focus on the needs of real algorithms is important.

4.5 Further Refinements

One of the best known Branch and Bound algorithms for TSP is Little's algorithm[19]. This algorithm relies for its efficiency on a heuristic that causes the most promising nodes to be expanded first. The *most promising* value judgement is based upon a statically computed lower bound on tour length. Nodes with the lowest lower bound are expanded first. The SADT required to implement this algorithm in parallel is a *priority queue*, that allows the tasks with the lowest lower tour-length bound to be extracted first. This would appear to be a very promising approach, but is currently left open for further work.

4.6 An SADT system

To program applications using SADTs requires the support of a library of useful SADTs. In the TallShiP project[1], we are investigating the population of such a library by identifying common modes of sharing and capturing these using SADTs. The SADTs in the library make use of a set of features of an underlying run-time system. This provides basic facilities for system-wide communication, synchronisation, storage management and multi-threading.

To support the effective use of general-purpose SADTs, a language for SADT programming should provide effective mechanisms for abstraction. As noted before, SADTs *appear* similar to objects, although their implementation differs. A language supporting object-like encapsulation should therefore provide a suitable basis for SADT application programming.

To enhance the versatility of a set of SADTs, polymorphism is a very attractive feature. Few modern languages, excepting functional languages such as ML provide support for polymorphism. Generics (Modula-3) and templates (C++) provide mechanisms for generating specific implementations of general-purpose abstractions and would appear to be suitable solutions to this problem.

As the basis for experimentation, we have chosen the Modula-3 language[21]. Modula-3 provides extensive support for multi-threading and network communications via its Network Objects package. This package permits us to construct SADTs consisting of many network objects distributed across the address-spaces of a system. In the sense of [5], these *representatives* co-operate to provide a uniform abstraction. Modula-3 has a well-designed Generic Modules facility, supporting the type of restricted polymorphism noted above. The

---

[1]TallShiP is an EPSRC-funded collaborative project between the School of Computer Studies at the University of Leeds, and Rutherford Appleton Laboratories.

facilities in Modula-3 for partial revelation offer additional support for re-usable implementation of generic features within SADTs whilst making these opaque to the application programmer. The run-time system we have implemented in Modula-3 to support this work is very compact, numbering less than 1000 lines of code. The use of high-performance messaging technology such as ATM and Active Messages[24] are being pursued to obtain good performance on workstation network systems as well as dedicated parallel systems.

5 Conclusions

This paper has presented a case study of the use of Shared Abstract Data-types (SADTs) for implementing a Branch-and-Bound algorithm for the Travelling Salesman Problem. As well as identifying the correctness and performance issues in the algorithm, a clean separation between the algorithm and the implementations of SADTs has been achieved. The discussion of the properties of the SADTs required has provided insights into how the semantic weakness/performance tradeoff can be exploited within the implementation of SADTs for this application.

5.1 Further work

SADTs provide a promising approach to encapsulating the details of communication and synchronisation, providing the programmer with more straightforward and problem-oriented abstractions. To develop these ideas further we are pursuing the following routes:

- The investigation of application kernels, and their implementation using SADTs.

- The design of SADTs, and the understanding of the influence of different design 'patterns' on semantics.

Acknowledgements

The authors would like to acknowledge the contributions of other members of the TallShiP project; Simon Dobson, Mourad Kara, Chris Wadsworth and Peter Dew.

References

[1] G M Amdahl. Validity of the single-processor approach to achieving large scale computing capabilities. In *AFIPS Conference proceedings*, pages 483–485, April 1967.

[2] Henri Bal. *Programming Distributed Systems*. Prentice-Hall, 1990.

[3] Henri E. Bal, M. Franz Kaashoek, and Andrew S. Tannenbaum. Orca: A Language for Parallel Programming of Distributed Systems. *IEEE Transactions on Software Engineering*, 18(3), March 1992.

[4] Robert Briggs. An Accumulator SADT: Implementation and Concurrent Semantics. Final Year Project Report (Unpublished), School of Computer Studies, University of Leeds, 1995.

[5] Andrew A. Chien. *Concurrent Aggregates*. MIT Press, 1993.

[6] M. Cole. *Algorithmic Skeletons: Structured Management of Parallel Computation*. Pitman/MIT Press, 1989.

[7] J. Darlington, A.J. Field, P.G. Harrison, P.H.J. Kelly, D.W.N Sharp, and Q. Wu. Parallel Programming Using Skeleton Functions. In *Parallel Languages and Architectures, Europe 1993*, 1993.

[8] Carla Schlatter Ellis. Concurrent Search and Insertion in AVL Trees. *IEEE Transactions on Computers*, C-29(9), September 1980.

[9] Don Goodeve, John Davy, Peter Dew, and Jonathan Nash. Concurrent Sharing through Abstract Data-types: A Case Study. In M. Kara et al., editor, *Abstract Machine Models for Parallel and Distributed Computing*. IOS Press, 1996.

[10] Don Goodeve, John Davy, and Chris Wadsworth. Shared Accumulators. In *Transputer Applications and Systems '95*, pages 518–528. IOS Press, 1995.

[11] A. Gottlieb, R. Grishman, C. P. Kruskal, K. M. McAuliffe, L. Rudolph, and M. Snir. The NYU Ultracomputer — Designing an MIMD Shared Memory Parallel Computer. *IEEE Transactions on Computers*, C-32(2):175–189, February 1983.

[12] Maurice P. Herlihy and Jeannette M. Wing. Linearizability: A Correctness Condition for Concurrent Objects. *ACM Transactions on Programming Languages and Systems*, 12(3):463–492, July 1990.

[13] T. Johnson. A Highly Concurrent Priority Queue. *Journal of Parallel and Distributed Computing*, 22(2):367–373, 1994.

[14] Nobert Kuck, Martin Middendorf, and Hartmut Schmeck. Generic Branch and Bound on Transputers. In R. Grebe et al., editor, *Transputer Applications and Systems '93*, pages 521–535. IOS Press, 1993.

[15] Sandeep Kumar and Dharma P. Agrawal. CORE: A Solution to the Inheritance Anomaly in Concurrent Object-Oriented Languages. In A. Kumar and K. Kamel, editors, *Parallel and Distributed Computing and Systems '96*, pages 75–81. ICSA, October 14-16, 1993.

[16] Ten-Hwang Lai and Sartaj Sahni. Anomalies in Parallel Branch-and-Bound Algorithms. *Communications of the ACM*, 27(6):594–602, June 1984.

[17] Leslie Lamport. How to make a Multiprocessor Computer that Correctly Executes Multiprocess Programs. *IEEE Transactions on Computers*, C-28(9):690–691, September 1979.

[18] Vladmir Lanin and Dennis Shasha. Concurrent set manipulation without locking. In *7th ACM Symposium on the Principlies of Database Systems*, pages 211–220, March 1988.

[19] John D.C. Little, Katta G. Murty, Dura W. Sweeney, and Caroline Karel. An Algorithm for the Travelling Salesman Problem. *Operations Research*, 11:972–989, 1963.

[20] G.P. McKeown, V.J. Rayward-Smith, S.A. Rush, and H.J. Turpin. Using a Transputer network to solve Branch-and-Bound problems. In P. Welch et al., editor, *Transputing '91*, pages 781–799. IOS Press, 1991.

[21] Greg Nelson. *Systems Programming with Modula-3*. Prentice-Hall series in Innovative Computer Science. Prentice-Hall, 1991.

[22] V.J. Rayward-Smith, S.A. Rush, and G.P. McKeown. Efficiency considerations in the implementation of parallel branch-and-bound. *Annals of Operations Research*, 43:123–145, 1993.

[23] Nir Shavit and Dan Touitou. Elimination Trees and the Construction of Pools and Stacks. In *7th Annual Symposium on Parallel Algorithms and Architectures*, pages 54–63. ACM Press, April 26th, 1995.

[24] Thorsten von Eicken, Anindya Basu, and Vineet Buch. Low-Latency Communication Over ATM Networks Using Active Messages. *IEEE Micro*, 15(1):46–53, 1995.

[25] Jeanette M. Wing and Chun Gong. Testing and Verifying Concurrent Objects. *Journal of Parallel and Distributed Computing*, 17:164–182, 1993.

Some Geographical Applications of Genetic Programming on the Cray T3D Supercomputer

I. Turton, S. Openshaw and G. Diplock

School of Geography, University of Leeds, Leeds, UK

email: ian@geog.leeds.ac.uk, stan@geog.leeds.ac.uk, gary@geog.leeds.ac.uk

April 15, 1996

Abstract

The paper describes some geographical applications of a parallel GP code which is run on a Cray T3D 512 processor supercomputer to create new types of well performing mathematical models. A series of results are described which allude to the potential power of the method for which there are many practical applications in spatial data rich environments where there are no suitable existing models and no soundly based theoretical framework on which to base them.

1 Introduction

The Geographical Information Systems (GIS) revolution together with the computerisation of management and administrative systems has produced large amounts of geographically referenced information covering many aspects of modern life. The challenge now is how best to use these databases to create new knowledge in areas where current theoretical understanding is weak, how to develop or discover new process models of the behaviour of the human systems that the databases reflect and how to invent new and more appropriate exploratory analysis systems. This paper deals with the task of developing new process models of geographical systems able to cope with the complex properties of spatial phenomena. This task is becoming increasingly urgent because of the difficulties of building geographical models by more traditional methods. Additionally, many of the existing models are old and predate the spatial data explosion that has occurred since the late 1980s.

Traditionally, mathematical models are specified on the basis of good or strong theoretical knowledge but in many social sciences the available theories are suspect and at best poor. Additionally, the geographical systems of interest are usually highly complex, non-linear, probably chaotic and currently are not fully or properly understood due to the immense complexity of the human and environmental systems that are involved. One way forward is to use artificial neural networks and fuzzy logic modelling as universal approximators in the hope that viable computer models can be obtained by these essentially black box methods ; see Openshaw (1992, 1996). These inductive approaches use machine learning techniques to create equation free representations that 'learn' how to map a set of inputs to one or more outputs and in the process provide good fits to observed data. However, these methods are far removed from the traditional equation based mathematical model building activities that geographers and the other social scientists have used.

The paper explores an alternative model building approach based on the application of Genetic Programming methods run on a Cray T3D with 512 processors. This has the advantage of retaining the algebraic symbolism of the traditional approach whilst removing the total dependency of the model design and model discovery process on the skills of the human being. Instead high performance computing is used to build new computer models using what might be termed a generic type of model breeding machine. Section 2 outlines the design of model breeders whilst section 3 discusses their implementation on the Cray T3D parallel supercomputer. The results of some of the early applications are presented in Section 4.

2 Early Model Breeding Machines

The idea of building models by computer is not new. For over 30 years certain classes of linear statistical models have been created by examining all permutations of the predictor variables; for instance, if there are M predictors there are 2^{M-1} possible linear regression models than can be built, explored, and the best one identified. There is no reason why a similar strategy cannot be used to build mathematical models except once the model form is no longer restricted to being linear the number of possible permutations becomes far too large to examine in an exhaustive manner. There are also other problems in that the parameters now have to be estimated using a non-linear optimisation procedure and this may well involve a three or four orders of magnitude increase in compute times for a single model.

The success of computer automated model design now critically depends on developing an efficient search process. For instance, how can you be reasonably confident that by creating and evaluating 10^4 models you have found the best or near best models from a search space that may well contain more possible model equations? Equally even if there exists an old model how can you be reasonably sure that this model is the best (or amongst the best) model that exists. One approach is to generate and evaluate as many randomly generated model equations as possible in a fixed period of compute time; see Openshaw (1986). This model crunching strategy would at least allow current conventionally produced models to be viewed in terms of a broader context. However, whilst surprisingly good levels of performance can often be achieved a much better approach is to base the model generation process on some kind of intelligent search or optimisation process. Early attempts involved the use of focused Monte Carlo search methods and simulated annealing (Openshaw, 1988).

It soon became apparent that it would be in principle far better to use a genetic algorithm to drive this model search process. This is investigated in Openshaw (1988) who developed what was termed an Automated Modelling

System (AMS). A basic genetic algorithm (BA) based on Holland (1976) was used to breed simple mathematical equation based models. The entire process was powered by various Cray IS and XMP supercomputers in the mid 1980's. These machine generated equation based models were evaluated in terms of their ability to fit a dataset. The problems were two-fold: (1) insufficiently powerful supercomputers and (2) difficulties in representing models as bit strings.

The basic idea is still relevant and it makes much sense to regard many model design problems as a search problem. In many modelling applications it is quite apparent that the available model pieces (variables, parameters, unary mathematical functions, binary operators, and rules of arithmetic equations) can be combined in many different ways to form an immense universe containing all possible model equations that could be built. In the original research the principal problem was how best to represent symbolic equations based on the range of available model pieces by a fixed length bit string that would nevertheless allow the GA maximum freedom to create and search the universe of all potentially possible model equations for good performing models. Two different representational schemes were used. The first assumed a very simple structure as shown in Figure 1. Note that each equation could have a number of unknown parameters and these were estimated using a non-linear least squares procedure which was embedded in the GA. However, the basic Darwinian, rather than Lamarckian, philosophy was retained and the optimal parameters were not stored as part of the bit string but merely used in computing the fitness function.

A more complex alternative coding scheme was developed whereby the bit string was decoded to form a reverse polish expression of the model equation. This was subsequently used in a commercial version developed from AMS system called OMIGA (Barrow 1993) . Figure 2 outlines this model representation. A model consists of a number of these genes. The genes are sorted by their status (providing position independence) and then used to create a model in a reverse polish form. The model equation that emerges is the longest complete equation that satisfies the reverse polish logic implicit in the ordering of the model pieces. The problem is that this type of implementation is hard for the GA to handle, due to the high probability of redundancy and unused bits, its variable length and its self defining nature. However, it does work, although there is a feeling that improved results might be obtainable if a better way of representing the problem could be found.

3 Genetic Programming based Model Breeders

3.1 Serial GP

In this paper we attempt to improve on AMS by using the newer technique of genetic programming (Koza, 1992). Figure 3 outlines the basic structure of a Genetic Programming approach. GP is basically a GA that applies modified genetic operators not to bit strings but directly to the symbolic equations. This method has the outstanding advantage that the problem representation is much

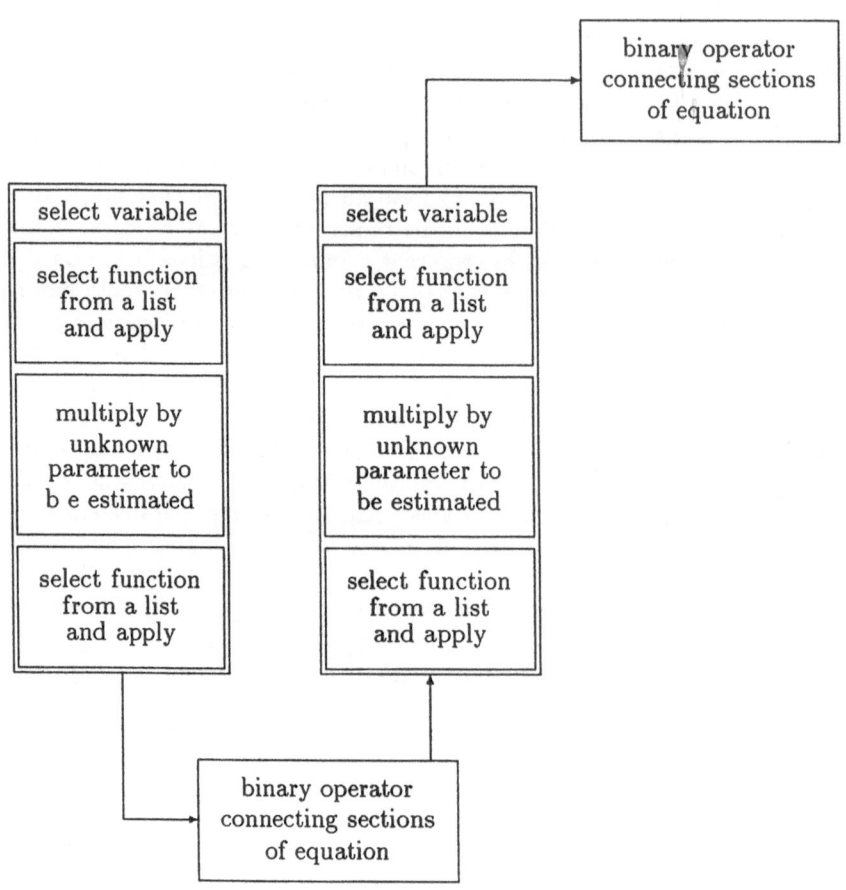

Figure 1: A simple model representation scheme

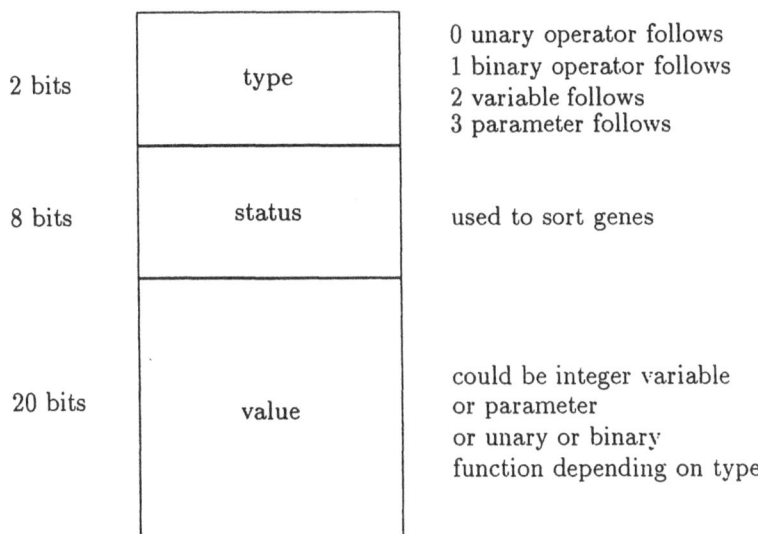

Figure 2: A more complex model representation scheme

more direct. There is no need for a bit string that has to be decoded to become a model equation. Instead the basic genetic operators of crossover and mutation are applied directly to the symbolic equations that explicitly represent the model. The trick is to ensure that these symbolic equations are manipulated in such a

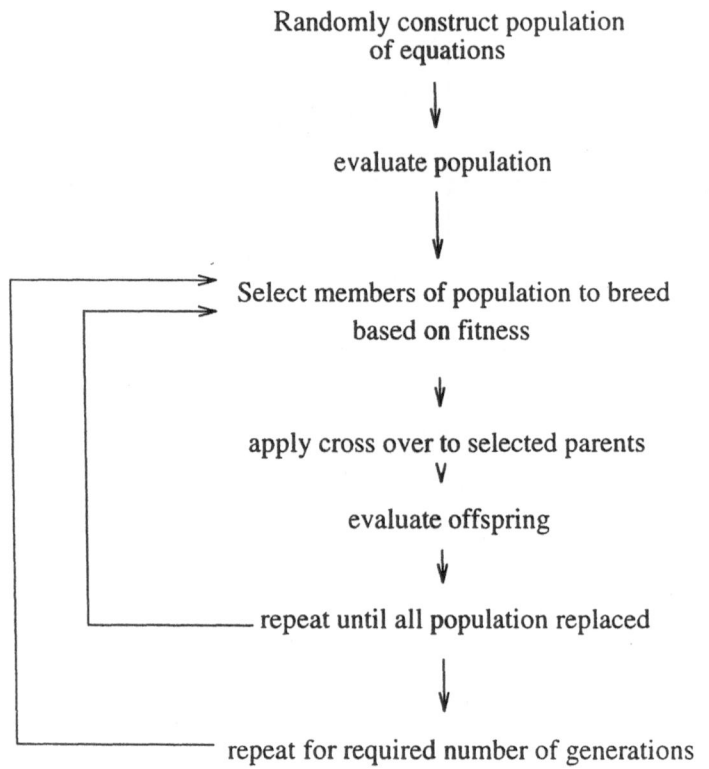

Figure 3: The genetic programming algorithm

way that valid models are always produced. This greatly simplifies the search task and should in principle yield a much more efficient model breeding machine. Koza (1992) based his GP on LISP S expressions (which he terms programs) and this is the key to understanding the tremedous flexibility provided by GP in an automated modelling context. Figure 4 illustrates this process using crossover on a simple S expression.

The genetic programming was carried out using two approaches, one a traditional method based on LISP S-expressions (Koza, 1992) and the second used a stack based representation that seemed to offer some benefits (Perkis, 1994). Both programs were written in standard FORTRAN 77 for convenience, since this allowed implementation on various high performance computer hardware.

A FORTRAN implementation may seem a little unusual but it is very

Parent 1: (*(V1)(-(V2)(V3)))   Parent 2: (/(+(V1)(V3))(*(V2)(V1)))

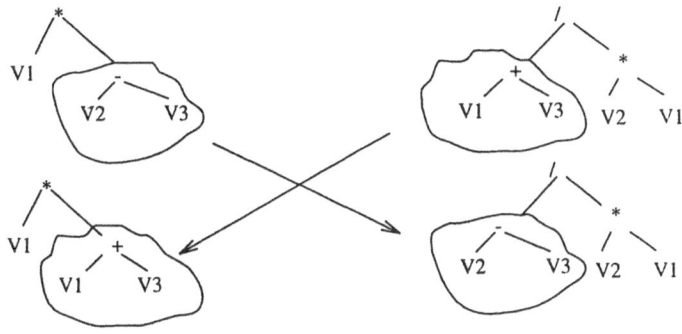

Child 1: (*(V1)(+(V1)(V3)))   Child 2: (/(-(V2)(V3))(*(V2)(V1))

Figure 4: Example of crossover on S expressions

straightforward. The LISP equations are handled as character strings which can only be crossed over at certain positions which generate well formed substrings, thereby completely emulating the LISP tree structure syntax. The equations contained in these character strings are then compiled into an efficient form for ease and efficiency of implementation. In this case the model is decomposed into a serial set of vector operations designed to maximise computational performance on large databases.

Figure 5 illustrates this process. An S expression in prefix form can be viewed as an infix expression. For ease of computation it is compiled into a quadruple structure. Note that here each of the operators work on vectors of data items; for example, $t1=v2+v3$ is actually implemented as $t1(i)=v2(i)+v3(i)$ $i=1....$ N; where N is the number of spatial zones or points. The next step is to tidy up this code to remove redundant expressions, to detect constants, and to apply standard arithmetic optimisation procedures (see Bergmann, 1994). This is important because the success of this GP approach, crudely put, depends on how million models can be evaluated per hour! The GP can be parallelised in various ways. The simplest is to exploit the vectorisation in the quadruple structure.

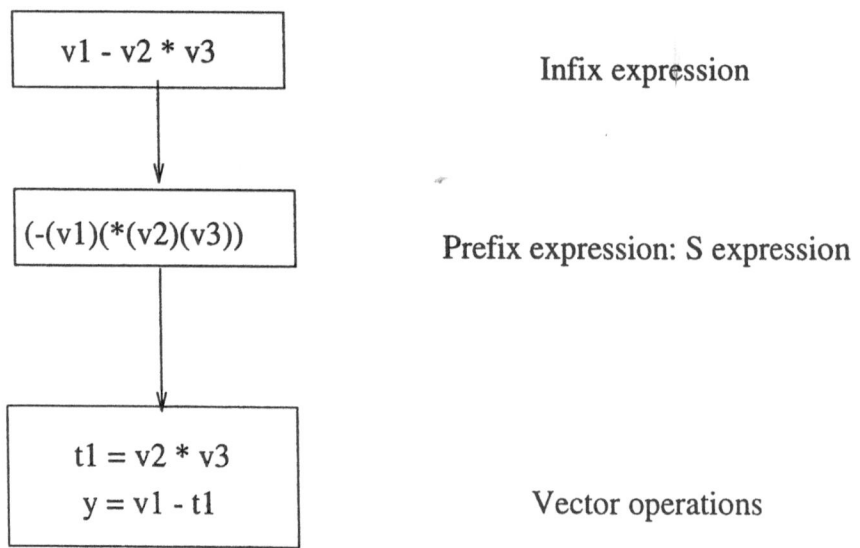

Figure 5: Infix equation, S expression and psuedo vector code

3.2 Parallel GP

The code was initially run on a Cray Y-MP and a Fujitsu VPX1200 vector supercomputer but whilst good levels of vector performance were obtained, it was quite clear that far more compute power was needed. It was subsequently ported onto the Cray T3D 512 node parallel supercomputer at Edinburgh University. The GP algorithm is naturally parallel because each member of the population of equations can be evaluated concurrently, see Figure 3. This requires that the population size is some integer multiple of the number of available processors. The initial code was parallelised in a data parallel form using CRAFT. The serial GP code could be parallelised at the vector loop level (but there was not much work here for a powerful highly parallel machine) or at the string evaluation (model level). The latter is best since there is considerable computation going on here with a non-linear optimiser being run to estimate values for the unknown parameters. Unfortunately, the compute times for each model equation are highly variable as it is a function of model complexity, the number of parameters to be estimated, and the nature of the mathematical function pieces used (e.g. a log takes much longer to compute than a multiply). This unevenness results in a large amount of idle processor time due to poor load balancing. It was obvious that a different form of parallel GP was needed if further progress was to be made.

It is necessary to develop a version of GP that uses what might be termed an asynchronous GP rather than the standard synchronous one; see Figure 6. This would allow a Message Passing (MPI) version to be developed that would ensure high levels of load balancing. The principal changes made to suit MPI are twofold: (1) the need to have a population size greater than the available number of processors being used (this is not a problem given the current trend towards highly (rather than massively) parallel systems) and the need for larger population sizes to ensure GP efficiency; and (2) the population updating needs to occurs asynchronously whereas in the serial GP it would be done synchronously when the complete population of equations had all been evaluated and their fitness ascertained. With this asynchronous approach almost perfect load balancing is achieved since as soon as a processor has finished evaluating an equation it is given another to work on using the latest fitness information available at the time. The task farm form of message passing parallel programming is very efficient at dealing with uneven computational tasks provided the individual tasks take more time than the communication overheads. In other words, the parallelism has to be relatively coarsely grained, which it certainly is in this modelling application.

3.3 Modified parallel GP

Other changes to the standard Koza (1992) form of GP are also necessary. A major departure was the replacement of the ephemeral constant by a parameter, the value of which is optimised using an embedded non-linear parameter estimation procedure. This increased execution times by a factor of between 100

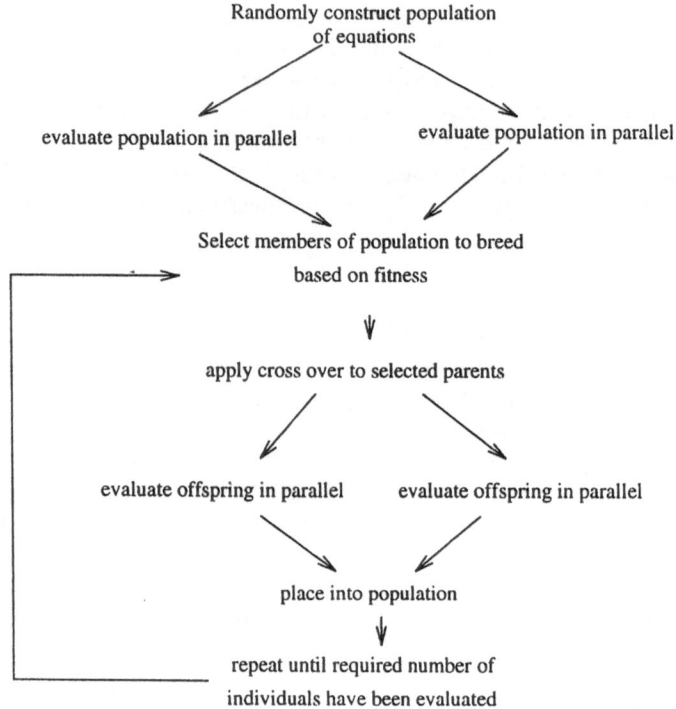

Figure 6: The parallel genetic programming algorithm

and 1000 times but it allowed the GP to concentrate on finding a good equation instead of also having to find optimal parameter values. It seemed quite unreasonable to expect the GP to do everything! This is also useful because it avoids a potentially good model being rejected because it has poor parameter values. However, the need to use a non-linear optimiser causes a number of additional difficulties in particular: (1) a risk of finding suboptimal solutions because of any underlying assumptions of continuously differentiable functions and parameter spaces need not apply; (2) arithmetic problems due to overflows, underflows, library exceptions and NaNs which can easily happen if you assemble a random equation with a divide by zero or a negative log function argument, the GP has to learn to avoid models with these problems implicit in them as part of the model building task rather than be presented with artificially protected versions of the functions; and (3) problems of computational efficiency since the non- linear optimiser used numerical derivatives which means that the computer code used to represent the equation has to be very efficient, since it is not unusual to perform 1000 or more equation evaluations with different parameter values, for datasets containing several thousand cases every time a new model is being evaluated. The non-linear optimisation used is based on a hybrid simulated evolution and quasi- Newton method. It is very straightforward with the simulated evolution method of Schwefel (1995) being used to provide good starting values for the quasi-Newton optimiser to fine tune. Both were hardened to handle arithmetic problems. This permits the parameter and GP optimisation process to continue without propagating erroneous results.

A final consideration is the need to optimise performance levels. Careful tuning of the code on a single processor resulted in a dramatic speed-up of about 140 times on a sample of benchmark equations. Most of the improvements came from the use of vector versions of the standard mathematical functions, use of BLAS routines wherever possible, and loop unrolling.

4   A Spatial Interaction Modelling Case Study

4.1   Data and model Pieces

The spatial interaction model is widely used to describe and predict flows of people, money, goods, migrants, etc. from a set of geographically distributed origins to a set of destinations. The modern form of these mathematical models was created by Wilson (1971) over 25 years ago and, from a broader historical perspective, their structure has changed greatly since their invention 150 years ago. The task of creating genuinely new and totally different models of spatial interaction has proven to be hard and there has been little significant progress since the 1970s.

The models used here are made up of the set of terminals as shown in Table 1. This reflects a desire to model spatial interaction data, such as journey to work flows between a set of origin and destination zones. The model pieces include those typically found in spatial interaction models so that the GP could re-discover the conventional model if relevant. The variables used are shown in

Table 1, along with the functions and operators that are also available to the GP runs. Most are self- explanatory; the competing destinations term is defined as the sum of competing destinations divided by their distance from an origin. The intervening opportunity term is expressed as a count of intervening destinations between each trip-pair. The data consists of a set of car sales for one of the Standard Metropolitan Statistical Areas of Seattle, in the United States, with 86 census tracts and 35 car dealers. The travel cost is measured as the drive time in minutes.

Table 1: Spatial interaction model pieces

Terminals		
	O	Origin size
	D	Destination size
	C	Travel cost
	X	Intervening opportunities term
	Z	Competing destinations term
Operators		
	$+, -, *, /, **$	
Functions		
	sqrt, log, exp	

4.2 GP runs

For operational convenience on the Cray T3D the parameters for the model breeding varied according to the size of the job being executed. When 128 processors were used, the populations size was set at 2000, with the number of generations set at 100. For smaller runs, such as using 64 processors, the size of the task was reduced accordingly, for example evaluating 50 generations of 2000 population members, or 100 generations of 1000 population members. Several runs of each were undertaken and the best results recorded.

4.3 Results

Table 2 illustrates that the GP bred models yield a small, though improved level of performance, again measured by the sum of squares error function, which is encouraging considering the experimental nature of the exercise. The models are also quite varied in their form, which is a reflection of not only differences between the number of potential model pieces, but also that the spatial interaction data exhibits more complex, non-linear relationships.

As a consequence, the interpretability of the GP results is problematic, with complex models being generated that are not readily understood. The models do not provide quick indicators of the stronger relationships within the data, and need a significant amount of simplification before they could be written in

Table 2: Spatial interaction model breeding results

Conventional models	Error
$T = O.D.C^{\beta}$	9.13
$T = O.D.\exp(\beta.C)$	9.21
$T = O.D.\exp(\beta.\sqrt{C})$	9.10
$T = O.D.\exp(\beta.\log(C))$	9.14
$T = O.D.\exp(\alpha.X + \beta.C)$	9.17
$T = O.D.Z^{\delta}\exp(\beta.C)$	9.08

GP Models	Error
$T = \left[\left(\frac{O}{6.01Z^{-1.21}D^{-3.97}}\right) + \left(\frac{D}{-7.52O-9.36}\right)\right].71,44C^{-0.77}$	8.06
$T = 11.58\left(\frac{D.C}{Z}\right)^{-1.13}.\left[13.41D + \frac{O.D^{1.14}}{C^{0.59}} + \frac{O-D}{C^{0.81}}\right] + O.C^{0.63} + 0.38$	7.93
$T = Z^{-0.8}\left[\left(\frac{D}{(O+2C)^{4.34}} + O - \log D\right).C^{1.05}\right]$	
$\quad - \left[C^{-0.72}.\left(\frac{O.D}{C^{0.04}} + \frac{X-D}{1.22}\right)\right]$	8.05

the form they possess in Table 2. These results suggest that a more rigorous investigation of the potential of breeding spatial interaction models over a varied number and type of data sets is necessary if the full potential of the method is to be realised.

5 Subglacial Water System Case Study

5.1 Data and Model Pieces

Our understanding of the basal hydraulic system of glaciers and ice masses has traditionally been developed from theoretical models based on our physical understanding of the basal system (e.g., film flow, channelised flow, linked cavities, canals) with rather few observations allowing direct verification of model validity. With the advent of hot-water drilling technology it has become possible to densely instrument the glacier bed; as a result while the data sets that are available are still comparatively small it is clear that we are rapidly moving from an age of data sparsity to data richness.

During the summer of 1992 the bed of Trapridge Glacier, Yukon Territory was densely instrumented with sensors to measure hydrological parameters including pressure transducers which included five installed approximately transverse to glacier flow and approximately 5m apart. Two of these sensors were installed in bore-holes that connected to the basal water system of the glacier, and as a result these sensors were dubbed C1 and C2 (Murray and Clarke, 1995). Two other sensors were installed into bore-holes that did not drain on reaching the glacier bed, and were therefore assumed to reach unconnected regions of the glacier bed; these sensors were dubbed U1 and U2 respectively. The fifth sensor appeared to be installed into a region of the bed that altern-

148

ated between being in the connected and unconnected regions and so became dubbed A1. The pressures measured by these sensors have been described in detail by Murray and Clarke (1995). Important features of the data are (1) both the connected sensors (C1 and C2) and unconnected sensors (U1 and U2) show a diurnal response that we assume is forced by surface melt variations; (2) the connected sensors are out-of-phase with the unconnected sensors – at times when the pressure is high in the connected system it is low in the unconnected system, and vice versa; (3) the alternating sensor (A1) shows a semi-diurnal response such that when the pressure in the connected system is high the pressure measured at the alternating sensor is high, however when the pressure at the unconnected sensor is high the pressure measured by the alternating sensor is also high. These responses are clear during the summer 1992 data and continue to be displayed, at least during the early part of the winter period when the water system is presumably closing due to a lack of surface water input.

Taking the pressure recorded by sensor C1 in the connected system as the forcing Murray and Clarke (1995) derive a series of models to predict the water pressure within each of the three systems based on low-order differential equations. Using the final forms of these models they then describe some of the processes that they feel are important in driving the form of these models.

The models used here are made up from the set of terminals shown in table 3. The pressure record from sensor C1 is the only input variable for each model for compariability to the black box models of Murray and Clarke (1995).

Table 3: Subglacial system model peices

Terminals		
	C1	Pressure record
Operators		
	$+, -, *, /$	
Functions		
	sqrt,log,exp,sin,cos	

5.2 GP runs

For operational convenience on the Cray T3D the parameters for the model breeding varied according to the size of the job being executed. When 128 processors were used, the populations size was set at 1000, with the number of generations set at 100. For smaller runs, such as using 64 processors, the size of the task was reduced accordingly, for example evaluating 50 generations of 1000 population members, or 100 generations of 500 population members. Several runs of each were undertaken and the best results recorded.

5.3 Results

Table 4 shows the results obtained by GP compared to the blackbox models derived by Murray and Clarke (1995).

Table 4: Subglacial Modeling Results

Connected System		
Black Box	$R(t) = 1.01F(t) - 4.96$	0.2m
GP	$R(t) = F(t) - 3.75$	0.3m
Unconnected System		
Black Box	$a_2 \frac{d^2R}{dt^2} + \frac{dR}{dt} - a_0\left[R^\star - R(t)\right]$ $= b_1 \exp[D_0 F(t)] \frac{dF}{dt}$	2.1m
GP	$R(t) = \frac{0.86}{e^{0.04f(t)}} - 0.05.(-1384.5 - F(t))$	3.4m
Alternating System		
Black Box	$R(t) = F(t_i^s) + c_1\left[F(t) - F(t_i^s)\right]$	
or	$a_2 \frac{d^2R}{dt^2} + \frac{dR}{dt} - a_0\left[R^\star - R(t)\right] =$ $\left\{ b_1 \exp[D_0 F(t)] \frac{dF}{dt} + b_0\left[F(t) - R(t)\right]\right\}$	6.1m
GP	$R(t) = 3F(t) + \frac{18000}{F(t)} - \frac{242423}{F^2(t)} - 374$	3.1m

Again the GP results produce a better preformance and in this case while complex can be considered no worse than the black box models. It should also be noted that the black box model for the alternating system contains hardwired switches between the two states where as the GP model has no knowledge added.

6 Conclusions

From a GP perspective there is a feeling that the best achievable results have still not being produced. Whether this reflects a lack of sufficient compute power to investigate larger population sizes or a need for a more efficient parameter estimation procedure, problems with the GP itself are a matter for further investigation and debate. Indeed debugging a GP is actually quite hard because the GP will cleverly accommodate all manner of non-fatal errors in the code. Indeed a major research effort is probably needed to determine good ways of validating GP software. Nevertheless, the paper clearly provides a glimpse of the potential of GP as a generic tool for creating new models of complex geographical systems. In principle it would appear to offer the ultimate technology for implementing an inductive approach to knowledge creation from data. At a time when there is a vast explosion in all kinds of information it is useful to know that GP provides the basis for new sets of tools that are able, in principle, to convert at least some of these data riches into new knowledge. Whether this approach works well depends on the speed of the available high performance computers, the power of the GP method itself, and the subsequent skills of the modeller in interpreting the equations that are created and declared optimal.

References

Barrow, D. (1993) The use and application of genetic algorithms, *Journal of Targeting, Measurement and Analyses for Marketing* 2: 30-41.

Goldberg, D E. (1989) *Genetic Algorithms in Search, Optimisation and Machine Learning*, Addison Wesley, Reading Mass.

Holland, J. (1975) *Adaptation in Natural and Artificial Systems*, the University of Michigan Press, Ann Arbor.

Koza, J. (1992) *Genetic Programming: on the programming of computers by means of natural selection*, MIT Press, Cambridge, Mass.

Koza, J. (1994) *Genetic Programming II: Automatic Discovery of Reusable programs*, MIT Press, Cambridge, Mass.

Murray, T. and Clarke, G.K.C. 1995. Black-box modeling of the subglacial water system. *Journal of Geophysical Research*, 100(B7), 10231–10245.

Openshaw, S. (1976) An empirical study of some spatial interaction models, *Environment and Planning A* 8: 23-41.

Openshaw, S (1986) Modelling relevancy, *Environment and Planning A* 18: 143-147

Openshaw, S. (1988) Building an automated modelling system to explore a universe of spatial interaction models, *Geographical Analysis* 20: 31-46.

Openshaw, S. (1992) Some suggestions concerning the development of artificial intelligence tools for spatial modelling and analysis in GIS, *Annals of Regional Science* 20: 35-51

Openshaw, S. (1996) Fuzzy Logic as a New Scientific Paradigm for doing Geography, *Environment and Planning A* (forthcoming).

Perkis, T. (1994) Stack-based genetic programming, *IEEE World Congress on Computational Intelligence*

Schwefel, H.P. (1995) *Evolution and optimum seeking*, Wiley, New York

Wilson, A.G. (1971) A family of spatial interaction models and associated developments, *Environment and Planning A* 3: 1-32

Parallel Genetic Programming

Dimitris C. Dracopoulos
Department of Computer Science
Brunel University
London, UK

Duncan Self
Department of Computer Science
Brunel University
London, UK

Abstract

A parallel implementation of Genetic Programming using PVM is described. Two different topologies for parallel implementation of GP are examined. Both of them are based on the island model for evolutionary algorithms. It is shown that considerable speedup of the GP execution can be achieved and that the parallel versions of the algorithm are very suitable for complex, time consuming problems.

1 Introduction

The newly created field of Genetic Programming (GP), has recently received a lot of attention and expands rapidly its application to new domains. Although several parallel implementations of genetic algorithms exist, currently there is no parallel implementation for genetic programming (only some preliminary work done by Koza [5]).

The Genetic Programming process often involves the processing of very large numbers of data structures when applied to a complicated problem. In addition to that, the individual processing of each data structure can be CPU time intensive. For these reasons, it comes of little surprise that Genetic Programming can take a considerable amount of time to arrive at a solution. This paper describes a parallel Genetic Programming implementation, using PVM. The aim of this work is to speedup the Genetic Programming process, used for the automatic discovery of computer programs. The implementation described here is based on the island model of evolutionary algorithms [3]. The parallel GP is tested on the truck backer upper problem, a well known problem in control theory. It is shown that considerable speedup of the GP execution can be achieved.

2 Genetic Programming

Genetic programming (GP) [6] is an extension of the genetic algorithm (GA) function optimization method. Both methods are based on the evolutionary process of the Darwinian natural selection.

In a genetic algorithm [2], an initial population of potential solutions is generated randomly. Each solution is represented as a data structure that is often a character string (something which is an abstraction of nature's chromosome structures). The quality (goodness) of a solution is measured by evaluating a function, referred to as the fitness function. This function is evaluated by considering a member of the population and testing its ability to solve the problem. The value (fitness) returned from the fitness function, is then used to guide the chance of the particular individual to survive for the next generation. The aim is to evolve the population, so that the overall fitness will be increased and ultimately finding the optimal (or near optimal) solution to the given problem. The evolution of the population is achieved with the application of various genetic operators. Commonly used genetic operators are: reproduction (asexual), crossover (sexual recombination), and mutation (figure 1).

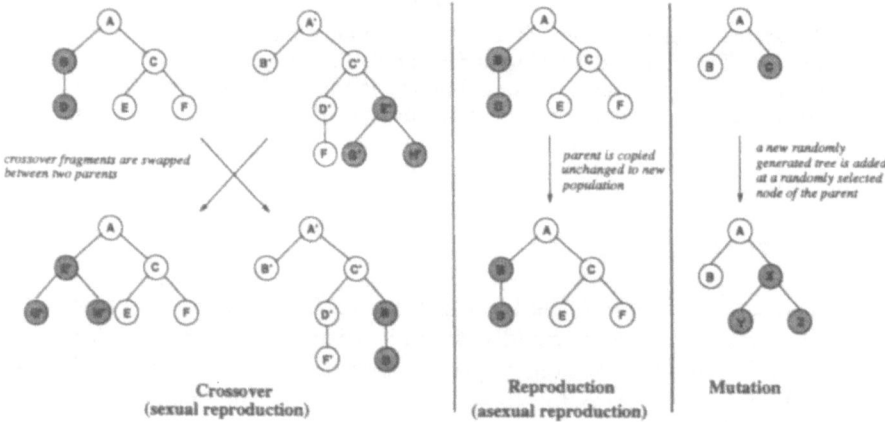

Figure 1: Basic Genetic Operators used in Genetic Programming

These are applied to the individual structures of the population, with an individual having a probability to be selected (to participate in a genetic operation), proportional to its fitness value (although other selection methods can be used as well). The convergence of the algorithm is governed by the "Schema" theorem [4].

Genetic Programming uses the same concepts, however the chromosome abstraction is a more complex structure (and thus having a much more powerful representation of a solution to a particular problem). As its name implies the structure used is a hierarchical computer program. The representation of the program can be of variable length and shape. A program consists of a composition of functions and terminals which are specific to the problem domain. Each program is represented as a tree structure where the roots are functions and the leafs are the terminals. The flowchart of the whole process can be found in figure 2.

Genetic programming is parallel in its very nature of operation, because of the way in which the population is evolved. A parallelisation approach for the GP process is proposed in this paper. Although the parallelisation described in this work is general, the particular implementation is based on PVM.

3   PVM

Parallel Virtual Machine is a package for the implementation of parallel programs using heterogeneous networked UNIX computers. PVM was originally prototyped at Oak Ridge Laboratory and further developed at the University of Tennessee where it is still a current project. The parallel GP implementation in this paper uses C with PVM version 3.3.9.

4   Parallel GP implementation

The aim of this work is to parallelise the GP process, and to measure the speedups achieved using different parallel configurations. The island model [3] of parallelisation is used. According to this model, a set of non overlapping populations is kept in different processors. The GP procedure is applied independently to each processor, but from time to time individuals (solutions) migrate to an island next to them. The convergence of the algorithm can be improved using this island model and the total GP execution time is reduced significantly due to the parallelisation of the task.

4.1   Parallel Configurations

The particular implementation measured the different speedups achieved with up to 8 processors. Two different parallel configurations for the island model are used. The first one assumes that processors (and islands) are connected in a ring configuration. A copy of the two best individuals is allowed to migrate in every generation. Thus, each island will receive four immigrants per generation. The coarse grained parallelisation method attempts to reduce the communication between processes, thus reducing overhead, and improving speedup.

The second configuration assumes a full connected graph, thus each island is close enough to each other, allowing immigrants from any island to any other. In every generation two individuals are allowed to migrate according to their fitness.

In all the topologies a number of processes are started, each with their own private population, which they are responsible for initialising, evaluating and evolving. The necessary addition to the GP process is that of a migration operator. Each of the individual processes is considered to be an island, detached from the other processes. Every few generations, after the fitness evaluation phase, migration occurs, whereby certain individuals are moved between processes, thus distributing the genetic material throughout all the process 'islands'. There is great scope here for varying the frequency of the migration, the number of individuals transferred, and the method by which individuals are chosen for migration. This paper does not seek to provide an exhaustive investigation into all possible variations of the parameters.

Again, this is obviously not an exhaustive investigation of topologies, and the two presented here are examples rather than suggestions of optimal topologies.

PVM does not restrict which tasks communicate however to facilitate our model we have used static PVM groups. The PVM group ids are used to map the tasks onto the island model. The first task to join the group spawns the other tasks. pvm_barrier() is used to ensure all the tasks have joined the group. Each island assumes a population size of ($500/$*number of islands*). Each island randomly generates its initial population using the ramped half-and-half grow method.

Each task carries out a depth first traversal of each individual to migrate. The contents of each node is packed into the send buffer. The fitness of the individual is also packed if available. In the ring topology we have stored the task ids for each islands neighbours in an array. The array is then passed to pvm_mcast() when migrating. In the fully connected topology we use pvm_bcast() when migrating. Each individual is unpacked in the same order in which it was packed. Each individual has a flag to save re-evaluating the fitness of those reproduced.

We have used pvm_barrier() to synchronise the processors at two stages (as shown in figure 4).

5 Test problem

The parallel GP software produced and the speedup measurements are for a well known difficult control theory problem: the "truck backer upper" problem, as described by [6]. The basis of the problem is to reverse a tractor-trailer truck up to a loading dock. The truck moves at a constant speed, steering with the front wheels of the tractor unit. The aim is to line the midpoint of the rear of the trailer up with a point on the loading dock, without crashing the truck. The parallel GP seeks to find a control program (strategy) for backing up the truck, in an optimum way.

The dynamic system is described by the following equations of motion:

$$
\begin{aligned}
A &= r \cos u(t) \\
B &= A \cos(\theta_c(t) - \theta_t(t)) \\
C &= A \sin(\theta_c(t) - \theta_t(t))
\end{aligned}
\tag{1}
$$

and

$$
\begin{aligned}
x(t+1) &= x(t) - B \cos \theta_t \\
y(t+1) &= y(t) - B \sin \theta_t \\
\theta_c(t+1) &= \tan^{-1}\left(\frac{d_c \sin \theta_c(t) - r \cos \theta_c(t) \sin u(t)}{d_c \cos \theta_c(t) + r \sin \theta_c(t) \sin u(t)} \right) \\
\theta_t(t+1) &= \tan^{-1}\left(\frac{d_s \sin \theta_t(t) - C \cos \theta_t}{d_s \cos \theta_t(t) + C \sin \theta_t(t)} \right) \\
\theta_d(t+1) &= \theta_t(t) - \theta_c(t)
\end{aligned}
\tag{2}
$$

$$
\tag{3}
$$

According to this, x and y are the horizontal and vertical distances, respectively, of the midpoint of the trailer to the point $(0,0)$ on the loading dock, θ_t is the difference in angle between the trailer and the loading dock and θ_d is the difference in angle between the tractor and the trailer which may not exceed 90. The difference in angle between the tractor and the loading dock is denoted by θ_c, while $u(t)$ (the control variable) is the difference in angle of the tires of the tractor to the tractor. The tractor can only move backwards, in an r rate.

The parallel GP uses a population size of 500 for each island and the following function set F and terminal set T:

$$F = (+, -, *, \%, ATG, IFLTZ) \tag{4}$$

$$T = (x, y, \theta_t, \theta_d, R) \tag{5}$$

ATG is the arctangent function representing $\tan^{-1}(x/y)$ and $IFLTZ$ stands for IF Less Than Zero, which is a comparative operator. R is the constant random generator.

The fitness of each individual is measured by running each control strategy from eight different start points (initial conditions) and summing the squares of the differences between the x, y, and θ_t and their target values. Figure 5 describes the state variables of the dynamic system.

It is shown that considerable speedup can be achieved, using the parallel GP PVM implementation. The results suggest that GP researchers should consider such an implementation when they deal with complex, time consuming problems.

6 Results

The workstations used to run the software were a number of SUN SPARCstation™ 5 machines with 70MHz microSPARC-II processors, and running SOLARIS 2.4, each with 32Mb of RAM. These machines were connected on a common subnet with ethernet cabling. Communication between processors was achieved using TCP/IP.

The recorded speedups are shown in two graphs. The speedup for the fully connected graph is shown in Figure 6, and the ring topology speedups are shown in Figures 7.

Although the size of the problem was not very large, one can see that the achieved speedup of the GP run is significant. As the size of the problem increases, one can expect to see that for the global parallelisation version the achievable speedup of the PVM GP system will be improve, as the communication overhead will be small compared with the actual parallel computational time. Apparently, given a problem of fixed size, there is an optimum number of processors with which a maximum speedup can be achieved. Therefore, to optimise the performance of the parallel GP system, the choice of the number of processors must be decided carefully.

Results for the actual solution of the described problem are not considered here, as the main aim of the paper is to show the speedups of the GP process that can be achieved. However, many typical solutions of the truck backer problem using a sequential version of the GP can be found in [6].

7   Conclusions

A parallel implementation of a Genetic Programming system was described, using PVM. Two topologies for parallelisation were examined. The first was based on a fully connected graph while the second implemented a ring. Both of them were based on the island model for evolutionary processes. This can also improve the convergence of the GP algorithm. Although the size of the test problem was quite small, the speedups achieved were significant. The implementation is portable to a number of different platforms

Using the implemented PVM GP system, higher speedups can be achieved in large problems. In addition, the time required to parallelise evolutionary algorithms with the PVM model is insignificant, compared with the achieved speedups, when the problem is a complex and time consuming. The parallel implementation proved to be very suitable and efficient for the solution of GP process, so as to suggest its use for algorithms of similar nature.

References

[1] A. Geist, A. Beguelin, J. Dongarra, W. Jiang, R. Manchek, and V. Sunderam. *PVM: Parallel Virtual Machine A Users' Guide and Tutorial for Networked Parallel Computing.* MIT Press, 1994.

[2] David E. Goldberg. *Genetic Algorithms in Search, Optimization and Machine Learning.* Addison Wesley, 1989.

[3] V. Scott Gordon and Darrell Whitley. Serial and parallel genetic algorithms as function optimizers. In Stefanie Forrest, editor, *Proceedings of the 5th International Conference on Genetic Algorithms.* Morgan Kaufmann, 1993.

[4] John H. Holland. *Adaptation in Natural and Artificial Systems.* The University of Michigan Press, 1975.

[5] John Koza and David Andre. Parallel genetic programming on a network of transputers. Technical Report CS-TR-95-1542, Stanford University, 1995.

[6] John R. Koza. *Genetic Programming.* MIT Press, 1982.

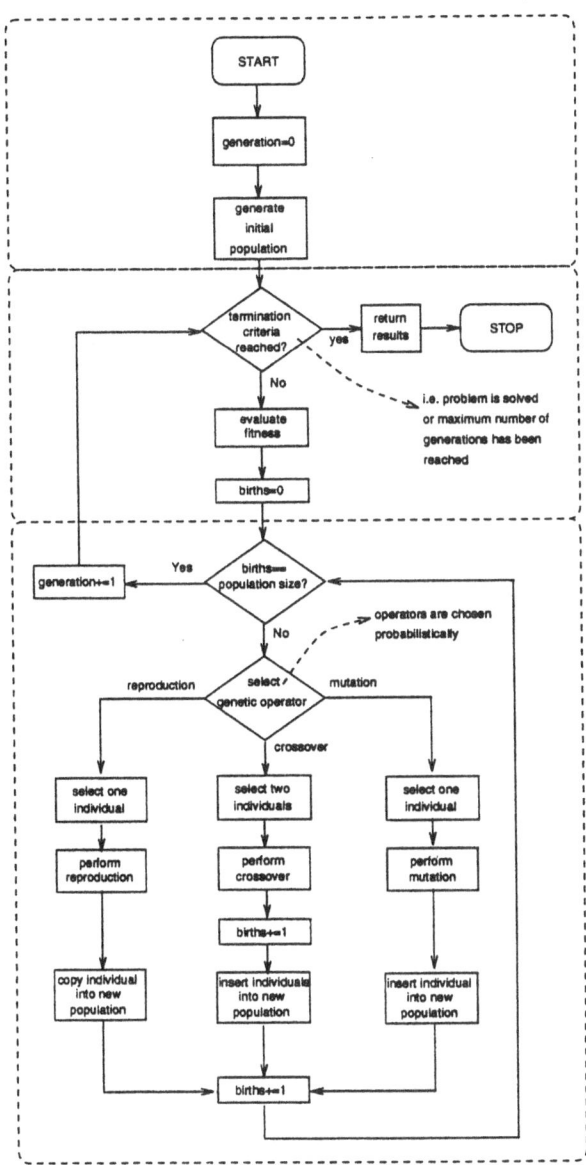

Figure 2: Flowchart of the process used in Genetic Programming

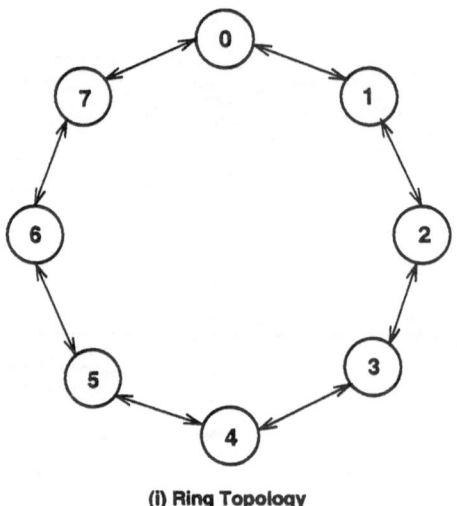

(i) Ring Topology

Figure 3: Topologies with the island model GP implementation.

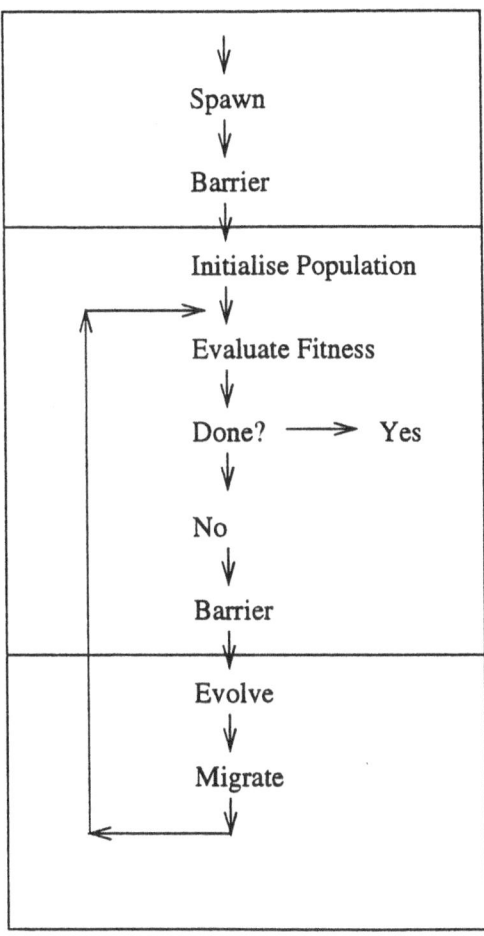

Figure 4: Synchronisation of the parallel PVM GP system.

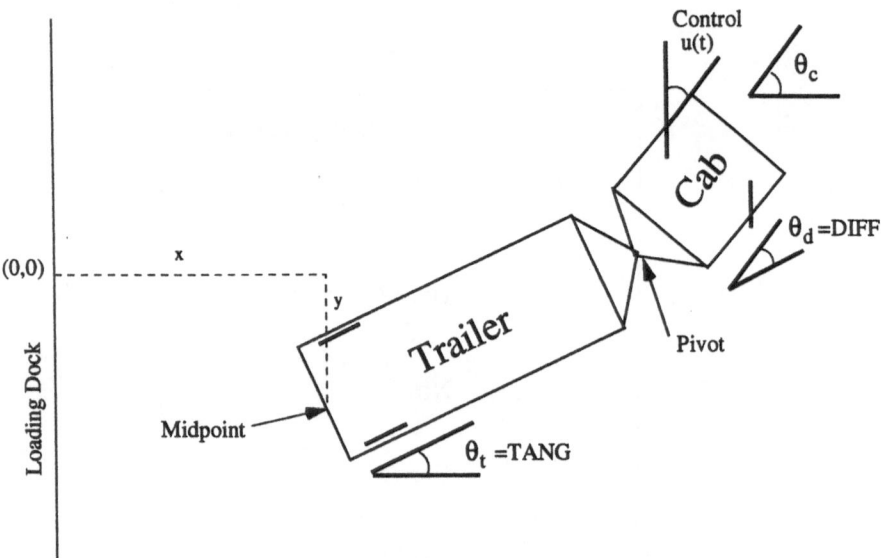

Figure 5: The truck backer upper problem

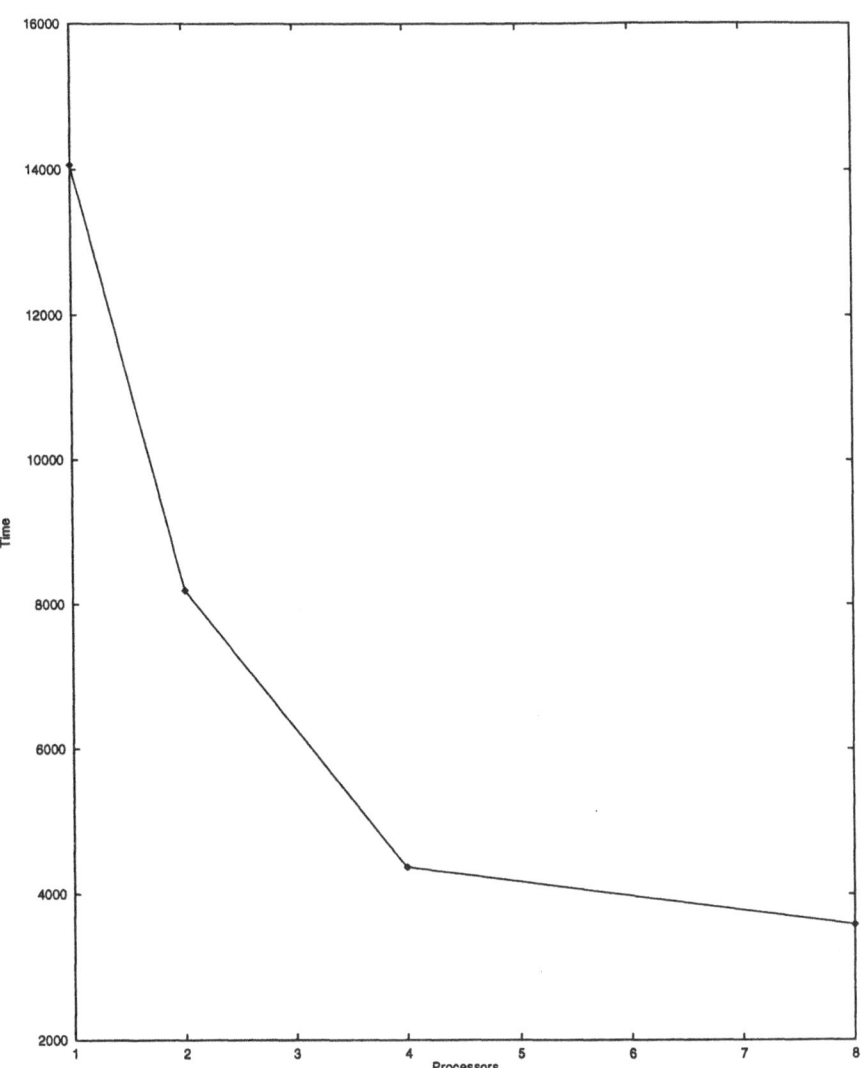

Figure 6: Times achieved with fully connected graph.

162

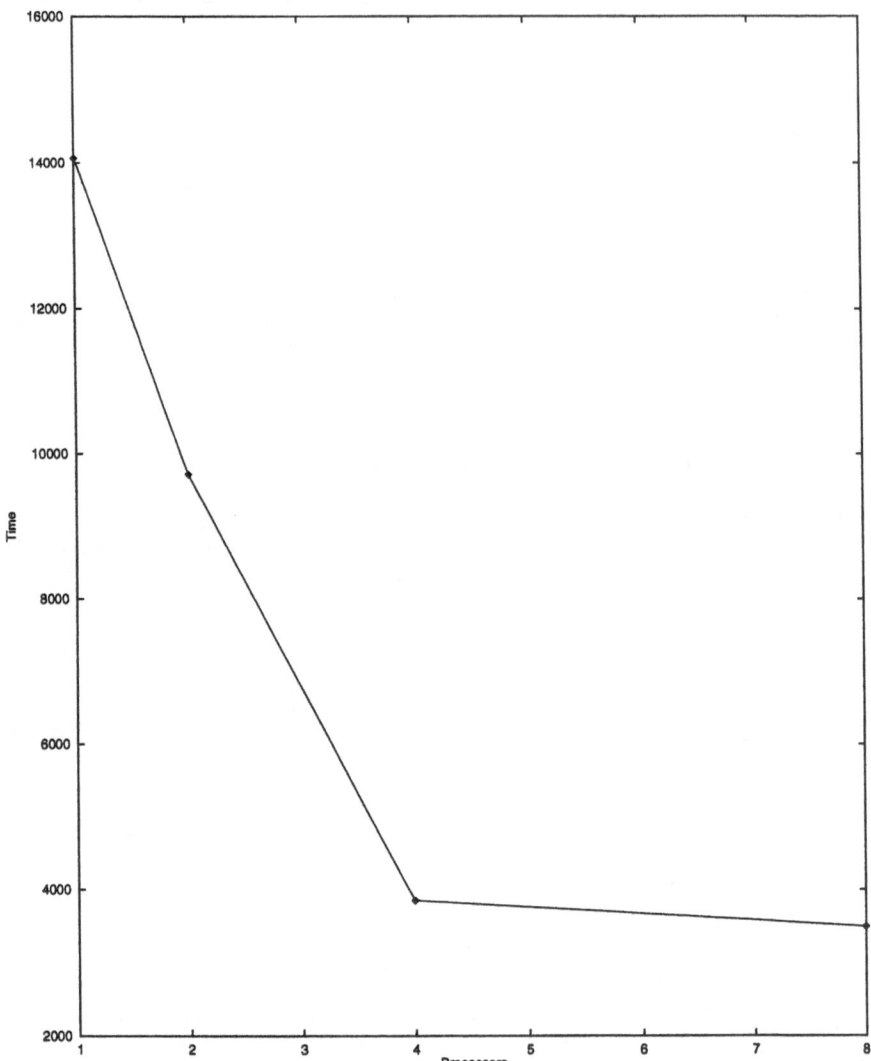

Figure 7: Times achieved with ring topology.

Designing and Instrumenting a Software Template for Embedded Parallel Systems

M. Fleury

Dept. of Electronic Systems Engineering, Essex University

Colchester, U.K

H. P. Sava

Dept. of Electronic Systems Engineering, Essex University

Colchester, U.K

A. C. Downton

Dept. of Electronic Systems Engineering, Essex University

Colchester, U.K

A. F. Clark

Dept. of Electronic Systems Engineering, Essex University

Colchester, U.K

Abstract

This paper considers the design of a reusable software template for a parallel data-farm which uses demand-based load-balancing. A feature of the farm is integral instrumentation. A design example is given for a hybrid processor message-passing machine (the Paramid) in which monitoring is accomplished by an instrumented interface program. Other aspects of the design are use of buffering to mask communication latency, an asynchronous multicast provision, and a controlled interface to the worker functions. Trace material is discussed from two examples when the template design was used to monitor real-time, continuous-flow applications. The template is a component of the Pipelined Processor Farm (PPF) methodology.

1   Introduction

This paper describes the design of a software 'template' which supports construction of embedded parallel applications that utilise multiple data farms. A template restricts the scope of the software thereby making the design easier to develop. The data farm is intended to enable rapid prototyping of applications developed according to the Pipelined Processor Farm (PPF) methodology [1]. PPFs are suitable for the class of continuous-flow embedded systems, which commonly have a time and/or ordering constraint imposed upon the output. The methodology proposes three forms of decomposing the workload in a component farm: by means of temporal multiplexing; through algorithmic parallelism; or through data parallelism. Demand-based farming utilising data parallelism enables the pipeline traversal latency to be reduced and permits incremental scaling of the farm throughput. It is therefore more flexible and popular as a design technique than the other two forms of decomposition, and hence provides the basis of this initial template design.

Unlike some other template designs [2, 3], our design includes instrumentation as an integral part of the software. Experience [4] shows that instrumentation is difficult to include at a later stage and that a static design will need to be tuned after an initial implementation [1]. In Tmon [5] instrumentation is included but requires a hardware monitor to provide time pulses, which may improve the accuracy but naturally limits the portability. Tmon also requires user annotation of the source code, whereas the present system intercepts communication events by means of a monitoring sub-system, implemented as part of the template. The PIE Environment [6] includes instrumentation provision in software but is less constrained in its applicability and is aimed at machines supporting a global address space. The concept of providing performance evaluation facilities as an integral part of the environment is present in Jade [7], though otherwise the similarity stops as this environment attempts to hide the details of parallelism from the programmer.

The design principles for our data-farm template can be summarized as:

- a demand-based load-balancing algorithm;
- latency regulation by the use of buffering, which is transparent to the message size and type;
- a multicast mechanism (on a per-farm basis), which can be called on at any time;
- graceful termination, which also allows a reset for reconfiguration purposes;
- a controlled interface to the functions offered by each worker process;
- instrumentation of all communication events.

These criteria are developed in succeeding sections. Though the major part of this paper is couched in the form of a case study, in fact most of the material presented is general (i.e., Sections 2.2, 2.3, 2.4 & 2.6) and can be transferred to other message-passing environments. Reference is made to two applications: a handwritten postcode recognition application and an H.263 image coder parallelization. Output from a trace visualizer for the two applications is included in Section 3. The final part of the paper, Section 4, summarizes and draws some conclusions.

2 An Instrumented Template on a Hybrid Machine

The initial target architecture for this implementation was the Paramid parallel processor from Transtech Ltd. [8] which is a distributed-memory message-passing machine built up from twin-processor modules. In our case, we were using an eight-module machine, with transputer communication processor (running at a nominal 30MHz, with link speed set to 20Mb/s and 4Mbytes RAM) and i860 computation engine (50MHz and 16Mbytes RAM). From the user perspective, the machine appears as a transputer machine with attached accelerator onto which jobs are allotted on a first-come-first-served basis by a host-based scheduler. The i860-XP is a superscalar RISC processor with pipelining of the integer and floating point computational streams. The i860 [9] is primarily suited to the processing of regular structures, such as matrices. Interprocessor communication is effected in the first instance by the i860 interrupting the transputer (via the transputer event pin) to signal a request. The transputer inspects a common memory area in order to service the request, releasing a software lock after fulfilling the request.

2.1 System Software Organization

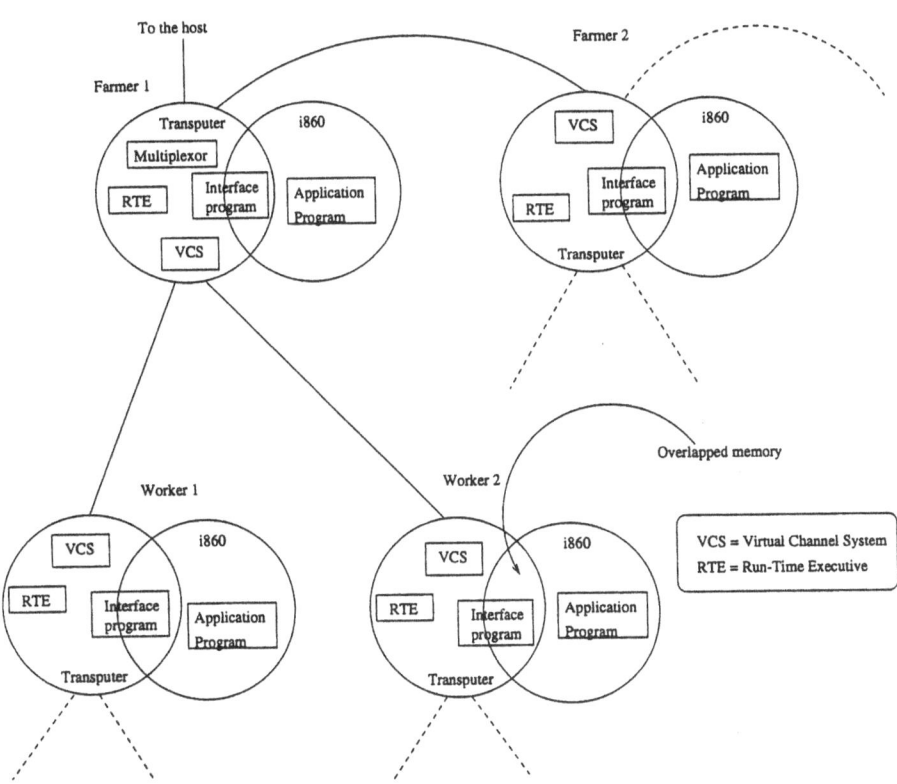

Figure 1: System Software

The existing system software (Figure 1) includes servicing of run-time I/O requests on all modules by means of a run-time executive (RTE). I/O is multiplexed onto the SCSI link to the host. The multiplexor channels are set up conveniently by means of a virtual channel system (VCS) which acts on each processor as an external communication link sentinel. VCS software is important in limiting the complexity of the communication software that is provided by the application programmer; but it also makes direct communication as required for multicasts awkward to guarantee (Section 2.4). Ideally, one would like to have both virtual and actual communication in the same application. The transputer provides efficient internal concurrency by manipulation of a process stack [10] but only one process running on the i860 can communicate with the system interface program running on the transputer. This restriction neatly meets the design methodology in that one process can be written with a public interface and a set of protected services, which thereby take the place of multiple processes on the i860 (Section 2.2). Note that 3L Parallel 'C' and Inmos Parallel 'C' for the transputer both distinguish between tasks on the same processor, which may communicate only by channels, and processes (equivalent to threads [11] or light-weight processes) which are internal to tasks and can communicate either by common memory or by channels.

Two versions of the data-farming template are necessary for this machine: one in which all application processes are sited on the i860s; and another in which the data-farmers are placed on transputers. The precise arrangement is application-specific as it depends on the degree of centralized processing necessary. In the H.263 encoder application [12] there were serial bottlenecks which made it important to place the data-farmers on the i860s: this produced a performance gain of a factor of 2 compared with placing the farmer processes on a transputer. In contrast, the three data farmers used in the postcode recognition application [13] were all placed on transputers as their computational load was small. This still allowed the real-time, ordering and latency constraints of the postcode specification to be met.

2.2 The Generic Worker Module

In designing the worker an initial consideration is the nature of the message traffic. Messages occur in two parts: a tag and the body of the message. The tag must include: the size of the message to follow; a type indicating whether a message is a multicast or a request for processing; and a message number. The message number is intended to signal to the receiver which data structure to position for the accommodation of the second part of the message. It might also be used for other purposes. The body of the message should include a function number as the first field of the message, but otherwise the message record structure is undetermined. If a sequential version of a program exists, it may involve excessive data movements to form messages into logical message structures. The application programmer will need to balance utility with complexity. The potential for a large number of different messages is a reason for confining oneself to a rigid message format. Unlike occam, the 'C' computer language does not offer guidance in this respect. C++ has the difficulty that there is not yet an ISO standard. Each work request message is serviced by one worker-module function (Figure 2). For reasons explained in Section 2.4, multicast messages generate no processing. In 'C' it is possible to use an array of function pointers to which the function number forms an index. Though not entirely satisfactory, data and parameters are passed to the function as globals. This means that each function can be referenced simply by a number. From the figure it will be seen that the worker module is divided between a public interface and a private part into which different functions can be slotted. This makes it possible to extract the functions from sequential code constructed with structured programming and place them into the slots.

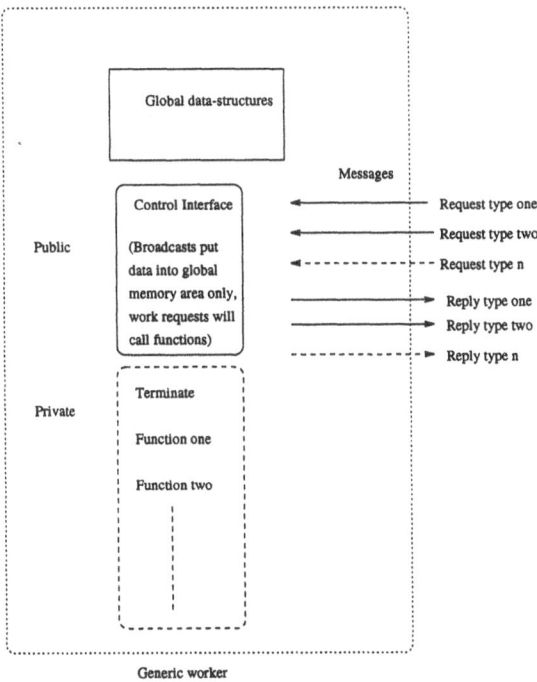

Figure 2: The Worker Module

2.3   The Buffer Design

While there has been considerable exploitation of parallel slackness (by means of concurrent or pseudo-parallel processes) as a way of masking communication latency, rather less attention has been given to using buffers for the same purpose [14]. Historically this situation arises because the XPRAM model [15] was part of an attractive plan for a universal programmer's model for parallel machines that could work on the two broad classes of MIMD, shared- and distributed-memory machines. Providing internal concurrency may not however be cost-free. If overlapped register windows are used, the cost of context switching may become large as the register set is exhausted. If a process is descheduled on one processor at a time when a process on another processor wishes to communicate, multiple delays can occur [16]. Buffering on the other hand was an important part of an early pipelined design where there are non-deterministic flows between the pipeline stages [17]. There is a substantial literature on queueing theory which can be applied selectively to particular buffering problems [18].

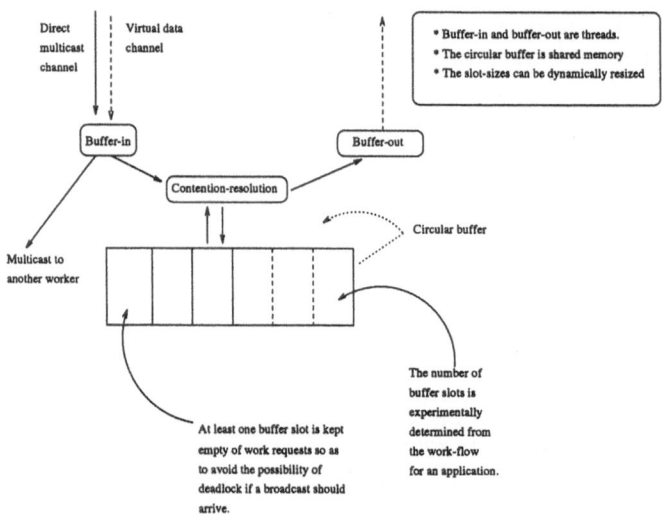

Figure 3: A Generic Buffer

In the template design, in-going (Figure 3) and out-going buffers service each application process. Additionally, buffers are placed between the stages of the pipeline. All buffers have the same generic form though they may differ in the number of buffer slots. To avoid internal data movements a shared address space is needed. The control of access contention is a standard problem in concurrency [19]. On transputers, software semaphores can be utilised by missing out any assembly language statement which might allow a context switch by the firmware. So that the buffer slot size should remain transparent to the message arrival size an initial buffer slot size is set which can be expanded by dynamic memory allocation on the arrival of too large a message. Separate buffer slots are kept for tags, otherwise there is a danger of the small slots needed for tags being expanded to provide for larger messages. At present, there is no means of reducing the buffer size if that size should, in the general case, turn out to be too large. Diagnostic software for memory usage (such as Purify [20] on sequential, possibly multi-threaded, machines) is not readily available for parallel machines, though one would need to expand the basic facilities of malloc debugging and array bound checking in order to check inter-task memory usage interaction. To avoid the possibility of deadlock if a series of multicast message were to arrive at asynchronous intervals, at least one extra buffer slot is provided over and above the number of messages sent out at loading time. This method is a variant of an algorithm which is proven in [21]. Trust in the implementation was established by sending multicasts at randomly (with a uniform distribution) determined intervals against a backdrop of continuous message traffic. The number of multicasts at each distribution time was also randomly determined.

2.4 The Multicast Sub-System

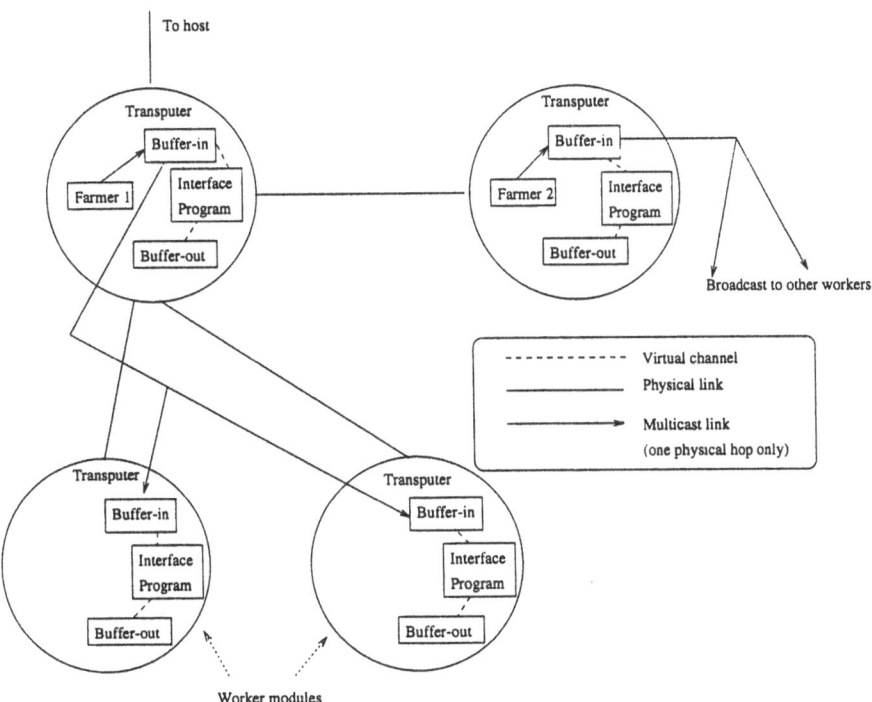

Figure 4: The Multicast Sub-System

In the expanded PPF methodology, multicasts can occur within each processor farm. Broadcasts (such as for initial parameter passing) obviously occur by inter-farmer communication. A multicast reduces message traffic, though in fact it breaks the paradigm of preventing worker to worker communication. When a VCS is employed it becomes necessary to specify point-to-point links and, if need be, set weightings to guide channel placement on the physical links available. The use of a tree-topology makes this easy to do but since a farm is not limited to a particular topology this is not generally the case. The tree topology also makes routing of multicasts trivial to arrange, since the in-going buffer need 'know' only how many ports it should send the multicast out to.

Other topologies may require the use of time-to-live (TTL) counters to avoid endless circulation. If multicasting is to be asynchronous then the possibility exists of a multicast being blocked because of a circuit between farmer and worker. In Section 2.3 an extra buffer slot is prescribed, but two further restrictions are needed to guarantee deadlock avoidance: a worker process can only act as a sink of multicast messages; and each work request can be met by one processed-work reply.

An alternative is barrier synchronization [22], but this option is rejected because of the overheads. Either all messages have to be absorbed by the farmer before broadcasting, in which case a per-worker process message count is needed, or a supervisory kernel is needed to wait for all workers to reach a barrier point.

2.5   The Monitoring Sub-System

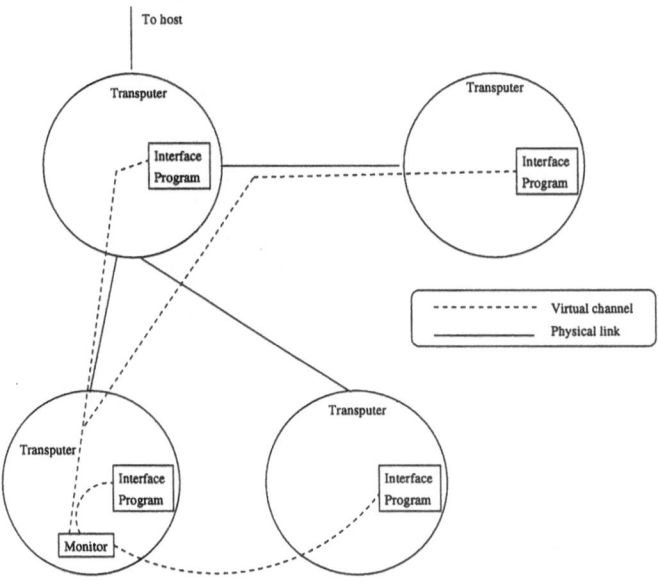

Figure 5: The Monitoring Sub-System

In the template version in which all application processes are placed on i860s, a monitor process synchronizes the clocks of all processes (Figure 5) by means of virtual channels. The monitor process can be placed on any processor, which avoids overloading the processor directly linked to the host. Virtual links are sufficient as the software global clock relies on the relative time differences between local clocks and a centrally maintained clock in order to synchronize to the central clock. Optionally at the start and definitely at the end, the monitor process synchronizes with the master data-farmer, at which time trace collection occurs. If transputer-based farmers are employed, the monitor process can be subsumed in the farmer. This is less satisfactory if the objective is to provide transparent monitoring, as the communication primitives must directly make the trace. PICL [23] communication calls were mimicked for this eventuality. In fact, the PICL trace file format [24] is also used as this enabled us to test the post-mortem output on the ParaGraph visualizer [25]. The PICL format includes a broadcast field but does not include multicast, which is understandable as the destinations are difficult to specify if the record size is restricted but which made it necessary to emulate multicasts by creating multiple message records in the trace file. Multicasts were stamped with the source and a code not used elsewhere. Post-processing changed the multicast message to a set of messages with the same timestamps but different destinations (Paragraph does not assume a monotonic clock). Initialization and termination messages could also be removed at post-processing time.

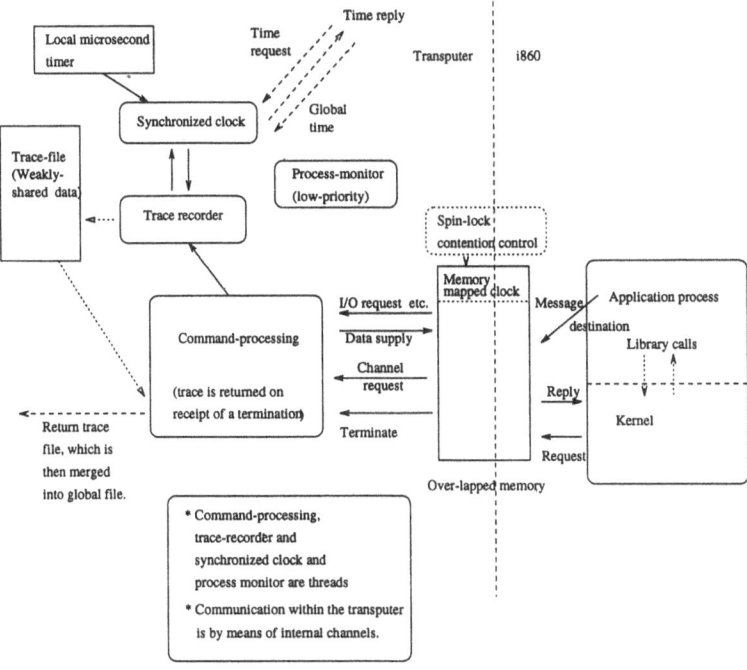

Figure 6: The Monitoring Layout

The interface program was enhanced with a trace recorder and synchronized clock process (Figure 6). To substitute the new interface program the application object code is booted onto the i860 network and in a second loading phase the transputers are booted up. The interface program then restarts the i860. The local clocks are updated by periodic pulses from the monitor. An adjustment algorithm is used to compensate for local clock drift. On receipt of a command from the i860 application program, a trace record is also generated, timestamped by a call to the local clock. All the processes mentioned run at high-priority as it is important to service the i860. Where a trace is made on a transputer-based process the clock should run at high priority so as to reduce the interrupt latency, which for a single high priority process is 58 processor cycles ($2\mu s$). If need be an additional process is run at low priority [26] with the purpose of monitoring processor activity. The process simply counts each time it is activated before descheduling itself. If the processor-monitor is called relatively frequently the processor can be assumed to be relatively idle. Internal monitoring of processes is not necessary if there is limited competition for the processor's time. If the interface program could determine the destination or source of a message by its contents these arrangements would be enough. At present, the communication primitive on the i860 is augmented to include these details. (The Paramid shared-memory data structure can be changed usually without disturbing the pre-compiled kernel routines.)

The synchronization algorithm, discussed in detail in [27], involves sending three messages. Unlike a generalized tracing system, initiation and subsequent maintenance of the clocks can be performed from a central point, the monitor process. In order to reduce disruption to the pattern of messages during normal working, all worker processes are synchronized at approximately the same time by a round-robin poll. The monitor computes the relative time difference between an averaged central time and the local times. The local clocks will receive the estimated difference at a later time. Between synchronization points, local clocks are adjusted by a local estimate of the relative drift between the clocks. Because crystal clocks are used linear drift is a good approximation (for experimental evidence see [28, 4]). The interval between synchronization pulses, before drift causes an error greater than the resolution of the intended visualizer, is calculated by an heuristic adaptation of a method due to [29]. No ordering errors were generated for the postcode or H.263 applications when the trace files were fed through ParaGraph's consistency checks though the runs lasted for several minutes. The time taken up by the clock synchronization messages was in the region of 5% for an application with mean per-message computation time of 0.1s for 1000 messages. Larger mean computation times (with the times forming a truncated Gaussian distribution) result in a lower percentage cost.

2.6   Other Features

Correct termination of the farm is necessary both for the collection of outstanding results and the gathering in of trace files. It is anticipated also that the farm may need to be reconfigured if the workload alters during the course of a run. On termination, the data farmer employs a sink process, which is broadly in line with the methods discussed in [30]. The first function in the worker modules is reserved for termination.

Pipelines are developed in an incremental fashion by adding one farm at a time. To allow a farm to be developed in isolation, source and sink processes may be needed. These process stubs collect files that can be used as a comparison with a correctly-running sequential version. If a feedback path exists then this development cycle may not be possible, as was discovered with the

H.263 encoder. However, for complex systems it is strongly recommended that an incremental testing procedure is thought out before commencing.

The implementation of the guarded indeterminate communication operator in the firmware of the transputer favours those channels found first in order of textual declaration. To provide 'fair' selection of input channels, a channel shuffling routine is provided. Experiment shows that for demand-based farming, avoiding locking out worker requests does improve performance when requests are closely synchronized.

3   Analysing the Results from Two Real-Time Systems

Our goal in providing visualization as a built-in feature was to diagnose the communication behaviour for differing regimes of the parallel application. Accuracy is not of primary concern for a top-down approach to performance tuning, but it was apparent that an accurate trace could also serve to debug an application (at a future date). Presently, real-time debugging messages can be turned on at the interface program.

```
Master3: No. = 287 read Filename=ts50335.1 countAddrLine=4 postcode=C0111RU, address[0]=WELHAMS WAY
Sending out rank vector no. 297.
Filename ts50346.u No. of characters is 6 sequence no. is 297
Master3: No. = 288 read filename=ts50336.u countAddrLine=4 postcode=C057PU, address[0]=HALL COTTAGES
Sending out rank vector no. 298.
Filename ts50347.1 No. of characters is 7 sequence no. is 298
Sending out rank vector no. 299.
Filename ts50348.1 No. of characters is 7 sequence no. is 299
Master3: No. = 290 read filename=ts50338.u countAddrLine=2 postcode=C0440S, address[0]=CLOUGH ROAD
Master3: no. = 290 read filename=ts50339.u countAddrLine=3 postcode=C0106BA, address[0]=GREGORY STREET
Master3: no. = 291 read filename=ts50340.u countAddrLine=3 postcode=C0148UB, address[0]=CLAYS ROAD
Master3: no. = 292 read filename=ts50341.1 countAddrLine=3 postcode=C0168XT, address[0]=MYTCHETT CLOSE
Master3: no. = 293 read filename=ts50342.u countAddrLine=2 postcode=C028JB, address[0]=HYTHE QUAY
Master3: no. = 294 read filename=ts50343.1 countAddrLine=3 postcode=C064PL, address[0]=PLOUGH LANE
Master3: no. = 295 read filename=ts50345.1 countAddrLine=4 postcode=C057BQ, address[0]=CHURCH GREEN
Master3: no. = 296 read filename=ts50344.u countAddrLine=3 postcode=C0167DD, address[0]=PRIMULA CLOSE
Master3: no. = 297 read filename=ts50346.u countAddrLine=2 postcode=C0280R, address[0]=QUEEN ELIZABETH WAY
Master3: no. = 298 read filename=ts50347.u countAddrLine=3 postcode=C0153AR, address[0]=STANNYN AVENUE
Master3: no. = 299 read filename=ts50348.1 countAddrLine=4 postcode=C0124HA, address[0]=PARKESTON ROAD
Dictionary stage terminated.
Farmer1 'wall-clock' time is 25.922048 secs.
This is a throughput of 11.573160 postcodes/sec.
With a success rate of at least one match of 79.666668.
```

Figure 7: Postcode Diagnostics

3.1   A Postcode Recognition System

The postcode recognition application is intended to read automatically hand-written British postcodes in time for the envelopes to be coded with the correct postcode (using a phosphorescent dot code) as they reach the end of a mechanical conveyor belt. Diagnostic output from the tail end of the application from the final dictionary search farmer (master 3) is shown in Figure 7. The throughput easily meets the specification even when a trace is included (10.60 postcodes/sec. with trace and 11.57 postcodes/sec. without). There is no direct comparison because due to the number of trace records generated the run for a trace was limited to 100 postcodes. If one of the processes, in this case the initial postcode image extractor, sends a relatively large number of short messages it will fill its trace buffer up quickly. At visualization time the display can be cluttered by messages from verbose processes, though this may be solved by post-processing the trace file.

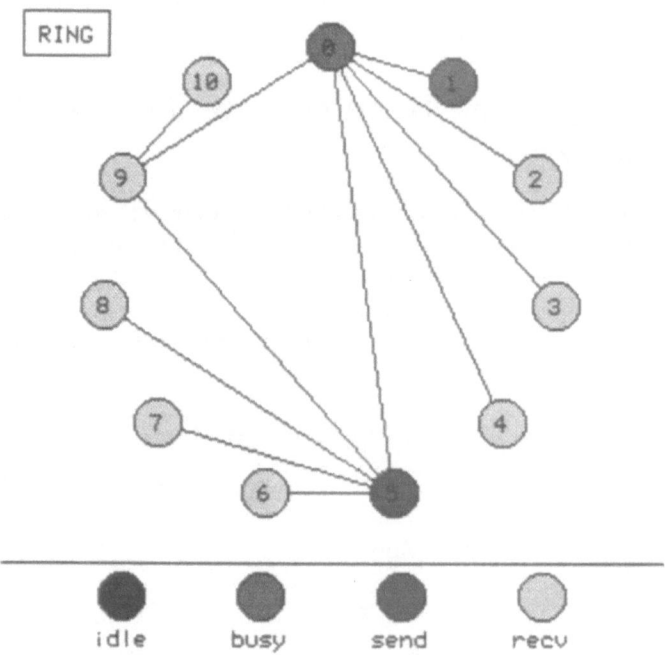

Figure 8: Animation of the Postcode Application

In the example chosen, there are three stages to the pipeline. The first pre-processing farm has three workers (processors 2, 3, & 4) and an initial image extractor (processor 1), with three workers (processors 6, 7, & 8) in the classification stage and one for the dictionary stage (processor 10). The arrangement is shown in a screen shot from ParaGraph's animation display (Figure 8). Note that, though the Paramid has eight modules, the three farmers are placed on transputers, giving eleven processes in all. Less clear is Figure 9, showing a time-space display at full magnification. Paradoxically, because the particular partition of the pipeline kept the processors running with limited idle time the display is cluttered. Had the buffer processes also been instrumented the impression would be cramped further. The trace does not show the operation of system software, which in some cases might be helpful. As communication is taking place simultaneously at various stages of the pipeline there is a good overlap. ParaGraph's display is not proportionate to the time taken by the application but is dependent on the display exigencies (as naturally some applications would take too long to display). The information from a display of the type in the figure gives a broad-brush impression but for some applications traffic-flow statistics would need to be extracted from the trace as a basis for a complementary analytic analysis.

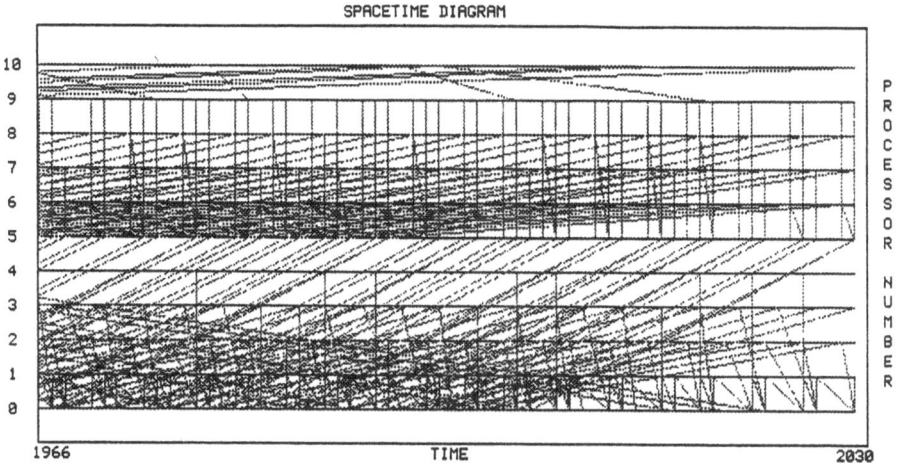

Figure 9: Time/Space Display of the Postcode Application

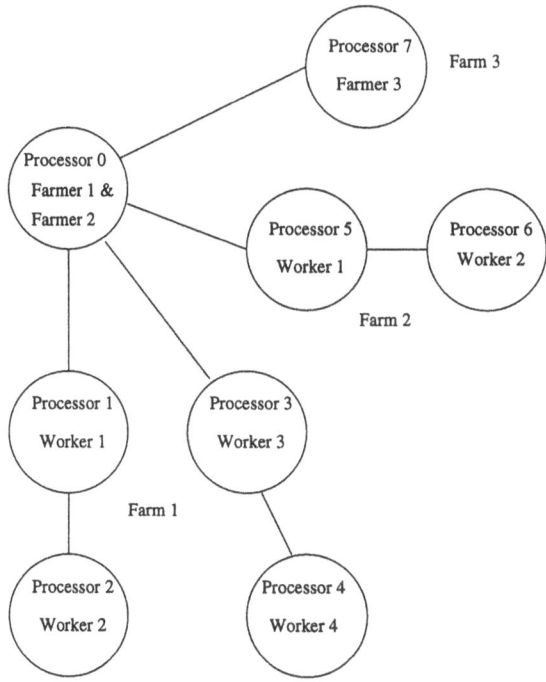

Figure 10: H.263 Physical Layout

176

3.2 The H.263 Video Encoder

The H.263 encoder, which is a standardized algorithm, is intended for real-time encoding of video frame sequences for very low bit-rate videophones or video conferencing [12]. The H.263 encoder was tested using three physical farms. However, because of the sequencing constraints imposed by the algorithm two of the data-farmers were combined into one, leading to the physical arrangement portrayed in Figure 10. Farm 1 has four workers, farm 2 has two workers and the worker on farm 3 is actually the farmer.

Figure 11 shows a portion of a trace for a typical run. The slope of the lines indicates the direction of travel. Unfortunately, for short messages even at highest magnification this is not apparent, as the first message to processor 7 shows. This is a tag message, with the body of the message following later. Running diagonally across the figure to meet at processor 0 are the messages from the first worker set, which farmer 1 cannot respond to until it has received work back (in the guise of farmer 2) from the second farm. The processor-monitor revealed a 30% idle time. The three farm arrangement was later abandoned in favour of a simpler setup.

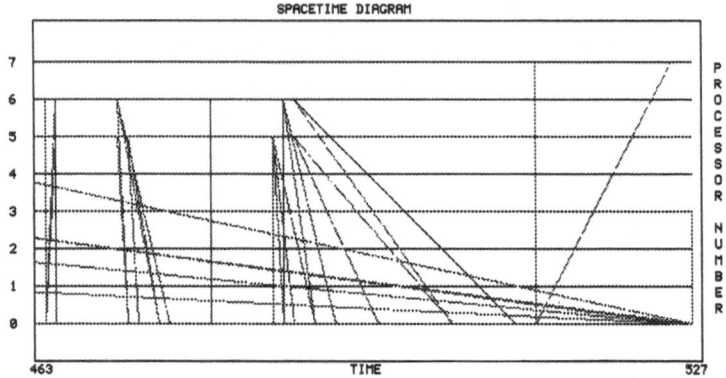

Figure 11: Time/Space Display for H.263

Because ParaGraph was intended for a hypercube machine it gives the principal topologies that can be embedded in a hypercube. The hypercube display (Figure 12) is helpful in the respect that non-hypercube communication is obvious on a colour screen. Thus, one can see whether a port would succeed. Though the range of displays and the display options offered by ParaGraph is very convenient and cost-effective, a more focussed approach would be helpful. ParaGraph is too unconstrained, offering the user limited guidance, which is a point also made in [31]. From the PPF perspective, construction of multiple tree topologies would be useful, showing message flow constrictions. If the displays were written in a language that was in the first instance interpreted (such as Java [32]) then display prototyping would be quicker. A further advantage is that the display formats could be user modifiable, without the extensive parameterization of the X Window system.

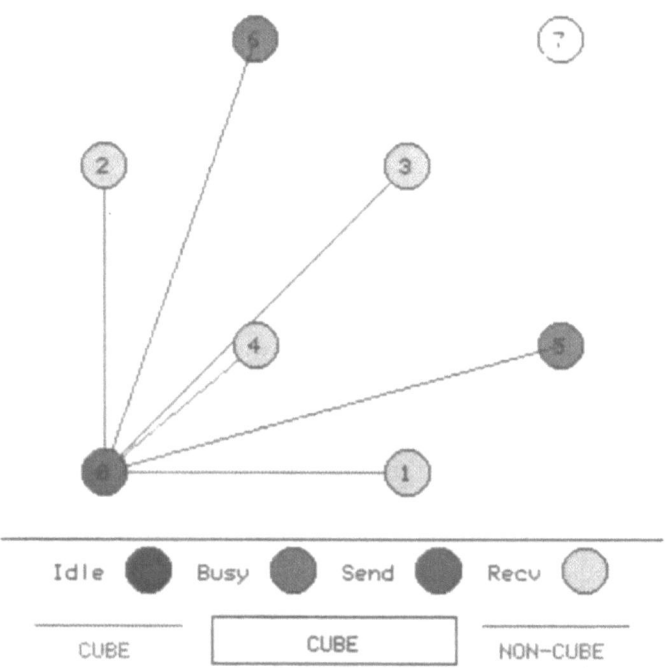

Figure 12: Hypercube Display Screen Shot

4 Conclusion

This paper has described the design of a farm template which includes software instrumentation as an integral part. The template is at a prototype stage and does not include measures to reduce the trace flow (such as semantic compression, throttling of the flow or user indication of events of concern). The principles behind the design of the template have been tried out in two applications involving a pipelined design. Interim results are shown in the form of trace displays. Data for the displays are collected by interface processes which are largely transparent to the application source code. The template has been constructed upon object-oriented design principles, which means that rather than produce generalized software all software consists of a collection of self-contained building blocks. The worker module with its controlled interface and private functions is not unlike earlier approaches, for instance the Actors' model [33]. It has been necessary to include a per-farm asynchronous multicast facility. Trace visualization is modified so as to add multicasts. The displays can be used to show communication traffic flow. The partition of the pipeline is then adjusted accordingly. On the micro level the expected traffic flow is used to balance memory requirements for buffering, which is also an essential part of the template design. A customized visualizer, capturing the features of the PPF method, is a future intention. A template for the other two parallel decomposition paradigms also may be part of forthcoming work. Finally, if 'repeatable' runs can be achieved as part of a debugging cycle [34] then an integrated parallel debugger can share the timing data.

Acknowledgement

This work is being carried out under EPSRC research contract GR/K40277 'Portable software tools for embedded signal processing applications' as part of the EPSRC Portable Software Tools for Parallel Architectures directed programme.

References

[1] A. C. Downton, R. W. S. Tregidgo, and A. Çuhadar. Generalized parallelism for embedded vision applications. In A. Y. Zomaya, editor, *Parallel Computing: Paradigms and Applications*, pages 553–577. Thompson, 1996.

[2] S. Ahmed, N. Carriero, and D. Gelernter. The Linda program builder. In A. Nicolau, D. Gelernter, T. Gross, and D. Padua, editors, *Advances in Languages and Compilers for Parallel Processing*, pages 71–87. Pitman, 1991.

[3] D. Feldcamp and A. Wagner. Using the Parsec environment to implement high-performance processor farm. In 28th *Annual Hawaii International Conference on System Sciences*, pages 212–221, 1995.

[4] D. A. Reed. Performance instrumentation techniques for parallel systems. *Lecture Notes in Computer Science*, 729:463–490, 1993.

[5] J. Jiang, A. Wagner, and S. Chanson. Tmon: A real-time performance monitor for transputer-based multicomputers. In D. L. Fielding, editor, *Transputer Research and Applications 4*, pages 36–45. IOS, 1990.

[6] Z. Segall and L. Rudolph. PIE: A programming and instrumentation environment for parallel processing. *IEEE Software*, pages 22–37, November 1985.

[7] M. C. Rinard, D. J. Scales, and M. S. Lam. Jade: A high-level machine-independent language for parallel programming. *IEEE Computer*, pages 28–38, June 1993.

[8] Transtech Parallel Systems Ltd., 17-19 Manor Court Yard, Hughenden Ave., High Wycombe, Bucks., UK. *The Paramid User's Guide*, 1993.

[9] M. Atkins. Performance and the i860 microprocessor. *IEEE Micro*, page 24, October 1991.

[10] D. A. P. Mitchell, J. A. Thompson, G. A. Manson, and G. R. Brooks. *Inside the Transputer*. Blackwell Scientific Publications, 1990.

[11] A. D. Birrell. An introduction to programming with threads. Technical report, Digital Systems Research Center, 130 Lytton Avenue, Palo Alto, Cal., 1989. Research Report 35.

[12] H. P. Sava, M. Fleury, A. C. Downton, and A. F. Clark. A case study in pipeline processor farming: Parallelising the H.263 encoder, 1996. In this volume.

[13] A. Çuhadar and A. C. D. Downton. Structured parallel design for embedded vision systems: An application case study. In *Proceedings of IPA'95 IEE International Conference on Image Processing and Its Applications*, pages 712–716, July 1995. IEE Conference Publication No. 410.

[14] W. N. Rea. Performance of task farming with transputers. In T. S. Durrani, W. A. Sandham, J. J. Soraghan, and S. M. Forbes, editors, *Applications of Transputers 3*, pages 792–797. IOS, 1991.

[15] L. G. Valiant. General purpose parallel architectures. In J. van Leeuwen, editor, *Handbook of Theoretical Computer Science*, volume A, pages 943–972. Elsevier, 1990.

[16] R. H. Arpaci, A. C. Dusseau, A. M. Vahdat, L. T. Liu, T. E. Anderson, and D. A. Patterson. The interaction of parallel and sequential workloads on a network of workstations. In *ACM Sigmetrics Conference on Measurement and Modelling of Computer Systems*, pages 267–278. ACM, May 1995.

[17] S. Yalamanchili and J. K. Aggrawal. Analysis of a model for image processing. *Pattern Recognition*, 18(1):1–16, 1985.

[18] P. J. B. King. *Computer and Communication Performance Modelling*. Prentice Hall, 1990.

[19] G. R. Andrews. Paradigms for process interaction in distributed programs. *ACM Computing Surveys*, 23(1):49–90, 1991.

[20] R. Hastings and B. Joyce. Purify. In *Winter Usenix '92 Conference*, 1992. Preprint.

[21] A. W. Roscoe. Routing messages through networks: An exercise in deadlock avoidance. In T. Muntean, editor, 7th *Occam User Group Technical Meeting*, pages 55–79. IOS, 1987.

[22] H. F. Jordan. Problems in characterizing barrier performance. In M. Simmons, R. Koskela, and I. Bucher, editors, *Instrumentation for Future Parallel Computing Systems*, pages 185–200. ACM, 1989.

[23] G. A. Geist, M. T. Heath, B. W. Peyton, and P. H. Worley. A user's guide to PICL: a portable instrumented communication library. Technical report, Oak Ridge National Laboratory, Oak Ridge, TN, USA, August 1990. Report ORNL/TM-11616.

[24] P. H. Worley. A new PICL trace file format. Technical report, Oak Ridge National Laboratory, Oak Ridge, TN, USA, September 1992. Report ORNL/TM-12125.

[25] M. T. Heath and J. A. Etheridge. Visualizing the performance of parallel programs. *IEEE Software*, 8(5):29–39, 1991.

[26] A. Bauch, T. Kosch, E. Maehle, and Obelöer. The software-monitor DELTA-T and its use for performance measurements of some farming variants on the multi-transputer system DAMP. *Lecture Notes in Computer Science*, 634:67–78, 1992. Proceedings of CONPAR '92 - VAPP V.

[27] M. Fleury, A. C. Downton, A. F. Clark, and H. P. Sava. The design of a clock synchronization sub-system for parallel embedded systems, 1996. In preparation.

[28] R. Cole and C. Foxcroft. An experiment in clock synchronization. *The Computer Journal*, 31(6):496–502, 1988.

[29] T. H. Dunigan. Hypercube clock synchronization. *Concurrency: Practice and Experience*, 4(3):257–268, May 1992.

[30] P. H. Welch. Graceful termination — graceful resetting. In Bakkers A., editor, 10th *Occam User Group Technical Meeting*. IOS, 1989.

[31] C. Pancake. Visualization techniques for parallel debugging and performance-tuning tools. In A. Y. Zomaya, editor, *Parallel Computing: Paradigms and Applications*, pages 376–393. Thompson, 1996.

[32] J. Gosling and H. McGilton. The Java language environment. Technical report, Sun Microsystems, Inc., 2550 Garcia Avenue, Mountain View, Cal., 1995.

[33] G. Agha, C. Houck, and R. Panwar. Distributed execution of Actor programs. In U. Banerjee, D. Gelernter, A. Nicolau, and D. Padua, editors, *Languages and Compilers for Parallel Computing*, pages 1–17. Springer, 1992. Lecture Notes in Computer Science Volume 589.

[34] T. J. LeBlanc and J. M. Mellor-Crummey. Debugging parallel programs with instant replay. *IEEE Transactions on Computers*, 36(4):471–481, April 1987.

Dynamic Data Management for Parallel Volume Visualisation

Cemal Köse   Alan Chalmers

Department of Computer Science,

University of Bristol,

Bristol, United Kingdom.

kose@compsci.bristol.ac.uk   alan@compsci.bristol.ac.uk

Abstract

The parallel implementation of volume visualisation offers the potential of solving this computationally complex problem in reasonable times. This paper discusses the preferred bias strategy for allocating tasks to processing elements. This strategy is able to exploit both spatial and temporal coherence within the problem domain between successive frames to improve the effectiveness of the distributed memory management system and thus increase overall system performance. Tree and torus configurations are also investigated to determine the effect configurations have on the parallel implementation of volume visualisation on large multiprocessor systems.

1   Introduction

Volume visualisation has emerged as powerful tool in science and engineering providing a method of extracting meaningful information from volumetric data sets. Through the use of rendering techniques to produce interactive images, volume visualisation allows the user to "peer" into structures and understand their complexity and dynamics [3]. The computational effort required to render the images is significant. A single image of a complex volume may take many minutes, even hours, to render on a conventional machine. Parallel processing offers the potential of rendering these complex images in acceptable times.

Volumetric data sets are typically represented by a three-dimensional regular grid of volume elements (known as voxels). These data sets are very large - far larger than can be accommodated on a single processor. Thus, a parallel implementation of a volume rendering algorithm must be able to operate on data sets which are distributed amongst many processors. The correct distribution of the data, and the minimisation of the communication latency associated with a remote data fetch, are fundamental to any efficient parallel solution to volume rendering [4].

While volume rendering is concerned with the synthesis of a single image, volume visualisation entails rendering a sequence of images. Each image, or frame, that is produced is dependent on the current view point selected by the user. In a parallel implementation of volume visualisation, the data required by the individual processors to render one image may be quite different from that necessary to produce another image from a different view point. Thus the parallel implementation must include data management strategies which are capable of dealing with these dynamic data requirements efficiently if the visualisation is to be achieved in an acceptable time. This paper discusses these strategies and shows how any coherence in the data requirements can be exploited to improve significantly the overall performance of the parallel solution.

2 Volume Visualisation

Volume rendering is the conversion, or mapping, of a multi-dimensional volume data set which has been specified spatially, into a two-dimensional image. Volume visualisation, on the other hand, allows the user to manipulate the current view point, thereby rotating the volume to enable it to be studied from any direction. Volume rendering is used to produce the image from each of the altered view points.

The sequence of mapping for volume rendering can vary according to which method is adopted. An optimum sequence would be as follows: Firstly, the volume data is properly filtered, classified and sampled. Secondly, the volume data is reconstructed by using an interpolation technique such as trilinear or inverse weighted interpolation. This converts the volume data from a discrete to a continuous form so that it may be sampled correctly. The data is then transformed into the image space. Once in the image space the volume may now be re-sampled in the correct position for rendering.

Thirdly, the transformed volume, now represented as a continuous function may be shaded. The shaded volume can then be filtered using a low-past filter to remove any high frequency artefacts. Finally, the volume is re-sampled at a rate corresponding to the desired image resolution and a visibility function, with either back-to-front or front-to-back opacity integration, may be applied as the final step [2, 3].

A number of techniques have been developed for volume rendering. Some of these, for example the "splatting method", although frequently used for sequential implementations [9], exhibit strong dependencies, which make them ill-suited for implementing in parallel. Ray casting, on the other hand, is a simple technique, well suited for parallel processing [4, 5].

2.1 Ray casting

In this method, rays are cast from a viewpoint, through the pixels of the image plane, into the voxels of the volume data, as shown in figure 1. Ray casting maps the volume as voxels along the rays through image plane onto the pixel plane. The volumes are reconstructed from the discrete volume data to calculate the exact ray and volume surface intersection points.

When a ray hits a surface an intensity value is calculated involving the distance the ray has travelled from the view point through the volume. The simulation of transmission of light through volume and the model of reflectance from the layered volume is defined by the radiation transfer function with a single scattering approximation [5]. Opacity and inverse transparency as scalar functions are evaluated at the nearest face of each voxel along the ray's path. These opacity and intensity values are accumulated as the ray travels through

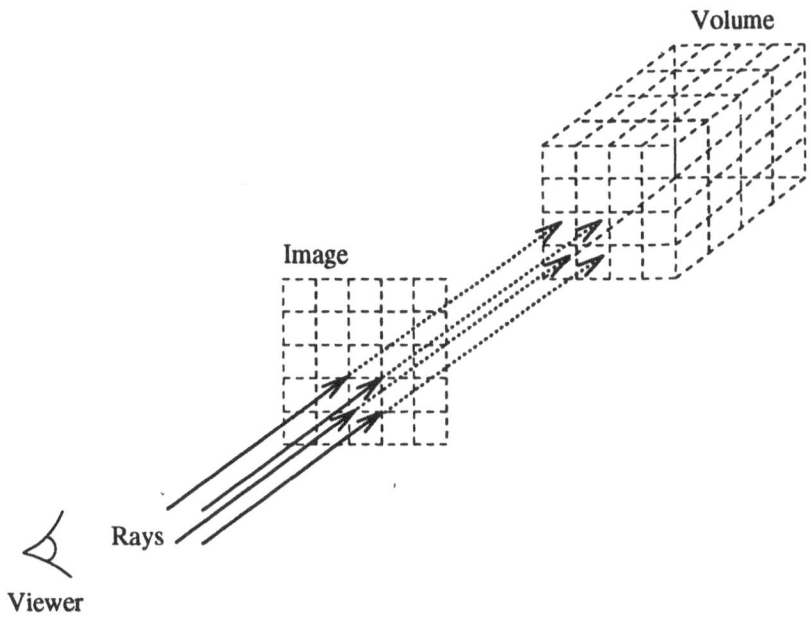

Figure 1: Ray casting

the volume. The path of a ray may be terminated when the ray has passed through the volume or the accumulated opacity along the ray exceeds a specified threshold. This early termination of a ray can be used to optimise the ray casting method [6].

3 Parallel Implementation

A single task of a parallel rendering algorithm may be chosen as the computation of the local colour and opacity contribution of an intersection of a voxel of the volume data with a ray cast through a pixel of the image plane. These tasks can be allocated to the processing elements of the parallel system by either:

Volume partitioning: Each processing element partially computes the tasks for a portion of the volume data; or

Image partitioning Each processing element computes all the tasks associated with rays cast through a sub-region of the image plane [7]:

The volume partitioning strategy has the advantage that processing elements are able to complete their partial tasks without the need to exchange any of the volume voxels that they hold. If the data requirements are so large that they can not be accommodated within the combined local memories of the multiprocessor system, then additional data may need to be fetched from secondary storage. This can be done in advance directly to the appropriate processing element. There is a communication overhead implicit in volume partitioning and that arises from the need to exchange the partially completed tasks so they may be compositted prior to rendering the final image.

A parallel implementation of volume rendering using volume partitioning does have a further significant disadvantage: this technique is unable to exploit the "early terminating" optimisation of ray casting. Early terminating may occur if an opaque layer hides the rest of the volume from a cast ray or the opacity accumulation exceeds a certain level. A front-to-back opacity accumulation technique is able to determine this situation and thus stop any further computation of tasks on the path of the considered ray. Such early termination can save a significant amount of computation, especially when considering high density objects [6].

Image partitioning schemes allocate each processing element a portion of the image plane to compute. Any variations in computational complexity between different sub-regions of the image plane can result in significant load imbalances, with some processing elements standing idle while others struggle to complete their complex portions. A simple geometric decomposition of the problem domain does have the advantage that the data requirements of each portion are known *a priori*. Even though this known data may still be too large to be accommodated at the appropriate processing element, it can be *prefetched* by a resident data manager process. In this way the data should be available locally when required [1]. The *preferred bias allocation* strategy discussed in this paper combines the advantages to data management provided by a simple geometric decomposition of the problem domain with the flexibility of a demand driven approach to ensure even load balancing.

3.1 Preferred bias allocation

The preferred bias method of task management is a way of allocating tasks to processing elements which combines the simplicity of a balanced data driven model with the flexibility of the demand driven approach [1]. The differences between these two computational models is:

- Tasks are allocated to processing elements in a predetermined manner in the balanced data driven approach.

- In the demand driven model, tasks are allocated to processing elements on demand. The requesting processing element will be assigned the next available task packet from the task pool, and thus no processing element is bound to any area of the problem domain.

As no data-dependencies exist between different pixels of the image plane, the order of task completion is unimportant. Once all tasks have been computed, the image is rendered. In the preferred bias method, the problem domain, that is the image plane, is divided into equal regions with each region being assigned to a particular processing element, as is done in the balanced data driven approach. However, in this method, these regions are purely *conceptual* in nature. A demand driven model of computation is still used, but the tasks are not now allocated in an arbitrary fashion to the processing elements.

Rather, a task is dispatched to a processing element from its conceptual portion. Once all tasks from a processing element's conceptual portion have been completed, only then will that processing element be allocated its next task from the portion of another processing element which has yet to complete its conceptual portion of tasks. In order to minimise communication overheads, this task should come from a processing element which is physically "close". This will mean that the volume data associated with the task may be prefetched across a minimum distance.

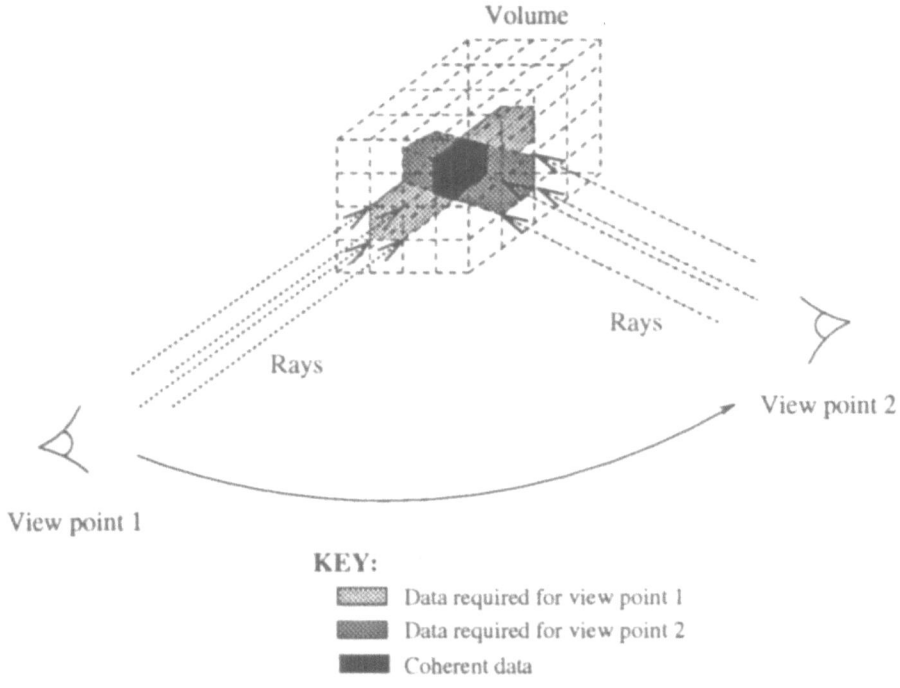

Figure 2: Coherent data requirement for two view points

The exploitation of data coherence between successive frames is essential if interactive volume visualisation is to be achieved. Preferred bias allocation of tasks ensures that tasks are allocated to those processing elements which are known to contain at least some of the requisite data to enable the processing element to start the computation, as shown in figure 2. Any additional data items can subsequently be prefetched, thus overlapping the communication with the computation.

3.2   Data coherence

In many problems the sequence in which references are made to data items is not random, but occurs in a somewhat predictable manner. This is due to a property which has been termed *coherence* (also known as *locality*); it is observed that the data item requests which are generated by a "typical" program tend to be restricted to a small subset of the whole problem. Conventional virtual memory management systems depend on exploiting this feature for their success. Coherence refers to three concepts:

1. Temporal coherence. If a problem has good *temporal coherence* it means that if task uses a data item at time T, it is likely that the task will use it again in the near future, at time $T + \delta t$.

2. Spatial coherence, in the problem domain. If a problem shows good *problem domain coherence* it means that if a data item at position A of the problem domain is accessed, it is likely that items in the neighbourhood of A ($A \pm \delta a$) will be accessed soon.

3. Spatial coherence, in the network. If a application has good *network coherence* it means that data items that are available on processing element PE_1 are more likely to be used at processing element PE_1 and the processing elements in the neighbourhood of PE_1 than on processing elements further away.

Ray casting exhibits spatial coherence in the problem domain. This is exploited using the preferred bias task allocation mechanism. In addition, when the volume data is rotated, that is when the view point is moved, then the temporal coherence between successive frames may be utilised, especially if angle of rotation between frames is small. Thus only a limited amount of additional data may need to be fetched to render the spatially coherent tasks for the next frame.

3.3 Configuration

The performance of a distributed memory multiprocessor depends in large part on the efficiency of the message transfer system that provides the interface between the co-operating processing elements. The choice of configuration can thus play a significant rôle in reducing communication overheads. To achieve the most efficient performance, the configuration chosen should be well suited to the communication patterns inherent in the parallel implementation [1]. Two configurations, the tree and the torus, have been considered for parallel volume visualisation.

The tree configuration has been widely used for solving a variety of applications in parallel. A tree of degree d and height h consists of a single processing element at the top level, the *root processing element*, connected to d other processing elements, each of which is a "root" processing element of a subtree of degree d and height $(h - 1)$. The processing elements at the lowest level of the tree, the *leaf processing elements*, are only connected to their "parent" tree. Any leaf processing element wishing to communicate with another leaf processing element must thus do so via branch processing elements further "up" the tree.

A torus configuration consists of rings of rings of processing elements. To minimise the diameter of the torus it is preferable that the number of processing elements within the horizontal rings is approximately the same as the number of processing elements in the vertical rings. Table 1 shows the comparison of the maximum distance between any two processing elements (the diameter) of ternary tree and torus configurations, while table 2 shows the average distances between any two processing elements for each of the configurations.

	Processors				
	8	16	32	64	128
Torus	3	4	6	7	12
Ternary Tree	4	5	6	8	10

Table 1: Comparison of configuration diameters

	Processors				
	8	16	32	64	128
Torus	1.50	2.00	3.00	4.00	5.64
Ternary Tree	1.97	2.91	3.93	5.01	6.25

Table 2: Comparison of average interprocessor distances

4 Data management

The distribution of the volume data across the multiprocessor system, means that any required data item which is not available locally must be acquired from elsewhere in the system during the course of the computation. If this data item is essential for the continuation of the task then the processing element will remain idle until it is fetched. The time to fetch this data item and, therefore, the idle time, can be significant. This *latency* is difficult to predict and may not be repeatable due to other factors, such as current message densities within the system. The overall aim of data management is to maximise effective processing element computation by minimising the occurrence and effects of remote data fetches. A data manager process is introduced alongside the application process (which is computing the tasks) at each processing element to manage the data requirements. The data manager may use a number of techniques to reduce the remote fetch latency by:

Hiding the Latency: - overlapping the communication with the computation, by:

> **Prefetching** - anticipating data items that will be required
>
> **Multi-threading** - keeping the processing element busy with other useful computation during the remote fetch

Minimising the Latency: - reducing the time associated with a remote fetch by:

> **Caching** - exploiting any coherence that may exist in the problem domain

4.1 Prefetching

If it is known at the start of the computation which data items will be required by each task then these data items can be *prefetched* by the data manager so that they are available locally when required. The data manager thus issues the requests for the data items *before* they are actually required and in this way overlaps the communication required for the remote fetches with the ongoing computation of the application process. This is in contrast with the simple fetch-upon-demand strategy where the data manager only issues the external request for a data item at the moment it is requested by the application process and it is not found in the local memory.

By treating its local memory as a "circular buffer" the data manager can be loading prefetched data items into one end of the buffer while the application process is requesting the data items from the other end the data items will be determined by the size of the local memory and the rate at which the application process is "using" the data items.

4.2 Multi-threading

Any failure by the data manager to have the requested data item available locally for the application process will result in idle time unless the processing element can be kept busy doing some other useful computation. One solution is to have more than one concurrent computational process at each processing element. Each of these application processes is known as a separate *thread* of computation. Now, although one thread may be suspended awaiting a remote data item, the other threads may still be able to continue. It may not be feasible to determine just how many of these threads will be necessary to avoid the case where all of them are suspended awaiting data. However, if there are sufficient threads (and of course sufficient tasks) then the processing element should always be performing useful computation. This multi-threading is similar to the Bulk Synchronous Parallel paradigm [8].

Multi-threading does however have serious limitations [1]. Previous work has shown that, for volume rendering, increasing the number of threads per processing element does produce a performance improvement until a certain number of threads have been added. Beyond this point, the overheads of having the additional threads are greater than the benefit gained, and thus the times to solve the problem once more increase [4]. The number of threads at which the overheads outweigh the benefits gained is lower for larger numbers of processing elements. This is because the more threads there are per processing element, the larger the message output from each processing element will be (assuming an average number of remote fetches per thread). As the average distances the remote data fetches have to travel in larger systems is greater, the impact of increasing numbers of messages on the overall system density is more significant and thus the request latency will be higher. Adding more threads now no longer helps overcome communication delays, but in fact, the increasing number of messages actually exacerbates the communication difficulties.

The number of threads that can be used in order to improve efficiency for volume rendering on a large system is small. An effective caching strategy must therefore be employed to reduce the number of remote data fetches [4].

4.3 Caching

In our distributed data management strategy, the local memory at each processing element, which we term the *local cache*, assumes the rôle of the cache memories of conventional processors. The combined local caches of all the processing elements are the equivalent of the "main memory" of conventional processors. The concept of *data sharing* provides the virtual shared memory environment [1]. However, the access time for a data manager to fetch data item from a remote "memory" location will be substantially higher than a fetch from its local cache. Coherence is used to ensure a high "cache-hit" ratio.

The spatial coherence in the problem domain and the temporal coherence together with the preferred biased task allocation provides the data manager with a good estimate of the future data requirements of the tasks being computed at a processing element The data manager can now use this information to *prefetch* those data items which are *likely* to be used by subsequent tasks being performed at that processing element. If the data manager is always correct with its prediction then a data item will always be available locally when required by the computational thread and thus this thread is never delayed awaiting a remote fetch. Note in this case there is no need for multi-threading.

5 Results

The data and computational requirements for volume visualisation are significant. To show the performance improvements that preferred bias allocation can provide by increasing data coherence, two volume data sets: a volume frame of the Mandelbrot set in the quaternion, shown in figure 3; and, a medical MRI scan of a human head, figure 4, were visualised. The results have been obtained on a Meiko system of sixty four T800 transputers arranged in both tree and torus configurations with a volume data size of $128 \times 128 \times 128$ voxels. In all cases the volume data was rotated about an arbitrary axis.

The advantages of a preferred bias task allocation strategy can be seen in figure 5. This graph compares the speed-up obtained using a random task allocation strategy with the preferred bias method on tree configurations. The inherent bottlenecks for global communication in the tree configurations has an increasing effect on the system performance as the number of processing elements is increased. Nevertheless, the benefits of exploiting coherence with the preferred bias strategy can clearly be seen.

Figure 6 shows how the choice of configuration influences overall system performance. The graph shows speed-up obtained using the preferred bias method on both tree and torus configurations. For lower numbers of processing elements the choice of configuration has little effect. However, for the larger systems, the lower diameters and average interprocessor distances of the torus configurations, and their lack of bottlenecks provides a significant improvement in system performance.

Finally, figure 7 shows the speed-up obtained for the preferred bias allocation strategy on the torus configurations, compared with the random task allocation method on the tree systems. The "preferred bias - torus" implementation on the 64 processing element system was approximately three times faster than the other "random - tree" implementation.

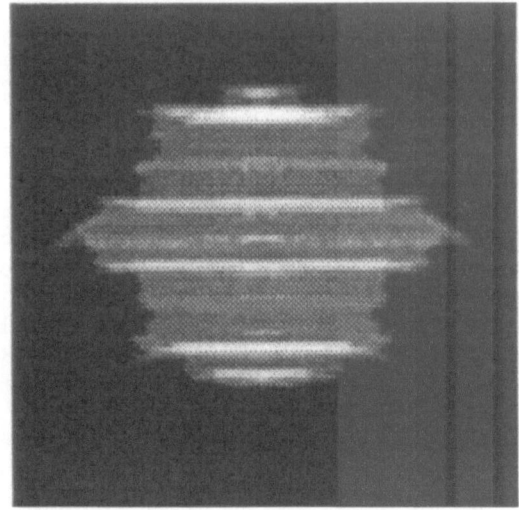

Figure 3: Fractal image in the quaternion

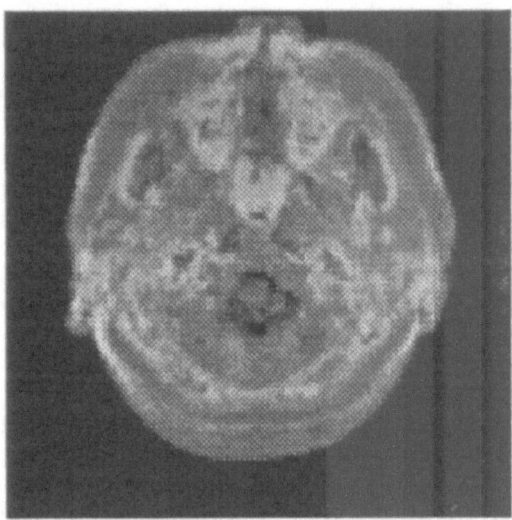

Figure 4: Medical scan of a slice of a human head

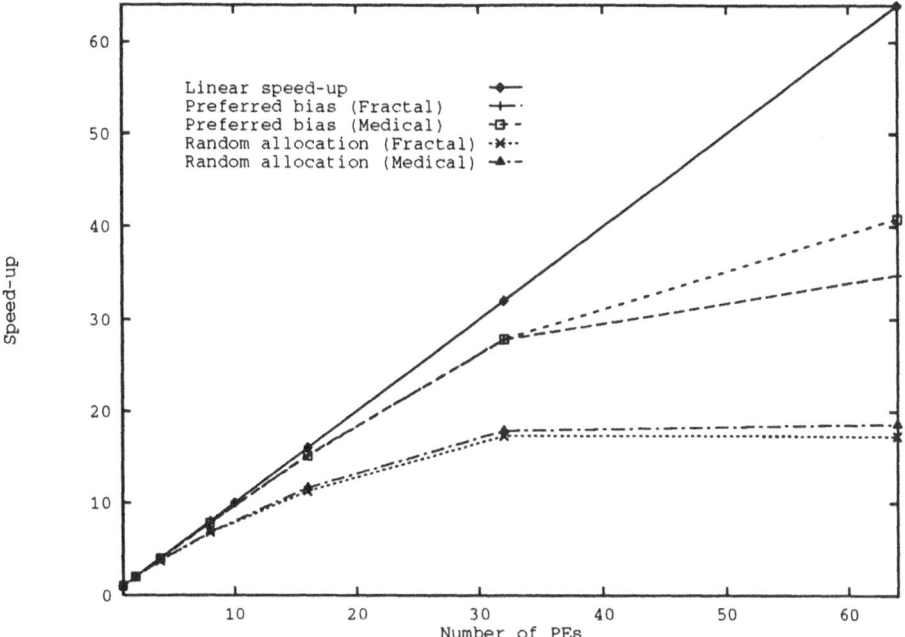

Figure 5: Task allocation strategies on tree configurations

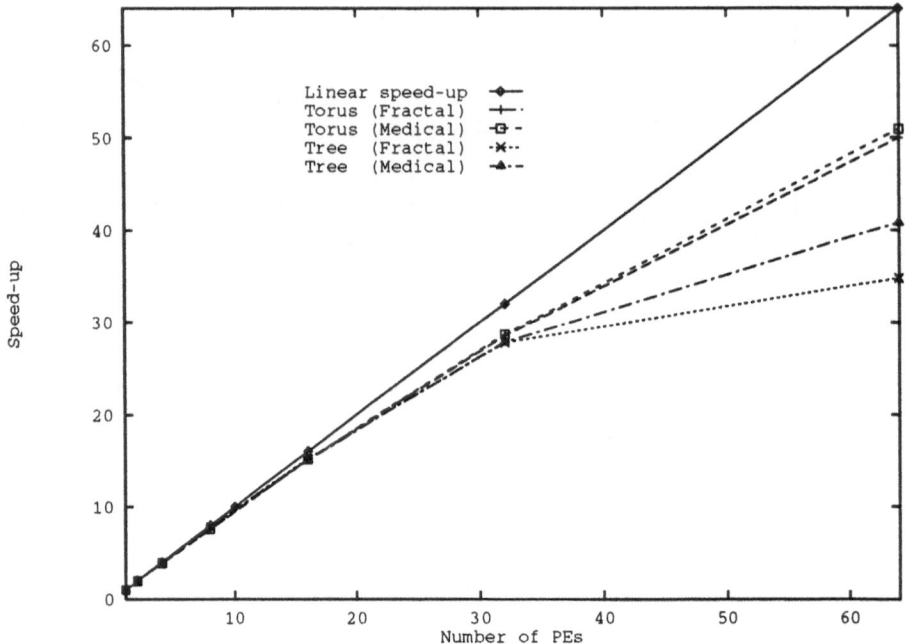

Figure 6: Preferred bias allocation on tree and torus configurations

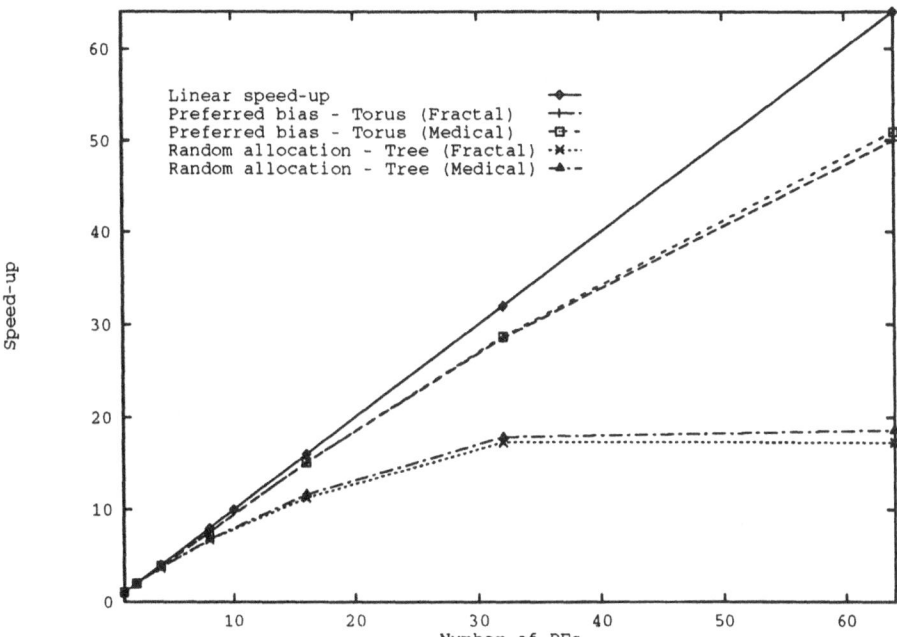

Figure 7: A comparison of strategies

194

6 Conclusions

The results presented in this paper confirm that it is possible to implement volume visualisation on a distributed memory multiprocessor system efficiently. A preferred bias allocation of tasks to processing elements allows spatial and temporal coherence in the data domain to be exploited between successive frames. This enables the remote fetching of data items to be overlapped with computing the desired image and reduces the possibility of a data item not being available locally when required.

The very large memory requirements for the volume data necessitates distributing this data amongst all the processing elements. This results in the need for every processing element to communicate with every other processing element. As the results show, for large multiprocessor systems, torus configurations are better suited than tree configurations for such a global communication need. Future work will also consider the irregular minimum path (AMP) configurations which have been shown to be very efficient configurations for global communication [1].

Despite the system performance improvements that can be achieved by exploiting the coherence within the data domain (a speed-up of over 50 for both volume data sets on 64 processing elements), improvements will still need to be made if *interactive* volume visualisation is to be achieved. Future work will examine complexity reduction schemes which will render an approximation of the volume data between successive view points. Once the desired new view point has been reached, progressive refinement techniques will be used to obtain desired image quality from these approximations.

Acknowledgements

We would like to thank the Black Sea Technical University, Turkey, for supporting Cemal's research in the UK.

References

[1] A. G. Chalmers and J. P. Tidmus. *Practical Parallel Processing: An introduction to problem solving in parallel.* International Thomson Publishing, London, 1996.

[2] R. A. Drebin, L. Carpenter, and P. Hanrahan. Volume rendering. *Computer Graphics*, 22(4):65–74, Aug. 1988.

[3] A. Kaufman, K. Höhne, and P. Schröder. Research issues in volume visualisation. *IEEE Computer Graphics and Applications*, 63–67, March 1994.

[4] C. Köse and A. G. Chalmers. Memory management strategies for parallel volume rendering. In B. O'Neil, editor, 19th *World Occam and Transputer User Group meeting*, IOS Press, Nottingham, March 1996. To appear.

[5] M. S. Levey. Volume rendering: display of surfaces from volume data. *Computer Graphics and Applications*, 8(3), May 1988.

[6] M. S. Levoy. Efficient ray tracing of volume data. *ACM Transactions of Graphics*, 9(3), July 1990.

[7] U. Neumann. Communication cost for parallel volume rendering algorithms. *IEEE Computer Graphics and Applications*, 49–58, July 1994.

[8] L. G. Valiant. A bridging model for parallel computation. *Communications of the ACM*, 33(8):103–111, Aug. 1990.

[9] L. A. Westover. *Splatting: A parallel, feed-forward volume rendering algorithm*. Technical Report, The University of North Carolina at Chapel Hill, Department of Computer Science, July 1991.

A Case Study in Pipeline Processor Farming: Parallelising the H.263 Encoder

H. Sava,

Department of Electronic Systems Engineering, University of Essex,
Wivenhoe Park, Colchester CO4 3SQ, U.K

M. Fleury,

Department of Electronic Systems Engineering, University of Essex,
Wivenhoe Park, Colchester CO4 3SQ, U.K

A. C. Downton

Department of Electronic Systems Engineering, University of Essex,
Wivenhoe Park, Colchester CO4 3SQ, U.K

A. F. Clark

Department of Electronic Systems Engineering, University of Essex,
Wivenhoe Park, Colchester CO4 3SQ, U.K

Abstract

This paper describes the parallelisation of the H.263 hybrid video encoder algorithm based upon a pipelines of processor farms (PPF) paradigm. In addition, a data-farming template, which can be very useful for several image coding algorithms, was incorporated in the PPF model. A variety of parallel topologies were implemented in order to obtain the best time performance for an eight processor distributed-memory machine. Results show that, due to communication overheads and algorithm constraints, the speed-up performance is below the value predicted by static analysis. However, the design examples indicated how to modify the PPF methodology in identifying those algorithm components which restrict scaling performance. The paper highlights the problems associated with the parallelisation of sequential algorithms and emphasises the need for generic tools to facilitate such conversion.

1   Introduction

H.263 is a new standard for very low bit-rate videocoding (<64kbps) which is in the process of ratification by ITU-T. One key application will be PSTN videotelephony, i.e. videotelephony on normal analogue telephone lines. The standard has been developed collaboratively by researchers in telecommunications organisations around the world, and algorithms for an H.263 decoder and encoder implemented by Telenor (Norwegian Telecom) are freely available over the Internet [1]. On a Sparcstation 20, the decoder runs in real-time, though the encoder runs at only about 2 frames/s. In the short term, before real-time VLSI hardware implementations become widely available, there is therefore significant interest in parallelising the encoder algorithm to obtain real-time performance in distributed- or shared-memory multiprocessor environments.

This paper describes a case study which applies a pipeline processor farming (PPF) methodology [2] to parallelise the Telenor H.263 image encoding algorithm. The goal is to obtain a portable, parallel, real-time H.263 encoder which is capable of running in a range of multiprocessor environments (e.g., i860-based MIMD machine, TMS320C40 parallel DSPs, multiple workstations running PVM [5], shared-memory multiprocessor workstations) with minimal software changes. The paper not only describes the architecture of the parallelisation solution adopted for this application but also addresses general issues related to the conversion of sequential algorithms to parallel ones and emphasises the need for generic tools to facilitate such conversion.

2   H.263 algorithm characteristics

Figure 1 shows a block diagram of the H.263 encoder.

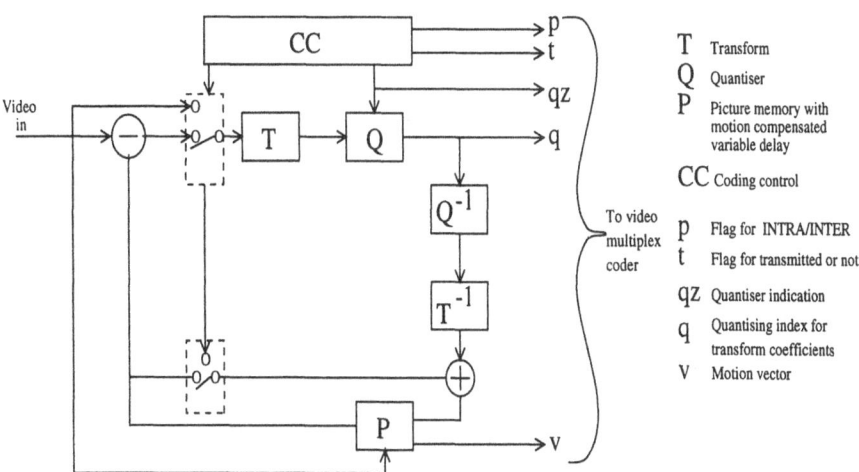

Figure 1: Block diagram of the structure of the H.263 encoder

The basic configuration of the video source coding algorithm has been developed from ITU-T recommendation H.261 and is a hybrid of inter-picture prediction to utilise temporal redundancy and transform coding of the remaining signal to reduce spatial redundancy [1, 7]. In addition to the basic video source coding algorithm, four negotiable coding options are available: Unrestricted Motion Vectors, Syntax-based Arithmetic Coding, Advanced Prediction and PB-frames. The coding method uses 16×16 macro-blocks, 8×8 sub-blocks, motion estimation and compensation, DCT transform of prediction errors, run-length coding and variable-length codewords.

3 Parallelising the H.263 algorithm

3.1 Parallel design model

The PPF design methodology can be used to decompose existing sequential applications onto any type of parallel processor network with any communication model [2]. The methodology proceeds from the observation that embedded signal processing systems with continuous data flow may be characterised as consisting of a series of independent processing stages. It therefore maps the sequential algorithm structure to a generalised parallel architecture based upon a pipeline of stages with well-defined data communication patterns between them. Each stage of the pipeline then exploits parallelism in the most appropriate way, for example, data parallelism applied at various levels, algorithmic parallelism, or temporal multiplexing of complete data sets. This decomposition has been applied successfully to similar applications in the past [3, 6].

3.2 Static analysis of H.263 algorithm

The first step of the design model is to decompose the sequential software into pipeline stages using top-down profiling data derived from sequential execution. This stage identifies the individual stages and their relative computational requirements and allows the required number of processors in each stage to be calculated directly. In its simplest form, the model ignores communication overheads between processors and assumes static task execution times. Although practically not achievable, this is useful in determining speed-up trends.

Analysis of the execution profile of the H.263 encoder using the *gprof* profiler on test sequences such as "Mother and Daughter" and "Car Phone" shows that only three functions have execution times large enough to be measurable at the sampling accuracy used. One of these functions, *CodeOneIntra*, is called only once to code the initial frame using intra-frame coding alone. Therefore, this function was excluded from the analysis, although it is structurally similar to the inter-frame coding used for other frames and so could in principle be included in the encoder/decoder stage of the pipeline. The analysis of the other two major functions, *CodeOneOrTwo* and *ComputeSNR*, shows that 98% of the execution time is spent on *CodeOneOrTwo* regardless of the coding options chosen.

Table 1 shows the breakdown of the execution time of the main function *CodeOneOrTwo* into sub-functions, and includes the 8 most significant sub-functions which constitute 97.9%of the execution time of *CodeOneOrTwo*.

Function Name	% CodeOneOrTwo execution time (default mode)	% CodeOneOrTwo execution time (full options)
MotionEstimatePicture	63.8	64.8
MB_Decode	13.1	9.1
MB_Encode	12.8	9.4
PredictP	2.6	5.2
InterpolateImage	1.9	1.9
MB_Recon_P	1.3	5.1
Clip	1.2	1.1
ReconImage	1.2	1.3

Table 1: Top-down profiling data for the 8 most intensive functions within the CodeOneOrTwo function of the H.263 coder

Nearly 64% of the execution time of *CodeOneOrTwo* is expended in the motion estimation function and the remaining time on the *Encoder-Decoder* function. From the above analysis it was concluded that these two functions should be placed in separate PPF pipeline stages within the frame feedback loop, and each image frame subdivided into half-frames for processing concurrently in consecutive pipeline stages. Comparison of the execution times of the two stages shows that their static execution times are approximately in the ratio 2:1; hence a balanced pipeline can be achieved by populating the respective processor farms with workers in this ratio. An implementation based on this architecture is shown in Figure 2.

According to Amdahl's law, the speed-up which can be achieved is defined largely by any residual sequential elements within an application's algorithm [4]. Hence, an implementation based upon this architecture would result in an overall speed-up of up to six according to Amdahl's law.

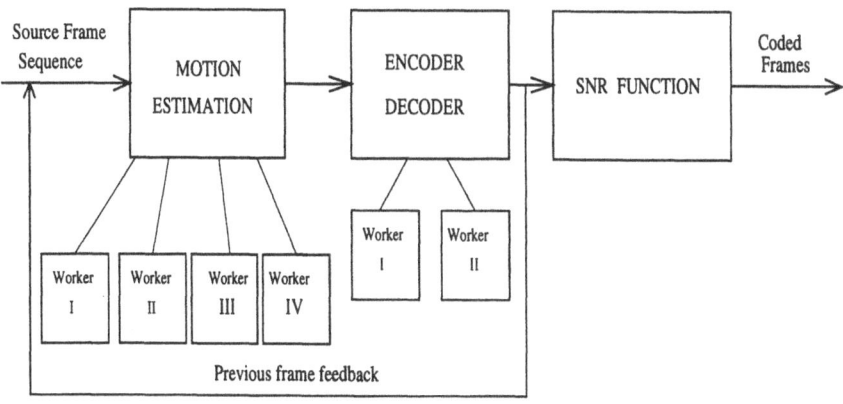

Figure 2: Pipeline architecture of H.263 encoder

In the present study, the scale of the structure was restricted to eight processors because of the number of processors in the Transtech Paramid machine used. The Paramid [8] consists of compound processor nodes comprising a transputer communication co-processor and i860 computational engine [9]. The processes were implemented on i860s which run at 50 MHz, the transputer communication links being set at 20 MHz. The "Car Phone" image sequence, comprising some 74 frames, was used as a test data.

4   General parallel design issues

Although the overall structure of processors in the parallel implementation was determined directly from the execution time of the sequential program, the conversion to a parallel algorithm suitable for distributed-memory processors presents numerous software conversion problems. In the case of a single processor, where shared memory is used, efficient inter-function communication is generally provided by passing pointers to data structures. However, to support the general case of distributed-memory MIMD processors (e.g., the Paramid machine), required data must be explicitly passed down the pipeline and distributed to worker processors in each farm. Thus, to support parallelisation of existing application codes, generic analysis tools are required to track memory use and to convert communication at application partitioning points from referential to explicit. Subsequently, generic design tools are needed to support and simplify the partitioning process and to enable the application to be rescaled easily.

At this stage, *Purify*, a memory usage analyser, was found to be useful when modifying the sequential code. The *Purify* software minimises debugging time due to its capability of identifying when an error occurs, the origin of the error and the relevant line number in the source code. These features are very useful, especially when dealing with complex and large software applications such as H.263 algorithm. Furthermore, most of the bugs occuring at this stage are related to memory leaks as a result of converting pointer reference variables to statically allocated variables. In this context, the availability of *Purify* was found very useful.

Table 2 shows comparative execution for Sparc 20, Sparc 5 and single i860 of the sequential program.

Processor	Execution speed(secs./frame)
Sparc 20 (passing pointers)	0.40
Sparc 5 (passing pointers)	3.12
i860 (passing pointers)	3.20
i860 (passing data)	4.47

Table 2: Comparative overall performance of Sparc 20, Sparc5, and i860 for H.263 algorithm

The results presented in Table 2 suggest that a practical implementation using up to eight i860 nodes is unlikely to exceed the performance of a Sparc 20, as the i860 has a somewhat lower computational performance than the Sparc 20. However, such an implementation would at least give an insight to parallelisation of H.263 on a more powerful machine.

Another issue that requires particular attention, especially in the case of data-intensive applications, is that of data distribution. To handle this problem, a data-broadcast primitive was incorporated into the PPF model.

5 PPF Primitives

In order to facilitate the application of the PPF model to a wide range of embedded applications, and to minimise the debugging time for each new application, processor farm primitives are required.

Although there are cases (e.g., 3L Parallel C) where such primitives already exist, this was not the case for the Paramid system. Furthermore, existing primitives are largely designed to support only single processor farms, rather than the pipeline processor farm model required for embedded applications with continuous data flow. Thus, to support the PPF model a generic, reusable, demand-based processor farm primitive was developed [10].

Another evident problem associated with parallel image processing applications is that of immense data communications. Functions like *MotionEstimatePicture* or *EncodeDecode*, which constitute the bulk of hybrid coding algorithms, require several images and motion vectors which in themselves contain large amounts of data. One way to reduce the data communication would be to send to each worker only the required data for processing. However, this would lead not only to a complicated software structure, but, moreover, to an unscalable solution. To tackle this problem a data-farming template incorporating a multi-cast facility was implemented. This template distributes the data from the master processor to all workers simultaneously and can easily be scaled to the required number of processors. Furthermore, a buffering facility was designed in order to hide communication latencies. The data-farming template can also be adapted to use a data-flow synchronisation mode between workers during the initial phase of multi-casting. This type of synchronisation was used in this application at the start of processing each half-image by all the workers of a master.

6 Results and discussion

Due to the complexity of the H.263 algorithm, an incremental approach was adopted during the parallel implementation of the algorithm. Figure 3 depicts the developing stages of the parallel implementation and Table 3 presents the corresponding results on a time-per-frame basis. In all these cases the image frame is sub-divided so that, while one half-frame is being coded, motion estimation is simultaneously being carried out on the next half.

202

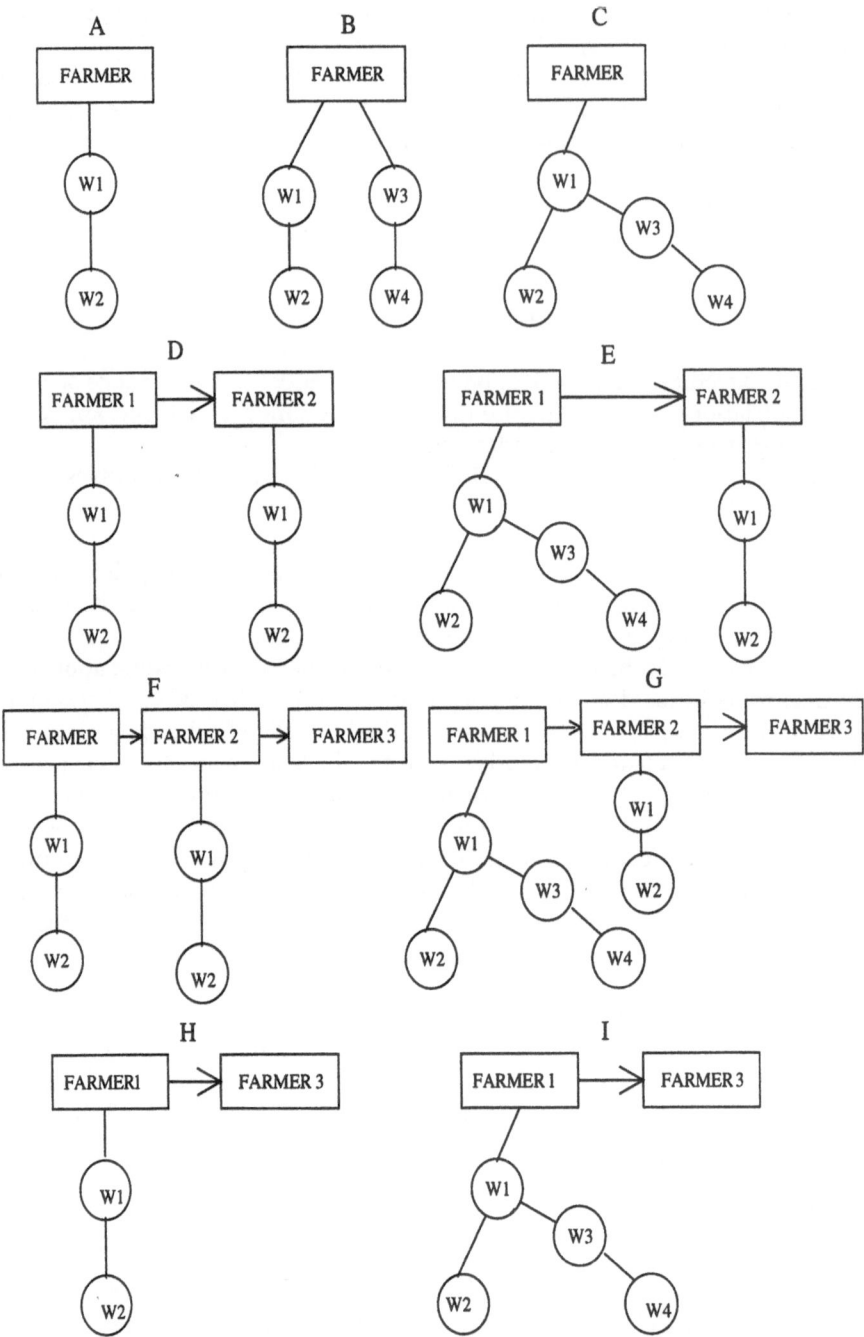

Figure 3: Implemented parallel topologies for the H.263 encoder

Parallel Topology	Execution speed(secs./frame)
Single i860 (passing pointers)	3.20
Single i860 (passing data)	4.47
Figure 3(a)	2.04
Figure 3(b)	2.2
Figure 3(c)	2.05
Figure 3(d)	2.52
Figure 3(e)	2.6
Figure 3(f)	2.46
Figure 3(g)	2.48
Figure 3(h)	1.86
Figure 3(i)	1.89

Table 3: Comparative overall performance of several parallel topologies for H.263

From Table 3 it is easy to see that the proposed topology from the static analysis (Figure 3g) does not match the speed-up predicted accorded to Amdahl's law. Indeed, the speed-up achieved in this case is about three times less than the theoretically predicted speed-up. This is mainly caused by the large amount of data that has to be communicated between farmers and respective workers. From Table 3 it can also be seen that the extension to a second farmer, which pipelines the encode-decode part of the algorithm, deteriorates the performance of the parallel structure. This can easily be seen from the comparison of time performance of Figure 3a-c with Figure 3d-e. In the latter case a 25% increase in per-frame processing time is measured. This is mainly caused by an inherent restriction within the H.263 algorithm which requires a row-by-row update of the quantisation variable. This constrains the encoder and decoder to process on only a row-by-row basis and increases the number of messages sent from the the workers to the relevant farmer. The measurement of the processing and communication times spent in the second farmer showed that both these times are equal. This finding suggests that, for the present hardware system, the extension to a second farmer is inappropriate. However, for another machine with higher communication bandwidth, a second pipeline stage utilising a greater number of processors may be worthwhile. Furthermore, the requirement for row-by-row update of quantisation can be relaxed in many cases and, if this is possible, the communication overhead of using a second pipeline stage could be reduced further.

According to Table 3, the best results are achieved by the topology described in Figure 3h. In this case the processors are entirely balanced and a further reduction in time is achieved from the introduction of a third farmer. However, it must be said that even for this case the time performance is far below the upper-bound speed-ups required for real-time implementation.

7   Conclusions

This paper has presented an application of the PPF methodology to parallel-ising the H.263 encoder. Although a real-time version of H.263 has not yet been achieved, this is largely due to communication bandwidth constraints of the current parallel machine. Work is currently under way to port the present parallel implementation to a TMS320C40 parallel DSP environment which has an order of magnitude higher communication bandwidth. This porting process is assisted by the use of a generic design methodology utilising data-farming templates developed specifically to support continuous data-flow embedded applications. The application highlights the impact of the communication overheads and inherent coding restrictions in achieving the upper-bound speed-ups predicted by a static analysis of the algorithm. These algorithm constraints are also relevant in designing real-time VLSI implementations of H.263.

8   Acknowledgements

This work is being carried out under EPSRC research contract GR/K40277 'Portable software tools for embedded signal processing applications' as part of the EPSRC PSTPA (Portable Software Tools for Parallel Architectures) directed programme.

References

[1] "ITU-T Recommendation H.263", *Technical Report*, 1995.

[2] A. C. Downton, R. W.S. Tregidgo, A. Cuhadar "Top-down Structured Parallelisation of Embedded Image Processing Applications", *IEE Proc. Vis. Image Signal Process.*, Vol. 141, No. 6, pp. 431–437, Dec. 1994.

[3] A. C. Downton "Generalised Approach to Parallelising Image Sequence Coding Algorithms", *IEE Proc. Vis. Image Signal Process.*, Vol. 141, No. 6, pp. 438–445, Dec. 1994.

[4] G. M. Amdahl, "Limits of Expectation", *Int. J. Supercomput. Appl.*, pp. 88–94, No. 2, 1982.

[5] A. Geist, A. Beguelin, J. Dongarra, W. Jiang, R. Manchek, V. Sunderam, "PVM: Parallel Virtual Machine—A Users' Guide and Tutorial for Networked Parallel Computing", *The MIT Press, Cambridge*, MA, USA, 1994.

[6] A. C. Downton "Speed-Up Trend Analysis for H.261 and Model-Based Image Coding Algorithms Using a Parallel-Pipeline Model", *Signal Processing: Image Communication*, Vol. 7, pp. 489–502, 1995.

[7] D. Bailey, M. Cressa, J. Fandrianto, D. Neubauer, H. Rainnie, Ch-Sh. Wang, "Programmable Vision Processor/Controller for Flexible Implementation of Current and Future Image Compression Standards", *IEEE Micro*, pp. 33–39. Oct. 1992.

[8] Transtech Parallel Systems Corporation "The Paramid Users Guide", 1993.

[9] M. Atkins "Performance of the i860 Microprocessor", *IEEE Micro*, pp. 24–78, Oct. 1991.

[10] M. Fleury, H.P. Sava, A.C. Downton and A.F. Clark "Designing and Instrumenting a Software Template for Embedded Parallel Systems", *In this volume.*

AUTHOR INDEX